Homeland Security and Intelligence

Homeland Security and Intelligence

KEITH GREGORY LOGAN, EDITOR

PRAEGER SECURITY INTERNATIONAL

 PRAEGER

AN IMPRINT OF ABC-CLIO, LLC
Santa Barbara, California • Denver, Colorado • Oxford, England

Library of Congress Cataloging-in-Publication Data

Homeland security and intelligence / Keith Gregory Logan, editor.
    p. cm.
    Includes bibliographical references and index.
    ISBN 978-0-313-37662-7 (hardcopy : alk. paper) — ISBN 978-0-313-37663-4 (ebook)
1. Intelligence service—United States.   2. Internal security—United States.
3. National security—United States.   I. Logan, Keith Gregory.
    JK468.I6H654   2010
    327.1273—dc22   2009051997

ISBN: 978-0-313-37662-7
EISBN: 978-0-313-37663-4

14   13   12   11   10   1   2   3   4   5

This book is also available on the World Wide Web as an eBook.
Visit www.abc-clio.com for details.

Praeger
An Imprint of ABC-CLIO, LLC

ABC-CLIO, LLC
130 Cremona Drive, P.O. Box 1911
Santa Barbara, California 93116-1911

This book is printed on acid-free paper ∞
Manufactured in the United States of America

To my wife Patricia, the only woman I have ever loved.

Contents

Acknowledgments

I would like to thank my wife Patricia and my son Drew for their support and encouragement; as always, it makes all the difference. I would also like to thank Kathryn Scarborough (Eastern Kentucky University), who brought me into this project, and Gary Cordner (Kutztown University) for their advice and counsel on the rigors of editing a homeland security book. There were several students who gave me their input on how this book might be received as a textbook; this was very helpful. In particular, Erika Wunderlich, a Kutztown University honors student, took time from her summer to read through many of the draft chapters to provide me with some additional insight.

INTRODUCTION

Connecting the Dots

Whenever someone mentions the discipline of intelligence, there is always a discussion of connecting the dots, which is part of what an *analyst* does. However, without the *collector*, there will not be any dots. Now consider that the dots are not always what they appear to be, nor are they static. Unlike those diagrams that we all completed as children when we were learning our numbers and letters, these dots move, change shape, change color, conflict with other dots that may change color, and sometimes disappear, then reappear in a different location. As children we were never confronted with two or three dots that had the same number or completed different figures. As the saying goes, "We are not in Kansas any more."

Providing homeland security is about identifying, collecting, interpreting, analyzing, communicating, and using the dots to create intelligence that can be used by strategists, policy makers, and military/security/ police forces and leaders. We know that the post-9/11 years do not represent our first foray into intelligence. Nor did it start in 1947 after World War II with the creation of the Central Intelligence Agency and the Department of Defense. For the United States, it goes as far back as our colonial days and our War of Independence, when we severed our relationship with Great Britain. George Washington was a strong believer in an intelligence program, and the results are obvious. Over the years, there have been highs and lows regarding our intelligence operations. While we have had many successes, we seem to remember those failures. There are two that stand out. The first was on December 7, 1941, in Pearl Harbor, and our most recent and significant failure was on 9/11 at the World Trade Center and Pentagon.

The collection and use of intelligence is as old as man. Some say that if only Adam had been more aware of the clues and connected the long string of dots, he would have seen the enemy slithering through the branches of that foreboding fruit tree. Were there clues? Were there changes in Eve's behavioral patterns that should have been noticed? Was there something different in the way she was looking at him and acting? What about that fig leaf that she was wearing? And what about that apple? The enemy is still out there. His form may change, but the destruction of peaceful society is still on his list. The methods have also changed. But the endgame remains the same. Over 2,000 years ago, Sun Tsu wrote about the art of war, discussing asymmetrical conflict and the use of spies and intelligence. Many of his rules still apply today. Many of the terrorists at home and abroad have read his book, and they have also found it useful.

The history and use of intelligence, whether political, military, or proprietary, is far too vast and complicated for one book. We have brought together a diverse group of authors, who are practitioners and educators, and who discuss intelligence in the United States and abroad, and the role that it plays in maintaining homeland security. The chapters are written for those who are new to the subject, as well for those who are working in the field. The writers take the reader through a short history on intelligence in America and an explanation of the new structure of the intelligence community in the post-9/11 world. The last section of the book will challenge the reader to take a critical view of the new homeland security initiatives. While we study intelligence, we also need to consider counterintelligence. Just as we all seek to identify and connect the dots, those who seek to do us harm will do the same thing. Part of our intelligence process is to be involved in counterintelligence, to lead the enemy in another direction by providing those misdirecting dots. Bear in mind that the misdirection works both ways. A good intelligence program is able to find the gold, to determine what is actually going to happen. A very significant piece of counterintelligence related to the misdirection during World War II was regarding the Allied invasion of Normandy, France. The Allied forces had broken the Axis codes and captured an enigma code machine. By providing misdirection, they ensured that the Axis forces were sent to the wrong locations, and the Allies were able to land and retake Western Europe. It was the connection of the wrong dots that facilitated the end of the war in Europe.

We will also look at how other nations approach homeland security, although most countries refer to this as *national defense*. It is important to note that from 1947 to 2001, there were only minor changes in the structure of the U.S. government and the national intelligence community (IC). After September 11, 2001, there were significant changes both to the structure of the IC and the government. There were also significant additions to the laws and tools that were available for use by government forces in fighting terrorists and others who sought to challenge free nations.

The authors were each asked to contribute a new writing. Each chapter reflects the opinions and findings of the authors and not the organizations with which they may be associated. Each contributor was given a free hand to write from his or her knowledge, experience, and heart regarding homeland security and intelligence. The only changes that were made reflect editorial efforts to maintain the size of each segment; there were no changes to the contributors' perspectives or their conclusions.

This book was written to *inform* the reader about changes in homeland security intelligence; *explain* the new structure of the IC; and let the reader, along with the contributing authors, *question* the effectiveness of the new intelligence processes.

As you will see, not every pass in this game has resulted in a touchdown, but we still have the ball, and we still have the lead. Effective intelligence collection and analysis will provide a reliable footing for homeland security. Freedom will prevail.

PART I

History and the Process of Intelligence

In this part, the authors review the history of intelligence, the structure of the intelligence community, and the fundamentals of intelligence. It concludes with a review of how the intelligence process works, followed by a case study of the events of 9/11.

CHAPTER 1: A HISTORY OF U.S. INTELLIGENCE

While the United States is a relative newcomer to the world of intelligence activities, it has advanced quickly. This has to do largely with the fact that for much of its history, the United States enjoyed relative isolation from the threat of foreign powers and was able to concentrate primarily on westward expansion and internal development. This does not mean that intelligence was completely ignored. During the Revolutionary War, George Washington served as an effective spymaster, and the Civil War saw the use of many forms of intelligence gathering, including aerial reconnaissance. Although the army and navy each had intelligence agencies in place by the end of the 19th century, there seemed to be no need for a national intelligence agency. World War I brought some tentative steps into intelligence and counterintelligence operations, but it was not until World War II that the United States intensified its intelligence efforts. The author notes that it was the onset of the cold war that finally led to the creation of a federal intelligence organization, the Central Intelligence Agency (CIA), along with other agencies over the following decades. Intelligence activities were critical to winning the cold war, and there is no longer any doubt about the need for a national intelligence community (IC) to help guard the nation's security. However, today's IC faces many challenges as it seeks to produce accurate assessments for our nation's leaders and policy makers.

CHAPTER 2: A BRIEF LOOK AT THE INTELLIGENCE COMMUNITY

The author presents a brief look at the IC in a post-9/11 environment. The IC is composed of 17 entities; some are parts of a larger organization, such as the Department of Homeland Security (DHS), and others are independent agencies, like the Drug Enforcement Administration (DEA). The lead organization is the newly created Office of the National Director of Intelligence (ODNI). This overview is not intended to make the reader an expert in the structure and operations of each entity, but to provide the reader with an understanding of exactly what is the IC. This is particularly relevant as one problem the pre-9/11 IC faced was its inability to effectively communicate with other organizations, including those at the federal, state, local, and tribal levels.

CHAPTER 3: INTELLIGENCE FUNDAMENTALS

The author makes the case that too little attention has been given to what the U.S. intelligence needs will be in the next decades. What kind of world will we live in? What kinds of threats and challenges are we likely to face? What can intelligence do to help the United States defend its open society? Given the current world security situation, it is timely to reissue Shakespeare's "warnings and portents of evils imminent" as well as to assist in dealing with them. The author is firm in his belief that intelligence must be dedicated to following evidence regarding foreign threats, whatever the direction, even if this leads to a refutation of accepted doctrines. The IC must collect and analyze data on all parts of the world, with primary emphasis on flash points and potential crisis areas. Advanced, sophisticated intelligence hardware—coupled to the most professional and powerful minds available in the country—is crucial to identifying future threats. The author advises that what is required is penetrating national intelligence and that no degree of conformity will allow such errors as the United States has suffered in the past.

CHAPTER 4: INTELLIGENCE ANALYSIS—A 9/11 CASE STUDY

In this chapter, the author labels the changes to intelligence analysis procedures in the post-9/11 years as revolutionary. Prior to 9/11, the main analytic approach to political-military intelligence, which includes terrorism analyses, was "unaided judgment"; this was based on the reasoned opinions of analysts experienced and well read in the subject. Today, the

IC employs a more formal analytic approach grounded in critical-thinking skills and structured analysis techniques. This makes today's intelligence analysis more science than opinion. This chapter provides a counterfactual case study of the 9/11 terrorism attacks on the United States, which reveals that if today's critical-thinking skills and structured analysis techniques had been used prior to 9/11, those catastrophic attacks would likely have been prevented.

A History of U.S. Intelligence

Gregory Moore

The experience of the United States with an established intelligence organization is relatively brief. Other major powers have had a much longer history of utilizing intelligence as a key component of their national security. Russian intelligence dates back to the time of Ivan the Terrible (1533–1584). English intelligence had its origins during the reign of Elizabeth I (1558–1603), and during the Thirty Years' War, Cardinal Richlieu, who guided French policy (1624–1642), was instrumental in establishing French intelligence. While intelligence played a significant role for the American cause in the Revolutionary War, it was not until the onset of World War II and the cold war that followed that the United States began to establish a formal intelligence community (IC).[1] For more than a century and a half, little attention was paid to intelligence gathering or analysis other than during wartime emergencies. Because the United States faced few legitimate threats from beyond its borders, the need to monitor the activities of other nations seemed to be of little necessity.

Through the beginning of the 20th century, the United States was focused primarily on westward expansion and internal development, and this may have further lessened any interest in establishing a formal intelligence process. Ironically, in his Farewell Address, George Washington, who understood and valued the importance of intelligence, had counseled the nation to avoid becoming involved in Europe's quarrels. Washington's advice became institutionalized as *isolationism,* whereby the United States sought to avoid entanglement in Europe's affairs and conflicts. If, beyond commercial relations, America intended to have as little to do with Europe as possible, then there seemed to be little need for a formal intelligence-gathering organization. As a nation conceived upon principles of liberty and freedom, there was also a sense that America represented a set of higher ethical and moral standards in the world. By refusing to engage in peacetime spying upon other countries, the United States was rejecting the self-serving and immoral practices of European diplomacy.[2] This does not mean, however, that the United States ignored intelligence completely. Intelligence activities that took place in the years leading up to the American Revolution were vital to winning independence and have been part of the government's function ever since.

INTELLIGENCE AND THE REVOLUTIONARY WAR

Passage of the Stamp Act in 1765 galvanized a protest campaign against the new law among the population of England's colonies in North America, especially around Boston and New York. Under the leadership of Samuel Adams and others, the Sons of Liberty became the vehicle through which an effective campaign of propaganda and street violence in opposition to the Stamp Act was carried out. When England repealed the Stamp Act the next year, the leaders of the Sons of Liberty recognized that they had won a significant victory. Parliament's enactment of the Townshend Acts provided the movement with an opportunity to increase its efforts, and over the next few years, the Sons of Liberty emerged as an important political force in the northern colonies. The level of violence and harassment of British officials and Loyalists increased so that Great Britain was eventually forced to station troops in Boston, which had become the center of much of the upheaval. This served only to increase tensions and culminated in the Boston Massacre in March 1770. Although the British soldiers involved in the incident were eventually acquitted, Adams was able to score a significant propaganda victory by creating a public perception of British responsibility for the killings through a series of newspaper articles in the Boston *Gazette*. Anti-British activities continued with increased propaganda and other activities.

In 1774 the Sons of Liberty created an intelligence organization known as the Mechanics. Under the leadership of Paul Revere, the Mechanics were to monitor the activities of British troops in Boston. Ultimately, they were able to develop sources within the administration of General Thomas Gage, the royal governor of Massachusetts, and once the Revolution began, some of the Mechanics would serve as intelligence agents operating behind British lines. The Mechanics were able to learn about British plots against Adams and other radicals and to facilitate the removal of military stores from British and colonial forts and installations. It was their discovery of Gage's intention to seize the stores of gunpowder and weapons the Sons of Liberty had stored in Concord that brought about the battle that launched the American Revolution. Adams and the other leaders of the movement that led to an open break with Great Britain were able to carry out a successful series of covert operations that helped motivate many influential leaders in the colonies that independence was preferable to remaining a part of the British Empire.[3]

The importance of intelligence to the American Revolution was understood by the Second Continental Congress. The Committee of Secret Correspondence was created in November 1775 to gather foreign intelligence. In a letter to one of its correspondents, Arthur Lee, then residing in London, the Committee wrote:

It would be agreeable to Congress to know the disposition of foreign powers towards us, and we hope this object will engage your attention. We need not hint that great circumspection and impenetrable secrecy are necessary.[4]

It was Washington, however, who took intelligence to the next level during the Revolution. Washington not only valued the importance of intelligence usage but was also actively involved in the process of intelligence gathering. He understood the importance of secrecy in order for intelligence operations to have any chance for success. Writing to one of his officers, Washington emphasized:

The necessity of procuring good intelligence is apparent & need not be further urged—All that remains for me to add is that you keep the whole matter as secret as possible. For upon Secrecy, success depends in most Enterprizes of the kind & for want of it, they are generally defeated, no matter how well planned.[5]

Throughout his command of the Continental army, Washington actively recruited agents (who were usually sworn to secrecy), organized and ran spy rings, and was often involved in tradecraft, including the use of codes and disappearing inks. He oversaw "deceit and deception" operations against the British and acted as his own analyst of the raw intelligence that he received. Washington was a demanding spymaster, often cajoling his *intelligencers,* as he referred to them, to find faster and better ways of communicating with him and even instructing them on the finer points of this tradecraft. Washington found it difficult to keep track of the many agents he had in the field. Although he did delegate some oversight to his aides, he was reluctant to do so in part because he had very few professional staff officers. His most successful operation may have been the Culper Ring, which gathered intelligence in British-occupied New York City. Washington's ability to provide the British with false information forestalled a British attack on French forces in Newport, and British dispatches intercepted by his agents were critical to the American victory at Yorktown. A schoolteacher from Boston, James Lovell, was instrumental in decrypting those documents and is now remembered as the "father of American cryptanalysis."[6] Overall, Washington's grasp and use of intelligence was generally superior to that of the British, and his efforts undoubtedly contributed significantly to the success of the American Revolution.

When he became the nation's first president, Washington brought his enthusiasm for intelligence with him. He took personal responsibility for the conduct of foreign intelligence, thereby creating the precedent of having the executive branch of the government oversee the intelligence function. In his first State of the Union message to Congress in January 1790, Washington asked for funding to conduct intelligence operations. Congress eventually authorized $40,000 for intelligence activities when it established the Contingent Fund of Foreign Intercourse (which became known as the Secret Service Fund) in July. By the third year of the fund's existence, the appropriation of funds had grown to a million dollars, which was approximately 12 percent of the government's budget. No funding appropriation for intelligence since then has come close to that percentage. (The 2007 budget of $43.5 billion represents about 1.6% of the federal budget, the same percentage as in 1999.)[7]

Washington used the money for a variety of purposes, not all of which were related to intelligence. The fund was tapped for the payment of bribes to foreign officials and for ransoming American hostages from the Barbary pirates. Although he was required to certify what amounts of money he spent, Congress did not require Washington to reveal the purpose of each expenditure or to whom he was paying the money; this, too, established a precedent. Although Congress challenged the practice in 1846, President Polk refused to release more detailed information, claiming the right to protect sources for purposes of national security. And when the CIA was established in 1949, the director of central intelligence was given similar authority.[8]

AN INTELLIGENCE FAILURE

After Washington, a long list of succeeding presidents tended to pay less attention to intelligence. Jefferson's authorization of the Lewis and Clark expedition might be viewed as an intelligence-gathering mission, since it was not clear exactly how much land the United States had purchased from France or what the geography was like. The War of 1812 saw a number of intelligence failures, including an act of British deception that forestalled an invasion of Canada, and the failure to discover that British forces were moving on the capital until they were only 16 miles away. The secretary of war had been certain the enemy would not attack Washington, and poor military intelligence reflected his view. Fortunately, President Madison and Mrs. Madison were able to flee the capital before British soldiers occupied the White House, which they looted and burned.[9] This debacle, however, did not lead to the creation of a permanent intelligence service, and succeeding presidents to the Civil War seem to have given intelligence little thought, other than to send individuals on secret missions from time to time. During the Mexican War, President Polk authorized funding for the Mexican Spy Company, which was composed of a Mexican outlaw gang. Paid $16,000 for their services, the gang provided intelligence from behind enemy lines about Mexican defenses.[10]

INTELLIGENCE REVIVAL AND THE CIVIL WAR

The Civil War restored intelligence activities to prominence. Although both sides built intelligence services, the North relied on a more decentralized intelligence-gathering process as each Union general tended to consider intelligence gathering a task for their individual commands. Allen Pinkerton, the self-styled "Chief of the United States Secret Service" actually worked just for General George B. McClellan, commander of the Army of the Potomac. Pinkerton collected intelligence only for McClellan and not the Union. Similarly, Lafayette C. Baker carried out counterintelligence operations and oversaw security for the commander in chief of the U.S. Army, General Winfield Scott. The level of decentralization was so great that President Abraham Lincoln hired his own agent and received intelligence reports from him.[11]

The Confederates focused much of their intelligence activities on Washington, D.C. The capital was filled with Southern sympathizers, and recruiting agents was not difficult. A branch of the Confederate Signal Corps, the Secret Service Bureau oversaw the movement of Confederate agents in and out of the North and forwarded messages from the Confederate government in Richmond to contacts in Europe and Canada. Confederate forces also relied heavily on scouts, usually cavalry units that rode behind enemy lines in uniform on reconnaissance missions. If these units were captured by Northern forces, they were treated as soldiers and prisoners of war. Other riders carrying out similar missions that were not in uniform, such as Coleman's Scouts, were treated as spies when they were captured by Union forces.[12]

Both sides were greatly interested in what today is called open source intelligence (OSINT). The Confederate Secret Service Bureau was charged with obtaining Northern newspapers. The Union was equally eager to obtain Southern papers. It is possible that the South may have benefited more from this source of intelligence as there were more newspapers being published in the North than in the South. With far fewer paper mills than the North had, the South was constantly short of newsprint. President Abraham Lincoln followed Northern intelligence activities avidly and would complain when he felt Southern press reports were not arriving swiftly enough. Ironically, each side complained that its own press was providing intelligence to the other side.[13]

While both sides utilized traditional elements of intelligence—espionage, covert activities, and cryptology—new methods appeared. Aerial reconnaissance made its debut on June 18, 1861, when Thaddeus S.

Lowe demonstrated the potential of balloons for this purpose. Lowe sent a telegraph directly from his aerial platform to President Lincoln, thereby becoming the first to send an electrical message from an aircraft to the ground; he was the first to communicate with the president of the United States in this manner and the first to transmit reconnaissance data in real time from an aircraft. Lincoln was sufficiently impressed and supported the formation of the U.S. Army Balloon Corps two months later. Although balloon flights occurred frequently over the next two years, the cumbersome process of moving the equipment necessary to support the reconnaissance flights eventually led to the disbanding of the Balloon Corps in 1863. Nonetheless, the Balloon Corps did provide some intelligence of value, especially when a large concentration of Confederate troops were identified preparing to attack at Fair Oaks, Virginia. The Confederates also made some attempts at aerial reconnaissance, but a lack of resources for manufacturing and supporting balloons led them to abandon the attempt. However, the Confederacy did learn to camouflage their camps in order to prevent Union balloonists from obtaining accurate observations of their strength.[14]

The telegraph also contributed to advances in intelligence gathering. The North used the telegraph to effectively link military commands with each other and with the War Department in Washington. The Confederacy likewise relied heavily on the telegraph for field communications and as a link to Richmond. Both sides routinely encrypted their messages and worked hard to crack the other's encryption systems. Code breaking was an intelligence activity that fascinated Lincoln, and he could often be found in the War Department's telegraph office observing the work of its cryptanalysts. Union code breakers scored an impressive success when they deciphered messages that revealed the existence of a Confederate counterfeiting ring in New York City. Wiretapping of telegraph lines was done by both sides, although capturing enemy telegraph stations usually proved to be a more reliable for intercepting messages. In addition, false messages could be transmitted from a captured station. Each side also utilized cipher disks for encoding telegrams.[15]

Possibly the most efficient intelligence agency established during the Civil War was the Bureau of Military Intelligence, formed by the new commander of the Army of the Potomac, General Joseph "Fightin' Joe" Hooker in January 1863. Hooker ordered his deputy provost marshal, Colonel George H. Sharpe, to organize an intelligence unit. Sharpe performed admirably, producing substantive reports from information gathered from a variety of sources, including agents, prisoners of war, Southern newspapers, and even documents taken from corpses on battlefields. Hooker, however, failed to make effective use of the intelligence he received, and this contributed to his defeat at Chancellorsville. His replacement, General George G. Meade, made better use of Sharpe's intelligence reports, as was evident at Gettysburg. In March 1864, Sharpe was made the intelligence officer for General Ulysses S. Grant, the new commander in chief of the Union armies. From this point on, Sharpe provided intelligence to both Grant and Meade. Operating out of Grant's headquarters at Point City, Virginia, Sharpe's operation provided Grant with intelligence that played an important role in the success of the Wilderness campaign. Sharpe's network of agents extended into the Confederate capital at Richmond, and he gave them much of the credit for the success of the bureau. Grant claimed that Sharpe's work allowed him to keep track of every Confederate move. The first really professional intelligence agency in America, the Bureau of Military Intelligence was disbanded shortly after the Civil War ended.

MILITARY INTELLIGENCE BRANCHES

Up to this point, the primary focus of intelligence activities had been to support military operations in wartime. The intelligence organizations that were established up through the Civil War were not meant to be permanent ones and were quickly disbanded once the conflict for which they were needed came to an end. The 1880s saw the creation of the first permanent intelligence organization. Founded in March 1882 within the Department of the Navy, the Office of Naval Intelligence (ONI) was tasked to gather intelligence on foreign navies during both war and peace. The impetus for the formation of the ONI was the War of the Pacific (1879–1882), fought by Chile against Peru and Bolivia. While introducing modern naval warfare to the Western Hemisphere, the conflict led to the disconcerting discovery that the Chilean navy was larger than that of the United States. This discovery, and concern about potential European meddling in Latin America and the Caribbean, led Congress to authorize the modernization of the American fleet. As part of this process, the ONI was organized and given an initial staff of four officers. Three years later, the establishment of the Military Intelligence Division (MID) authorized the Army to obtain foreign and domestic intelligence for both itself and the Department of War.[16]

Theodore Roosevelt recognized the value of ONI during his tenure as assistant secretary of the navy and, later, as president. Roosevelt believed ONI could serve as a valuable tool in promoting his vision of an American fleet that would not only be the dominant force in the Western Hemisphere, but would be the means by which the United States could project its growing power throughout the world. As president, Roosevelt utilized covert action to help bring about Panamanian independence from Columbia in order to build the Panama Canal; he also politicized ONI assessments to justify American naval expansion.[17]

Intelligence activities were primarily focused on increasing the nation's domestic intelligence capabilities. Charles Bonaparte, who served as Theodore Roosevelt's attorney general from 1905 to 1908, wanted to establish a group of special agents to investigate federal crimes. Up to this point, the Department of Justice (DOJ) had relied on hiring private detectives or borrowing Secret Service agents to conduct investigations. This frustrated Bonaparte, who had no real control over investigations under his jurisdiction; Secret Service agents reported to the chief of the Secret Service instead of the attorney general. When Congress enacted a law in May 1908 prohibiting the DOJ from borrowing operatives from the Secret Service, Bonaparte decided to build his own investigative department. With Roosevelt's support, the attorney general appointed 34 special agents of the DOJ and ordered them to report to the department's chief examiner. Before leaving the White House in March 1909, Roosevelt recommended that the agents become a permanent part of the DOJ. On March 16, 1909, the new attorney general, George Wickersham, named the unit the Bureau of Investigation (BOI).[18]

INTELLIGENCE AND WORLD WAR I

The United States was completely unprepared for the intelligence challenges that it would face in World War I. President Wilson did not seem to have realized that the nations of Europe all possessed secret services and routinely spied on one another. As a proponent of open diplomacy and transparency in foreign relations, Wilson could hardly conceive of an American intelligence service like those in England or Germany.[19] Once the war was underway, Germany initiated a massive effort of espionage, intrigue, and sabotage against the United States. Lacking a true national intelligence service, the nation's ability to respond to the clandestine activities of German agents was severely limited. Further hampering American countermeasures was the lack of any federal laws prohibiting espionage or sabotage during peacetime. Any foreign-directed conspiracy that violated the laws of multiple jurisdictions had to be investigated by federal, state, and local operatives because no federal agency possessed either the authority or resources to conduct an investigation on its own. Coordinating these efforts was both time consuming and inefficient. Attorney General Thomas Watt Gregory believed the BOI should investigate only those issues covered directly by federal law. However, as the number of incidents of sabotage rose, Gregory began to lobby for stronger laws to combat saboteurs and spies.[20] The Secret Service felt less constrained by the lack of specific federal laws regarding foreign espionage and covert activities against the United States. Treasury Secretary William G. McAdoo interpreted the Secret Service's investigatory powers more broadly than the attorney general did and, with the support of President Wilson, authorized increased surveillance of German diplomatic personnel. As the war continued, a growing bureaucratic rivalry over counterintelligence activities developed between the Secret Service and the BOI. The interagency conflict would continue until after the United States entered the war and was not fully resolved until 1918.

The BOI, which soon become the Federal Bureau of Investigation, was given the lead role in dealing with intelligence threats within the nation's borders.[21]

Covert activities carried out by Germany's agents proved significant in alienating American public opinion against Germany. Numerous bombings of cargo ships, munitions factories, and warehouses occurred in 1916. The most spectacular of these acts of sabotage was the July explosion at Black Tom Island in New York Harbor. The explosion was the result of a fire that began on a pier where over a thousand tons of ammunition scheduled for shipment to Great Britain, France, and Russia was stored. The fire set off an explosion so powerful that it awoke people in Maryland and shattered windows in Times Square. Over a two-year period, more than 40 acts of sabotage were carried out against American factories and warehouses, and some four dozen cargo ships were sunk. While these covert terrorist actions had no real impact on the Allied war effort or the American economy, they contributed to a growing anti-German sentiment among the American people as did the sinking of American ships by German U-boats.[22]

Great Britain's intelligence activities may have been far more important in bringing the United States into the war on the side of the Allied forces. The American government was poorly informed about German covert operations in the United States; the British were far better informed. In 1915, the British shared captured German documents that detailed elements of that nation's covert offensive against the United States. While returning to Berlin for consultations, Captain Fritz von Rintelen, who had run a German sabotage operation while posing illegally as a Swiss national, was apprehended by the British navy. Intelligence gathered from Rintelen's interrogation and passed on to American authorities revealed that German military attachés had also been involved in such operations. This led Wilson to order their expulsion. The British were able to search the luggage of one of the attachés, Fritz von Papen, and discovered documents that further confirmed his involvement in covert operations against the United States.[23]

Perhaps the most important contribution British intelligence made in bringing the United States into the war was the interception of a German cable in January 1917. When the coded telegram was decrypted, it revealed an offer to Mexico from the German foreign minister, Arthur Zimmerman, to declare war on the United States. If Germany won the war, Mexico would be rewarded with the return of Texas, California, Arizona, and New Mexico. The decoded cable was passed on to the president who, as the British expected, was infuriated. When made public in March, the telegram inflamed American public opinion against Germany. Wilson asked Congress to declare war on April 2. British intelligence undoubtedly provided Wilson with the final push he needed to bring the United States into the war against Germany.[24]

SIGINT

Shortly after American entry into the war, the first signals intelligence (SIGINT) agency was formed. Called MI8, the agency was established within the army and was given the task of decrypting military communications as well as creating codes for the military. In addition, the number of personnel in the ONI and the MID were substantially increased. The MID was also made one of the divisions within the War Department's General Staff. Meanwhile, the BOI concentrated on domestic counterintelligence. Some consideration was given to the establishment of a centralized intelligence organization, but at the end of the war, intelligence resources were substantially reduced or redirected.[25]

MI8 was transferred to the State Department and was called the Black Chamber. It now directed its activities to deciphering foreign diplomatic codes. While there were successes, it was not able to decrypt the codes of the major European powers after 1921. Ultimately, the role of the Black Chamber was reduced under President Calvin Coolidge and was dismantled by direction of President Herbert Hoover.[26]

FEDERAL BUREAU OF INVESTIGATION

The BOI saw its mission and workforce expand over the next two decades. J. Edgar Hoover was named its director in 1924. In 1935, the BOI became the Federal Bureau of Investigation (FBI) with a significantly broadened mission. The FBI directed its efforts mostly against organized crime in the 1920s and early 1930s; but as the Great Depression spawned increasing concerns about radicalism, the bureau began to investigate potential threats to American security from Fascist and Communist organizations. After the outbreak of war in Europe in 1939, the FBI became responsible for dealing with espionage, sabotage, and acts of subversion. A major spy ring, the Frederick Duquesne ring, was broken up prior to America's entry into the war, and in 1942, the FBI captured eight German saboteurs who had been brought to the United States by submarine.[27]

The FBI also undertook the gathering of foreign intelligence. Beginning in 1940, a select group of agents were organized into the Special Intelligence Service (SIS). Assisted by FBI legal attachés, these agents were assigned to gather intelligence on Axis activities in Latin America and to disrupt their propaganda networks. There were several hundred thousand Germans and numerous Japanese in South America, and many provided cover for or supported pro-Axis activity in the Western Hemisphere. By 1944, the SIS had rendered such actions impractical or impossible.[28]

INTELLIGENCE COORDINATION

During the late 1930s President Franklin D. Roosevelt (FDR) placed a great deal of reliance on information gathered by friends who were traveling abroad. Japanese aggression continued in Asia, and war clouds gathered over Europe. FDR was especially interested in assessments regarding the possible actions on the part of other national leaders. FDR sent his friend William J. Donovan, a New York attorney and veteran of World War I, on missions of inquiry to Britain and Italy in 1940 and 1941 to assess British stability and to gather information about Mussolini. Following these trips, Donovan began to lobby for the creation of a centralized civilian intelligence-gathering agency. In July 1941 Roosevelt made Donovan the nation's first coordinator of intelligence and instructed him to gather and analyze any information that might bear on national security. Donovan was forbidden from interfering with the president's military and naval advisers and was not allowed to get involved with the FBI's efforts in South America. Drawing heavily on the British model, Donovan created a staff to collect and analyze any information that might relate to national security. He also created a special board to review and test the conclusions of his staff, thereby establishing the principle of centralized analysis.[29]

WORLD WAR II

The ability of the Japanese to achieve a strategic surprise at Pearl Harbor on December 7, 1941, was largely the result of what has been called "a classic intelligence failure."[30] Intelligence procedures were both poorly carried out, and there was a lack of coordination among existing agencies, the army and navy in particular, so that critical information was not presented to critical decision makers in a timely manner. American analysts got caught up in mirror imaging, which led them to misconstrue Japanese actions by considering them from an American cultural perspective, and grossly underestimating their capabilities.[31] World War II brought about a multifaceted intelligence effort. Under the aegis of the newly created Joint Chiefs of Staff, William Donovan's unit was reorganized as the Office of Strategic Services (OSS) in June 1942. The OSS was tasked to collect and analyze information as required by the Joint Chiefs, and it also carried out clandestine operations against the Axis powers. The OSS was able to supply American policy makers with critical intelligence estimates, and it often provided direct assistance to various military efforts. The Joint Chiefs were never fully confident in the capabilities of the OSS or the value of the agency, and they refused to allow the OSS full jurisdiction over foreign intelligence activities. The FBI jealously guarded its intelligence responsibilities in Latin America, and the military services likewise protected their respective areas of responsibility. However, service in the OSS provided important training for an entire generation of intelligence operatives and analysts.[32]

The intelligence capabilities of the military services were significantly increased. Intelligence operations in the army came under the supervision of the MID. Its operations unit, the Military Intelligence Service (MIS), was organized in 1942. MIS conducted collections activities on a global scale, including signals interception and photoreconnaissance, and provided intelligence analysis to the United States and Allied commands. MIS intelligence agents also worked with units in the field. Army signals intelligence broke the codes used by the Japanese imperial army, producing intelligence that may have helped shorten the war in the Pacific theater. The ability of naval cryptographers to break the Japanese navy's codes contributed significantly to American victories at the battles of the Coral Sea and Midway. In the European theater, Army cryptanalysts worked with the British to decode German military communications. The intelligence produced by this effort, known by the code name ULTRA, was of considerable importance and hastened Germany's defeat. The U.S. Marines created and utilized the Navajo Code Talker Program with notable success, particularly at the battle of Iwo Jima.[33] And SIGINT may have contributed to the decision to use the atomic bomb on Japan in an effort to hasten the end of the war in the Pacific.[34]

By the end of the war, the nation's intelligence establishment had developed rather haphazardly, and President Truman understood that reforms were necessary. However, he did not have a clear idea about how best to create a peacetime intelligence organization. Donovan argued for the creation of a postwar civilian intelligence agency that would operate independently of the military and report directly to the president. Opponents of this plan favored retaining control of intelligence by the military. Following recommendations submitted by his budget director, President Truman disbanded the OSS in September 1945 and assigned its functions to the War Department and Department of State. The clandestine operations component of the OSS now shifted to the War Department, while the State Department assumed the research and analysis functions. At about this time, a study commissioned by the secretary of the Navy was released. This document recommended the creation of a national security council and central intelligence agency to coordinate the nation's intelligence requirements. Although President Truman did not act immediately on these recommendations, he did create the Central Intelligence Group (CIG) to oversee leftover OSS activities and to screen his incoming cable traffic.[35]

CENTRALIZED INTELLIGENCE

In January 1946, Truman instructed the CIG to begin evaluating intelligence from all parts of the government and to take over any remaining OSS espionage and counterintelligence activities. This directive was soon followed by an effort to unify the armed forces, another goal of the president. There was a proposal for a central intelligence agency as part of the unification process, and it had the support of the secretaries of war and the navy. However, CIG did not have full control over intelligence analysis or clandestine activities. Other cabinet departments and the military were not willing to subordinate their own collection and analysis capabilities to the new organization.[36] The FBI preferred a system whereby the armed services would be responsible for military intelligence, while the bureau would have jurisdiction over civilian activities.[37]

Truman's military reunification bill failed in 1946, and he submitted a new one early in 1947. The midterm elections of the year before had given the Republican Party control of Congress, and the limited provisions he had included in regard to intelligence quickly caught the eye of the new Congressional leadership. This section of the bill came under close scrutiny, and Congress considered the proposal for a Central Intelligence Agency (CIA) carefully. It soon became clear that Congress wanted the proposed CIA to provide the best possible foreign intelligence.[38]

The National Security Act of 1947 established the CIA as part of a national security framework. A director of central intelligence (DCI) was placed at the head of the CIA, and the agency's independence was guaranteed by congressional fiat. The agency was given access to departmental files and was kept apart from the policy-making functions of the federal government in order to assure the best correlation and evaluation of intelligence related to the nation's security. This act also created the National Security Council (NSC) to supervise the CIA. The CIA was authorized to conduct analysis and clandestine activities, but in addition to having no policy-making role, it was also denied any law enforcement powers. The DCI could be either a civilian or a military officer, and his appointment required Senate confirmation. To further assure the agency's independence, any time a military officer was selected to serve as DCI, he would be outside the chain of command of his branch of the service.[39]

Implementation of the intelligence provisions of the National Security Act continued through the Truman administration. Fifteen NSC Intelligence Directives (NSCID) established the parameters under which the CIA could operate and produce intelligence. In general, DCIs were confronted with the fact that they could coordinate intelligence but were prohibited from controlling it. This led DCIs to err on the side of loose oversight of common IC issues. The emphasis on coordination over control also kept the CIA from being able to integrate U.S. intelligence as the president and Congress had planned. The DCI could not serve as a manager of the IC, for example, and other elements of the federal government could conduct clandestine operations. Nor could the CIA obtain consensus from the rest of the IC on analytical issues that might come under dispute.[40] Later presidents would seek to improve the functioning of the IC by issuing directives calling for increased control on the part of DCIs over common IC issues and problems.[41]

The onset of the cold war created increasing concerns about threats to national security from within. Already charged with investigating suspected acts of sabotage and espionage during World War II, the FBI would turn its attention to the threat posed by the Soviet Union after the war's end. Fears of communist subversion led to an increased role for the FBI in terms of protecting the nation's security from suspected spies and saboteurs. The FBI was given authority to conduct background checks on prospective and current federal employees, and the Atomic Energy Act of 1946 gave the FBI responsibility for determining the loyalty of individuals who had access to atomic secrets. Both Presidents Truman and Eisenhower expanded this authority to permit the FBI to investigate allegations of disloyalty among federal workers. The FBI conducted the investigations; the departments requesting the inquiry made the final determination regarding the employee's loyalty.[42]

Concerns about Soviet espionage emerged during World War II, when the army's SIS began intercepting encrypted Soviet diplomatic communications. Aware that this traffic dealt with matters of espionage as well as diplomacy, the SIS began working to decrypt and translate these messages. Code-named VENONA, the project eventually revealed Soviet efforts to obtain information on the Manhattan Project and the atomic bomb, along with hundreds of communications between KGB residencies in the United States and Mexico with Moscow.[43]

KOREAN WAR

The outbreak of war in Korea in 1950 caught the United States by surprise once again. As with the intelligence failure in regard to the attack on Pearl Harbor, a lack of resources and administrative issues led to a failure to recognize the impending North Korean invasion. This problem was especially prevalent with SIGINT and contributed to the formation of the National Security Agency (NSA) in 1952. Responsibility for SIGINT had become divided between the branches of the military and the Armed Forces Security Agency (AFSA), which had been created in 1949. A decline in the quality of SIGINT during the Korean War led to a review of the existing establishment and resulted in a recommendation to unify SIGINT responsibilities in one agency. Acting on this proposal, Truman established the NSA by means of a classified memorandum. Placed within the Department of Defense, NSA assumed responsibility for the nation's SIGINT requirements.[44]

The 1950s also saw significant advances in image intelligence (IMINT). President Eisenhower had come to appreciate the value of IMINT during World War II, and he eagerly approved a project to build high-altitude reconnaissance aircraft in late 1954. Insisting on complete secrecy, Eisenhower combined the resources of the CIA and the air force to produce an aircraft (U-2) that would be difficult to detect as it flew reconnaissance

; over the Soviet Union. The success of these tests convinced
ver that the U-2 could carry out photoreconnaissance missions
ue Soviet Union. U-2 flights provided the Eisenhower administration with valuable IMINT as it dealt with the Suez crisis in the fall of 1956
and proved conclusively that the United States enjoyed a clear advantage
over the Soviets in both the development and deployment of strategic
weapons. However, in August 1960, the successful test of the photoreconnaissance capabilities of Discoverer 14 led to relying upon satellites
as the primary source of IMINT for the IC. To oversee satellite reconnaissance for the entire IC, Eisenhower approved the creation of the National
Reconnaissance Office. Although U-2 flights over the Soviet Union came
to an end, the aircraft continued to be used for other overflight missions
and played a critical role in providing images of Soviet missiles in Cuba
during the missile crisis of October 1962. The current version of the U-2
continues to fly occasional missions today.[45]

POST WORLD WAR II: COVERT OPERATIONS

Eisenhower also supported covert activities, although these had little
success. Ultimately, his administration would authorize about 170 covert
actions around the world, often in countries where operatives had little
knowledge of the language or customs. Eisenhower believed that such
operations were a viable foreign policy option in place of far riskier military interventions. While the president personally authorized each covert
operation, he was careful to make certain that no materials that might link
his decisions to the operations could be found in the Oval Office in the
event that something went wrong. Eisenhower's enthusiasm for covert
operations may have been fueled by the ability of the CIA to overthrow
governments. Eisenhower also sought to come up with a workable plan to
either assassinate or overthrow Cuban prime minister Fidel Castro. Eventually, a plan was developed to have Cuban exiles invade their former homeland in an effort to bring Castro down. This operation was not launched
until 1961, after John F. Kennedy had become president. The Bay of Pigs
failure led to the resignations of several top CIA leaders, including the DCI,
and clearly demonstrated the limitation of paramilitary operations.[46]

Shortly thereafter, President Kennedy found himself facing a crisis over
Berlin. In June of 1961, Kennedy met with Khrushchev in Vienna and
was shocked when the Soviet premier demanded an end to the American, British, and French presence in Berlin. The Soviets then erected a wall
between East and West Berlin in August. Throughout the crisis, Kennedy
stood firm on America's presence in Berlin. There were critical insights
about the Soviets that were provided by a Soviet penetration agent, Colonel Oleg Penkovsky, who was deputy head of the GRU, Soviet military
intelligence; he was a vital source of information about the USSR's military capabilities and Khrushchev's policies. Run jointly by the British and

the CIA, Penkovsky counseled Kennedy to take a tough stance, and, ultimately, Khrushchev backed down.[47]

President Kennedy authorized 550 covert operations ranging from providing secret funds to pro-American politicians to paramilitary operations. The president was especially anxious to avenge the failure at the Bay of Pigs and sought to find some way to remove or bring down Castro. He also instituted some reforms of the IC. The Defense Intelligence Agency (DIA) was created in 1961 to provide a greater level of oversight and co-ordination of the respective military intelligence departments. Kennedy also conducted regular meetings with the President's Foreign Intelligence Advisory Board (PFIAB). This group of consultants reviewed a wide range of intelligence issues and offered numerous recommendations for action, most of which Kennedy accepted.[48]

Although the resolution of the Cuban missile crisis may have been the greatest foreign policy success of the Kennedy administration, the United States was initially caught by surprise when Soviet medium-range ballistic missiles were discovered in Cuba. With the exception of DCI John McCone, the consensus of the IC was that the Soviet Union would not try something as reckless as placing missiles capable of delivering nuclear warheads in Cuba. However, the missile sites were discovered before they could be completed, which gave Kennedy the opportunity to resolve the situation without having to resort to using military force. Moreover, effective coordination between the intelligence agencies enabled them to provide Kennedy with good assessments of Soviet military capabilities, thereby enhancing his ability to manage the situation and come to the decisions necessary to defuse the crisis before it escalated further. In addition, the reputation of the IC received a needed boost after the Bay of Pigs episode.[49]

Lyndon B. Johnson became president following the assassination of President Kennedy. The primary foreign policy and intelligence problem that Johnson would face was Vietnam. Ignoring pessimistic CIA assessments of the conflict between North and South Vietnam, Johnson chose to believe that increasing American military pressure on the communist regime in North Vietnam would lead the communist government there to conclude that continuing the struggle would not be worth the effort. Confused and misleading reports in August 1964 regarding alleged North Vietnamese attacks on American ships enabled Johnson to persuade Congress to pass the Tonkin Gulf Resolution, which gave the president authority to escalate the conflict in Vietnam. Using raw SIGINT intelligence from the NSA, Secretary of Defense Robert McNamara convinced the president that the dubious reports claiming that the American destroyers had been attacked by North Vietnamese patrol boats were genuine.[50] The escalation of the war impacted the IC. Analysts, in particular, were concerned that their assessments were being politicized in order to support the administration's war policies.[51] In addition, disagreements arose between military and civilian intelligence analysts regarding such issues as the number of enemy troops in the field.[52]

DOMESTIC SPYING

Far more problematic was the fact that the CIA was called upon to spy on American citizens. The antiwar protests that flared up as the Vietnam War escalated led President Johnson to believe that the peace movement was being directed by the Soviet Union. The FBI dealt with the antiwar New Left as it had with Communists in the 1950s. Using its Counterintelligence Program (COINTELPRO) and traditional investigative techniques, agents worked to disrupt perceived domestic terrorist groups. Investigations of individuals and organizations that threatened violent activities were carried out, and in some cases, FBI agents infiltrated such groups and attempted to disrupt their activities even when little or no evidence existed that they were involved in unlawful activities. The FBI's efforts were revealed to the public and Congress following the burglary of an FBI office in Pennsylvania by radicals. As a result, the FBI came under fire for violations of First Amendment rights. Much more serious was the seven-year long domestic surveillance operation undertaken by the CIA. Authorized by President Johnson and code-named Operation Chaos, the program sent CIA operatives to infiltrate peace groups in the United States and Europe. An extensive computerized index of some 300,000 individuals and groups was assembled, and detailed dossiers were compiled on more than 7,000 citizens. Even the NSA was directed to eavesdrop on American citizens. Despite its best efforts, the CIA was unable to establish a link between the peace movement and Moscow.[53]

There were positives, however. Collection technology was revolutionized in this period. The first successful photoreconnaissance satellite, code-named Corona, was launched into orbit in 1960 and detected the first operational Soviet intercontinental ballistic missiles. The large number of images generated by Corona led to the National Photo Interpretation Center (NPIC), the forerunner of today's National Geospatial Intelligence Agency. The next generation of photoreconnaissance aircraft, the high-altitude, high-speed SR-71, became operational in 1962 and provided significant IMINT regarding the presence of surface-to-air missiles in North Vietnam. In a Special National Intelligence Estimate (SNIE) in May 1967, the CIA correctly predicted that war was imminent between Israel and Egypt and that the Israelis would win in a week to 10 days. In fact, Israel defeated Egypt in just 6 days.[54]

Johnson's successor, Richard M. Nixon, had a fundamental distrust of the CIA based on his belief that the agency was filled with liberals who had opposed him politically. Nixon even clung to the absurd belief that the CIA had somehow conspired to cost him the 1960 presidential election. The inability of the CIA to uncover proof that the antiwar movement was part of a Communist conspiracy only reinforced his views. Nixon continued to have the CIA violate its charter by spying on the leaders of the New Left. Both the NSA and FBI continued to monitor the antiwar movement as well. Despite his misgivings about the IC, Nixon understood that the SIGINT and IMINT capabilities the United States possessed would be important in helping to reduce strategic armaments. Both the Strategic Arms Limitation Treaty (SALT I) and the antiballistic missile (ABM) accord negotiated with the Soviet Union provided for the use of national technical means and verification procedures to assure compliance with the terms of the treaties.[55] Like his three predecessors, Nixon was a firm believer in covert activities. Nixon attempted to give the DCI greater control of the IC. The deputy director of the Office of Management and Budget (OMB), James Schlesinger, was tasked to determine how to improve the efficiency and effectiveness of the IC. Schlesinger determined that the IC was too fragmented and recommended a reform of the management structure. He called for strengthening the DCI's role so that costs could be controlled and the quality of intelligence products could be improved. Nixon followed through on Schlesinger's report and issued orders for more efficient use of resources and improvements in intelligence analysis. He made the DCI responsible for carrying out the directive and created a trio of committees and boards to assist him in doing so.[56]

The revelations of the Watergate affair kept these instructions from having much effect. Following Nixon's resignation in August 1974, reports began to appear in the media alleging that the CIA had been spying on American citizens. This led to passage of the Hughes-Ryan amendment to the Foreign Assistance Act in December 1974. The amendment required that the president report on any covert CIA activities in foreign countries to the relevant congressional committees.[57]

Under President Gerald Ford, the Rockefeller Commission was created to look into allegations that CIA employees had taken part in illegal activities within the United States. Chaired by Vice President Nelson Rockefeller, the commission determined that the CIA engaged in mail-opening activities and kept files on 300,000 citizens and domestic organizations, and that President Nixon had tried to use agency records for political purposes. The commission called for a joint congressional oversight committee, a stronger executive oversight procedure, and a maximum service time of 10 years for the DCI.[58]

Congressional committees also investigated the CIA's actions; these included the Church Committee, chaired by Senator Frank Church, and the Pike Committee, presided over by Congressman Otis Pike. In 1976 the Church Committee's six-volume report identified alleged CIA misconduct and made several recommendations. These included separating the DCI from the CIA; enhancing DCI authority over the IC; the creation of national statutory charters for the CIA, DIA, and NSA; publication of the intelligence budget; and the halting of clandestine support for regimes that disregarded human rights.[59] The Pike Committee's report was voted down by Congress and never officially issued.

Even before the Church and Pike committees completed their investigations, President Ford had begun to issue directives implementing most of the Rockefeller Commission's recommendations. Restrictions on the CIA's domestic activities were put in place, assassinations were prohibited, and executive oversight was increased. Congress joined in the oversight process, establishing the Senate Committee on Intelligence in May 1976, and the House followed suit in 1977 with the creation of the Permanent Select Committee on Intelligence. Congress continued to consider reforming the IC throughout the rest of the decade.

The Foreign Intelligence Surveillance Act (FISA) of 1978 established a special procedure for obtaining court orders authorizing electronic surveillance for purposes of intelligence gathering. The Intelligence Oversight Act of 1980 required the heads of the respective intelligence agencies to keep the Congressional oversight committees fully informed of any significant intelligence activities. Meanwhile, DCI Stansfield Turner established the National Intelligence Council (NIC) to oversee the production and quality of national intelligence estimates.[60] The exposure of misconduct on the part of the IC, the resulting investigations, and reform acts all combined to undermine the public's faith in government, especially the IC. From this point on, the nation's intelligence agencies would have to operate under a greater level of scrutiny than they had in the past.[61]

In 1973, FBI Director Clarence Kelly's emphasis on "quality over quantity" led to making foreign counterintelligence the FBI's top priority, followed by organized crime and white-collar crime.[62] Attorney General Edward Levi established specific doctrines for the collection of intelligence. Levi's guidelines for counterintelligence operations and domestic security investigations took effect in 1976.

In 1979, during the administration of President Jimmy Carter, the IC failed to recognize indications that trouble was brewing in Iran and Afghanistan. In the case of Iran, policy restrictions on intelligence gathering that had been implemented by previous administrations may have caused the CIA to miss the signs that the shah's reign in Iran was in jeopardy. Public demonstrations against the shah had begun in 1978, but there was no sense that they could mark the beginning of the process of his downfall. As the crisis steadily worsened, the president became certain that an intelligence failure had taken place. However, because intelligence activities in Iran had been limited in order not to offend the shah, the CIA's efforts there were hamstrung. When the shah was ousted in early 1979, the CIA would become the scapegoat for the failure to recognize the threat that Ayatollah Khomeini had posed to the regime. Perhaps more importantly, the overthrow of the Iranian monarchy cost the United States an important NSA listening post for the monitoring of Soviet missile development and testing.[63]

Indications that the Soviet Union intended to invade Afghanistan in late 1979 were also missed. Despite a rebellion against the Soviet-controlled Afghani government, the CIA rejected the premise that the Soviets might invade in order to put down the uprising. The agency monitored the steady buildup of Soviet forces on the Afghanistan border throughout 1979 and steadfastly concluded that the massing of troops there was not the precursor of a planned invasion. With some 40 million Muslims living in the central Asian republics of the Soviet Union, the spread of Islamic fundamentalism seriously worried Moscow. However, the CIA apparently did not understand these concerns and the conviction among Soviet leaders that control of Afghanistan had to be maintained at all costs. The CIA understood Soviet capabilities but lacked the imagination to deduce Soviet intentions in regard to Afghanistan. A few days before the invasion began, CIA analysts remained convinced that the Soviet Union had no intention of attacking Afghanistan. However, once the invasion was underway, President Carter determined to make the Soviets pay heavily. He swiftly authorized providing the Afghan Mujahideen resistance with Soviet-made arms and brokered a deal with Egyptian president Anwar Sadat to help smuggle them into Afghanistan.[64]

During the presidential campaign of 1980, Ronald Reagan promised that he would revitalize and "unleash" the CIA. As president, Reagan determined to follow through on his pledge. Reagan appointed William Casey, an OSS veteran, as his new DCI and upgraded the position to cabinet rank. This mandate from the president enabled Casey to secure higher budgets for intelligence and to initiate a program of personnel growth across the IC. Congress likewise enacted legislation to enhance and improve intelligence production. New laws provided protection for classified information used in criminal trials, made it illegal to reveal the names of covert intelligence officers, and exempted certain CIA files from disclosure under FISA. The Goldwater-Nichols Act of 1986 designated the DIA and Defense Mapping Agency (DMA) as combat support agencies and required the president to submit an annual report to Congress on national security strategy and an assessment of the IC's ability to carry out the strategy.[65]

Early in President Reagan's second term, a series of spy cases rocked the IC and led to new recommendations for overcoming deficiencies in the nation's counterintelligence and security policies. Various reviews and investigations resulted in a number of reports calling for a variety of improvements. However, nothing substantial had been done by the time Reagan left office and the fall of the Berlin Wall. Obvious changes within the Soviet Union reduced any sense of urgency regarding the dangers of espionage against the United States.[66]

Far more serious was the Iran-Contra affair. A number of Americans had been taken hostage in Lebanon in 1984, and the inability of the CIA to locate them and mount a rescue operation frustrated Reagan. Through an intermediary, the Iranian government indicated it could help arrange for the release of the hostages in exchange for American armaments. Reagan accepted the offer despite the fact that doing so violated his administration's policy of not negotiating with terrorists and not providing arms for Iran, which was involved in a war with Iraq. The Iranians received several shipments of missiles for which they paid inflated prices. The profits from these sales were then used to support anti-Communist insurgents in Nicaragua, despite the fact Congress had forbidden giving the rebels any assistance. Congress learned of these events in 1986 and launched an investigation. Eventually, 14 individuals were charged with criminal offenses and 11 were convicted, all of whom were later pardoned. The Iran-Contra affair exposed a number of problems, including limitations on oversight of the IC, the ability of the executive branch to ignore Congress if it chose to, and the dangers of having separate covert operations becoming entwined. Reagan's efforts to restore the nation's intelligence capabilities suffered a serious setback as well.[67]

A former DCI, George H. W. Bush was the first former head of intelligence to assume the leadership of a major Western nation. His administration would witness significant changes around the globe, many of which impacted upon the IC. The Berlin Wall came down in 1989, the reunification of Germany followed, and the Communist states of Eastern Europe began to move toward democracy. The invasion of Kuwait by Iraq in 1990 led to the Gulf War of 1991. At the same time, a number of Soviet republics declared their independence from the Soviet Union, and soon after, Communist rule came to an end in Russia. These events led to calls for major changes in the IC; some even questioned the need for the continued existence of the IC.[68]

The end of the cold war brought about changes in the FBI's role in guarding the nation's security. The National Security Threat list was created to identify all of the threats to the United States. Approved by the attorney general in 1991, this list concentrated not just on hostile intelligence services, but included those nations that might pose an ongoing intelligence risk to the country. The list identified risks such as the proliferation of biological, chemical, and nuclear weapons; critical technology losses; and the theft of trade or proprietary information.[69]

The brief Gulf War of 1991 alerted intelligence professionals to what were likely to be important changes in regard to the role of intelligence in wartime. Observers were amazed at how swiftly intelligence could be conveyed to the battlefield. The need to link intelligence systems to combat systems became apparent, along with the need to train combat personnel to use these systems to maximum effect. The creation of a Joint Intelligence Center allowed the major intelligence agencies to provide support to military operations and led to the creation of a National Military Joint Intelligence Center after the war came to an end. Certain problems were identified, such as dispensing imagery to troops in the field. In addition, military intelligence and the CIA disagreed on assessments of damage caused by allied bombing.[70]

CHANGES IN THE IC

In 1991, DCI Robert Gates undertook an exhaustive review of the IC. Fourteen separate task forces returned recommendations calling for major changes. These included making analysis more responsive to decision makers, a formal requirements process for human intelligence (HUMINT) collection, coordination of open source information, and improvements in CIA-military relations. Congress also got involved in the process of restructuring the IC. The end of the cold war led legislators to reduce defense spending, which, of course, meant less funding for the IC. Passage of the Intelligence Organization Act of 1992 defined the IC by law for the first time and spelled out the specific roles of the DCI. These included serving as both head of the IC and the CIA, as well as acting as the president's principal adviser on intelligence. The legislation also restricted the DCI's budgetary powers somewhat.[71]

President William Clinton continued the process of reviewing America's intelligence capabilities during his administration. A team from the Vice President's National Performance Review determined that the IC suffered from competition among agencies for new programs and budget allocations and suggested that collegiality could be achieved through a program of rotating assignments between agencies. Intelligence priorities were also reconsidered. Due to significant military deployments to trouble spots around the world, such as the Balkans, the Middle East, and Africa, Clinton determined that the primary responsibility of the IC was to provide tactical intelligence support for American forces abroad. Because budget cuts forced military intelligence to cut back on producing tactical intelligence products, this effort was passed on to the national intelligence agencies. The decision forced intelligence agencies tasked to provide this support to divert more and more of their increasingly limited resources to provide intelligence to an increasing number of peacekeeping missions.[72]

INTELLIGENCE REFORM

In 1994, a CIA officer named Aldrich H. Ames was accused of having been a spy for the Soviet Union since 1985. Ames passed on the names of almost all of the CIA's active Soviet agents, causing many of them to be executed or imprisoned. Ames and his wife entered guilty pleas at their trial; Ames was sentenced to life in prison, and his wife was sentenced to five years. The revelation of continued Soviet espionage activities against the United States, failures in American counterintelligence efforts, and problems in sharing information between the FBI and CIA all served to further undermine public confidence in the American IC, the CIA in particular. The arrest in 2001 of FBI agent Robert Hanssen, who had begun spying for the Soviet Union at about the same time as Ames, served to further illuminate these concerns.[73]

The Ames case led to a complete review of the IC. Six individual panels undertook a series of studies about the U.S. intelligence effort and generally agreed that a greater level of centralization and more authority for the DCI were called for. Congress acted on these recommendations by enacting the Intelligence Renewal and Reform Act of 1996, which enhanced the authority of the DCI in a number of areas. This reflected a growing consensus that greater centralization of the intelligence effort was necessary in order to produce better intelligence and minimize the problems that had occurred in the past. However, the dichotomy between the perceived need for strong centralized management of the intelligence process and the natural desire to preserve departmental independence had not been resolved at the time of the terrorist attacks of September 11, 2001.[74]

The attack on 9/11 once again raised the question of intelligence failure. In this case, the failure cut across all levels of government, from the White House to Congress to the CIA, FBI, and other federal agencies such as the Federal Aviation Administration. American intelligence was aware of Osama bin Laden's enmity toward the United States and the capabilities he possessed; what was missed was the method that his organization, al-Qaeda, chose in order to carry out its attack on America. DCI George Tenet immediately came under fire for this latest intelligence failure; despite calls for his resignation, President George W. Bush supported him. Congress, though, began a wide-ranging investigation into the performance of the IC.[75]

One immediate response to the attack was passage of the USA PATRIOT Act, which facilitated the collection of domestic and law enforcement intelligence and tried to improve coordination between these sectors. The mission of the FBI now included protection of the American people from further terrorist attacks. Newly appointed Director Robert Mueller immediately focused the FBI on counterterrorism, along with combating foreign intelligence efforts against the United States and dealing with cybercrime.[76]

The Intelligence Reform and Terrorism Prevention Act of 2004 (IRTPA) created a director of national intelligence (DNI) who replaced the director of Central Intelligence as the head of the IC and who assumed the responsibility of serving as the principal advisor on intelligence to the White House. The DCI now became the director of the CIA (DCIA). Prior to the passage of IRTPA, intelligence was considered to fall into two categories: foreign and domestic. IRTPA redefined intelligence as being simply "national intelligence" and identified three subdivisions: foreign, domestic, and homeland security. This served to give the DNI broader responsibilities and reflected the belief that the intelligence agencies did not share information effectively. The DNI has access to all intelligence and is responsible for its dissemination across the IC. He also is responsible for protecting intelligence sources and methodologies.[77]

John Negroponte, a career diplomat, was appointed as the first DNI in February 2005. Negroponte soon came under fire for not asserting his authority effectively. He did manage to get the newly revamped intelligence structure up and running, but Negroponte resigned as DNI in January 2007. His successor, former NSA Director Mike McConnell, an air force general, placed greater emphasis on resolving the problems he perceived as inhibiting greater integration of the IC. However, in 2008, newly elected President Barack Obama indicated that he would select his own DNI. McConnell resigned shortly after Obama's inauguration in 2009 and was succeeded by former Admiral Dennis C. Blair. Whether the creation of a DNI will prove successful in bringing about more effective integration of the IC remains to be seen. Ultimately, the success or failure of the DNI will depend upon presidential support, both real and perceived.[78]

As the war on terror got underway, intelligence collection improved through the use of new technologies, such as an unmanned aerial vehicle (UAV), which proved useful in providing real-time support to American combat units. The authority of the CIA was expanded in other areas as well, especially in regard to capturing suspected terrorists abroad and taking them to another country where they could be confined and interrogated. This practice proved controversial as questions were raised regarding the basis by which suspected terrorists were sent to other countries and the interrogation techniques that they might be subjected to in those nations.[79]

The Bush administration was certain that Saddam Hussein in Iraq was stockpiling weapons of mass destruction (WMDs). He opted for war in order to topple Hussein and his government, and to locate and remove the weapons Hussein was believed to possess. Although Hussein was overthrown, to date no evidence of any WMDs has been found. This failure set off another round of criticisms of the IC, which was castigated for reaching an erroneous conclusion. Furthermore, critics questioned the use of the prewar intelligence by policy makers and the collection and analysis of intelligence on Iraq's WMDs. The outbreak of a bloody insurgency in Iraq added to the controversy. Some former intelligence professionals revealed assessments that had predicted the likelihood of internal violence once Hussein was overthrown, thereby calling intelligence decisions on Iraq into further question.[80]

CONCLUSION

The Iraq war identified serious concerns regarding U.S. intelligence. Confidence in the analytical capabilities of the IC will only be restored as

more accurate assessments are produced. Issues regarding the politiciza-
tion of intelligence by elected officials in order to gain political advantage
are also disturbing.[81] Whether the latest reorganization of the IC will effectively address these issues remains to be seen. The United States will
face numerous challenges throughout the 21st century. Intelligence has a
role in providing solid, accurate analyses and in helping policy makers
anticipate future issues and potential problems. It is likely that the process
of trying to effectively integrate what is still a diverse and decentralized IC
will continue for the foreseeable future. The degree to which the obstacles
to centralization can be overcome may well determine the effectiveness of
American intelligence in the coming years.

NOTES

1. Mark M. Lowenthal, *Intelligence: From Secrets to Policy.* 4th ed. (Washington,
D.C.: CQ Press, 2009), pp. 11–12.

2. Christopher Andrew, *For the President's Eyes Only: Secret Intelligence and the
American Presidency form Washington to Bush* (New York: Harper Collins, 1995), p. 29.

3. See Kenneth A. Daigler, "Samuel Adams and the Covert Action Campaign
that led to the American Revolution," *The Intelligencer: Journal of U.S. Intelligence
Studies* 16, no. 2 (Fall 2008): 37–51.

4. Quoted in Andrews, *President's Eyes Only*, p. 7.

5. Quoted in Ibid., p. 8.

6. Ibid., pp. 7–11; a complete account of Washington's role as spymaster and
the intelligence activities he directed during the American Revolution is to be
found in Alexander Rose, *Washington's Spies: The Story of America's First Spy Ring*
(New York: Bantam Books, 2006).

7. Lowenthal, *From Secrets to Policy*, p. 12; Andrew, *President's Eyes Only*,
p. 11.

8. *The Evolution of the U.S. Intelligence Community—An Historical Overview*
(Washington, D.C.: Government Printing Office, 1996), http://www.fas.org/irp/
offdocs/int022.html; Andrew, *President's Eyes Only*, pp. 11, 13–14.

9. Andrew, *President's Eyes Only*, pp. 12–13.

10. Andrew, *President's Eyes Only*, p. 14.

11. Thomas Allen, *Intelligence in the Civil War* (Washington, D.C.: Central Intelligence Agency, Office of Public Affairs, 2007), p. 17, http://www.cia.gov.

12. Ibid., pp. 13–14.

13. Allen, *Intelligence in the Civil War*, p. 13; Andrew, *President's Eyes Only*,
pp. 14–15; *Evolution of the U.S. Intelligence Community*, p. 2.

14. Allen, *Intelligence in the Civil War*, pp. 31–33; Andrew, *President's Eyes Only*,
p. 20.

15. Allen, *Intelligence in the Civil War*, pp. 33–34.

16. Allen, *Intelligence in the Civil War*, p. 25; *Evolution of the U.S. Intelligence
Community*.

17. Andrew, *President's Eyes Only*, pp. 25–29.

18. History of the FBI, http://www.fbi.gov/libref/historic/history/origins.htm.

19. Andrew, *President's Eyes Only*, p. 30; *Evolution of the U.S. Intelligence Community*.

20. Michael Warner, "The Kaiser Sows Destruction" (2007), https://www.cia.gov/library/center-for-the-study-of-intelligence/csi-publications/csi-studies/studies/vol46no1/article02.html; John F. Fox, Jr., "Bureaucratic Wrangling Over Intelligence, 1917–1918" (2007), https://www.cia.gov/library/center-for-the-study-of-intelligence/csi-publications/csi-studies/studies/vol49no1/html_files/bureaucratic_wragling_2.html.

21. "Bureaucratic Wrangling over Intelligence"; Andrew, *President's Eyes Only*, pp. 38, 54–56.

22. Warner, "The Kaiser Sows Destruction."

23. Andrew, *President's Eyes Only*, pp. 33–36; Warner, "The Kaiser Sows Destruction."

24. Andrew, *President's Eyes Only*, pp. 41–46.

25. Andrew, *President's Eyes Only*, pp. 53–56; *Evolution of the U.S. Intelligence Community.*

26. Andrew, *President's Eyes Only*, pp. 68–74; *The Origins of NSA*, The Center for Cryptologic History, Fort Meade, Md. (undated), http://www.nsa.gov/about/_files/cryptologic_heritage/publications/misc/origins_of_nsa.pdf.

27. History of the FBI, http://www.fbi.gov/libref/historic/history/worldwar.htm.

28. Ibid.

29. *Evolution of the U.S. Intelligence Community*; Andrew, *President's Eyes Only*, pp. 85–86, 94–101.

30. Lowenthal, *From Secrets to Policy*, p. 19.

31. Lowenthal, *From Secrets to Policy*, p. 19; *Evolution of the U.S. Intelligence Community*; Andrew, *President's Eyes Only*, pp. 103–22.

32. "Central Intelligence Agency History," http://www.fas.org./irp/cia/ciahist.htm; *Evolution of the U.S. Intelligence Community.*

33. *Evolution of the U.S. Intelligence Community*; refer also to Andrew, *President's Eyes Only*, pp. 123–48.

34. Douglas A. MacEachin, *The Final Months of the War with Japan: Signals Intelligence, U.S. Invasion Planning, and the A-Bomb Decision* (Washington, D.C.: Central Intelligence Agency, Center for the Study of Intelligence, 1998), https://www.cia.gov/library/center-for-the-study-of-intelligence/csi-publications/books-and-monographs/the-final-months-of-the-war-with-japan-signals-intelligence-u-s-invasion-planning-and-the-a-bomb-decision/csi9810001.html.

35. Michael Warner, ed., *Central Intelligence: Origin and Evolution* (Washington, D.C.: Center for the Study of Intelligence, Central Intelligence Agency, 2001), https://www.cia.gov/library/center-for-the-study-of-intelligence/csi-publications/books-and-monographs/Origin_and_Evolution.pdf, pp. 2–3; *Evolution of the U.S. Intelligence Community.*

36. Warner, *Central Intelligence: Origin and Evolution*, pp. 3–4.

37. Tim Weiner, *Legacy of Ashes: The History of the CIA* (New York: Doubleday, 2006), pp. 12–19; "History of the CIA," http://www.cia.gov/about-cia/history-of-the-cia/index.html.

38. Warner, *Central Intelligence: Origin and Evolution*, pp. 4–5.

39. Ibid.

40. Warner, *Central Intelligence: Origin and Evolution*, pp. 4–5. See also, Andrew, *President's Eyes Only*, pp. 149–98; Weiner, *Legacy of Ashes*, pp. 20–26.

41. Warner, *Central Intelligence: Origin and Evolution.*

42. History of the FBI, http://www.fbi.gov/libref/historic/history/postwar. htm.

43. Robert L. Benson, *The VENONA Story* (Fort George Meade, Md.: Center for Cryptologic History, National Security Agency, 2001); James Bamford, *Body of Secrets: Anatomy of the Ultra-Secret National Security Agency* (New York: Anchor Books, 2002), pp. 20–21; Andrew, *President's Eyes Only*, pp. 178, 180–181, 185, 195, 219.

44. Bamford, *Body of Secrets*, pp. 23–31; Center for Cryptologic History, *The Origins of NSA* (Fort George Meade, Md.: Center for Cryptologic History, National Security Agency, 2002), http://www.nsa.gov/publications/publi00015.cfm.

45. Bamford, *Body of Secrets*, pp. 43–62; Andrew, *President's Eyes Only*, pp. 220–50; Weiner, *Legacy of Ashes*, pp. 158–60; *Encyclopedia of Espionage, Intelligence, and Information*, http://www.espionageinfo.com/Te-Uk/U-2-Spy-Plane. html; *Evolution of the U.S. Intelligence Community; U-2, Senior Year, Aquatone, U-2, TR-1 Overview*, Federation of American Scientists, http://www.fas.org/irp/ program/collect/u-2.htm.

46. Lowenthal, *From Secrets to Policy*, pp. 20–21; Weiner, *Legacy of Ashes*, pp. 74–77, 81–88, 93–104, 142–53, 160–66; Andrew, *President's Eyes Only*, pp. 202–11, 250–56.

47. Andrew, *President's Eyes Only*, pp. 267–71.

48. Andrew, *President'sEyes Only*, p. 272; DIA History, http://www.dia.mil/his tory/histories/origins.html; for the functions of the PFIAB, see Lowenthal, *From Secrets to Policy*, p. 200.

49. Weiner, *Legacy of Ashes*, 194–207; Andrew, *President's Eyes Only*, pp. 286–302; Bamford, *Body of Secrets*, pp. 95–126; Lowenthal, *From Secrets to Policy*, pp. 21–22.

50. Andrew, *President's Eyes Only*, pp. 314–22; Weiner, *Legacy of Ashes*, pp. 239–43; Bamford, *Body of Secrets*, pp. 291–301.

51. Andrew, *President's Eyes Only*, pp. 341–46; Bamford, *Body of Secrets*, pp. 332–40; Weiner, *Legacy of Ashes*, pp. 287–88; Lowenthal, *Secrets to Policy*, p. 22.

52. Andrew, *President's Eyes Only*, pp. 327–32; Weiner, *Legacy of Ashes*, pp. 266–69; Lowenthal, *Secrets to Policy*, p. 22.

53. Weiner, *Legacy of Ashes*, pp. 285–87; History of the FBI, http://www.fbi. gov/fbihistory.htm; DOJ/FBI, *Centennial History*, p. 57.

54. John H. Hedley, "The Evolution of Intelligence Analysis," in *Analyzing Intelligence: Origins, Obstacles, and Innovations*, ed. Roger Z. George and James B. Bruce (Washington, D.C.: Georgetown University Press, 2008), p. 26; Bamford, *Body of Secrets*, pp. 323–25; Andrew, *President's Eyes Only*, pp. 332–35.

55. Andrew, *President's Eyes Only*, pp. 364–70; Weiner, *Legacy of Ashes*, pp. 295, 319; Lowenthal, *Secrets to Policy*, pp. 22–23.

56. Warner, *Central Intelligence: Origin and Evolution*, p. 8; *Evolution of the U.S. Intelligence Community*.

57. *Evolution of the U.S. Intelligence Community*.

58. Ibid.

59. Ibid.

60. Ibid.

61. Lowenthal, *From Secrets to Policy*, p. 23.

62. History of the FBI, http://www.fbi.gov/libref/historic/history/water gate.htm.

63. Andrew, *President's Eyes Only*, pp. 438–42.

64. Weiner, *Legacy of Ashes*, pp. 365–67; Andrew, *President's Eyes Only*, pp. 447–48.

65. *Evolution of the U.S. Intelligence Community.*

66. Ibid.

67. *Evolution of the U.S. Intelligence Community*; Andrew, *President's Eyes Only*, pp. 479–83, 487–93; Weiner, *Legacy of Ashes*, pp. 397–98, 401–6; Lowenthal, *Secrets to Policy*, pp. 24, 168–69.

68. *Evolution of the U.S. Intelligence Community.*

69. History of the FBI: End of the Cold War, 1989–1993, http://www.fbi.gov/libref/historic/history/postcold.htm.

70. *Evolution of the U.S. Intelligence Community.*

71. Warner, *Central Intelligence: Origin and Evolution*, p. 12; *Evolution of the U.S. Intelligence Community.*

72. Warner, *Central Intelligence: Origin and Evolution*, pp. 13–14; *Evolution of the U.S. Intelligence Community.*

73. *Evolution of the U.S. Intelligence Community*; Lowenthal, *From Secrets to Policy*, pp. 24–25; Weiner, *Legacy of Ashes*, pp. 448–51. See also David Wise, *Nightmover: How Aldrich Ames Sold the CIA to the KGB for $4.6 Million* (New York: Harper Collins, 1995).

74. Warner, *Central Intelligence: Origin and Evolution*, pp. 13–18.

75. Lowenthal, *From Secrets to Policy*, p. 25.

76. History of the FBI, Change of Mandate: 2001–present, http://www.fbi.gov/libref/historic/history/changeman.htm.

77. Lowenthal, *From Secrets to Policy*, pp. 25, 29, 37.

78. Ibid., p. 301.

79. Ibid., pp. 25–26.

80. Ibid., p. 26.

81. Ibid.

A Brief Look at the Intelligence Community

Keith Gregory Logan

By 2010, the United States will have the largest structured intelligence program in its history. While most Americans think that the intelligence community[1] (IC) is composed of simply the Central Intelligence Agency (CIA) and the National Security Agency (NSA), it is far larger and more complex. Initially, the director of the CIA served not only as the head of an agency, but also as the director of intelligence for the United States from 1947 until 2004; that is no longer true. The signing of the Intelligence Reform and Terrorism Prevention Act of 2004 (P.L. 108–458) by the president created the Office of the Director of National Intelligence (ODNI). The paragraphs that follow present a basic picture of the current structure and primary purpose of the 17 agencies that comprise the IC. One of the recommendations of the 9/11 Commission was to unify "the intelligence community with a new National Intelligence Director."[2]

ODNI

The director of national intelligence (DNI) serves as the head of the ODNI; the principal advisor to the president, the National Security Council (NSC), and the Homeland Security Council (HSC) for intelligence matters related to national security; and the leader of the 16 other organizations that comprise the IC. The undersecretary of defense for intelligence also serves as an advisor to the DNI regarding defense intelligence matters.

As the 9/11 Commission, also known as the National Commission on Terrorist Attacks Upon the United States,[3] indicated in its investigation of the terrorist attacks in New York and Washington, D.C., there was *inadequate communication* among those federal, state, and local organizations that were responsible for national security and law enforcement. There has always been a high level of secrecy and compartmentalizing of information within the federal government, which has significantly hampered any effort at information sharing with state and local counterparts. This state of affairs is not new to the 21st century, but it has improved.[4] This communication problem was one of the factors that made the United States so vulnerable to terrorist acts in 2001. The creation of the Department of Homeland Security (DHS) and the creation of the ODNI are two significant steps designed to improve communication and security within the United States and the intelligence establishment.

In addition to the DNI and staff, there are several other key positions. The first is a principal deputy director, who is the second in command of the ODNI, and there are four deputy directors who are responsible for the leadership of the following areas:

- Office of the Deputy Director for Policy, Plans and Requirements
- Office of the Deputy Director for Collection
- Office of the Deputy Director for Analysis
- Office of the Deputy Director for Future Capabilities

There are three mission managers responsible for North Korea, Iran, and Cuba/Venezuela, and 10 functional mission support activities. Among those additional groups within the ODNI are the following:

- National Counterterrorism Center
- National Counterintelligence Executive
- National Counterproliferation Center
- Special Security Center
- National Intelligence Council
- National Intelligence University
- Intelligence Advanced Research Projects Activity
- Center for Security Evaluation
- National Intelligence Coordination Center
- Mission Support Center

There are also several organizations under the auspices of the DNI that serve several members of the IC. These organizations are as follows:

- Underground Facilities Analysis Center
- National Media Exploitation Center
- National Virtual Translation Center
- Open Source Center (OSC)

A key group in this new information age is the OSC; open source information is all of the available printed, electronic, digital, video, and other communication/information data sources that are in daily use around the world.[5] Even when governments are successful at blocking standard communication media, such as newspapers, radio, and television, the new digital media will find other routes. Cell phones, computers, and so forth, told the world what was really happening in Iran following their 2009 national elections. While the Iranian government sought to black out the postelection civil unrest, the people communicated with the rest of the world on the Internet and through the use of their cell phones. The OSC relies on the wealth of information that is available from commercial, private, and public databases, as well as other sources, such as scholarly works, brochures, papers, and so forth, that do not require special electronic devices, decoders, satellites, or other technical specialties. To illustrate this, Ambassador Kenneth Brill, director of the National Counterproliferation Center (NCPC), in his remarks at the NCPC Open Source Center Conference, quoted Tsar Nicholas I from the Crimean war, who said: "We have no need of spies. We have the *Times*."[6]

INTELLIGENCE COMMUNITY, ODNI

The ODNI serves as the center or hub of the IC, and each of the participating intelligence agencies represents a spoke or link on the intelligence wheel with the DNI. Their missions and purposes interconnect these entities with the ODNI and each other. They work independently in their specialized areas and together to protect the national security. The 16 entities listed below are the IC.[7] Although the CIA was created at the same time as the Department of Defense, it remains an independent agency within the IC. The 15 other entities are either part of or agencies affiliated with five cabinet-level departments.

CIA

The CIA is an independent agency known to almost everyone as America's Spy Agency; its counterpart in the UK is MI6 (Secret Intelligence Service), made famous by Ian Fleming's James Bond character. While the CIA is commonly referred to as the Company, its UK counterpart is called the Firm or Box 850, and the Israeli counterpart is the Institute or the Office. The CIA is the primary organization for the collection of all-source national security intelligence, and the CIA director is the national human intelligence (HUMINT) manager. The CIA does not have authority to conduct domestic intelligence collection. The basic components of the CIA are the National Clandestine Service (NCS), the Directorate of Intelligence, the Directorate of Science and Technology, and the Directorate of Support. When someone hears that the CIA has been involved in a particular espionage operation or counterintelligence activity, it has most likely originated within NCS.

The *Department of Justice* is not a direct participant in the IC. However, both the Federal Bureau of Investigation (FBI) and the Drug Enforcement Administration (DEA) have elements that are part of the IC. The director of the FBI and the administrator of the DEA report to the attorney general.

FBI

The FBI is primarily knows as a law enforcement agency, but even before 9/11, it had a role in America's national security. As a key member of both the law enforcement and intelligence communities, it walks a fine line separating the tools and authority that are available to those distinct aspects of its mission. During the cold war, the FBI played a key role as the domestic spy catcher, ferreting out those individuals who were Communist sympathizers and sought to sell strategic technology. But after 9/11, the FBI's primary focus was on combating the new terrorist threat and counterintelligence. It significantly increased its intelligence operations and created the *National Security Branch* (NSB). Another FBI priority is cybercrime, which is used by both criminals and terrorists. Within the NSB are the following: the Counterterrorism Division, the Counterintelligence Division, the Directorate of Intelligence, the Weapons of Mass Destruction Directorate, and the Terrorist Screening Center.

DEA

The newest organization to join the IC is the DEA; it is the only other IC organization that is primarily known for its law enforcement responsibilities. It is the DEA's *Office of National Security Intelligence* that directly interacts with the IC. DEA was one of the primary agencies responsible for starting and staffing the El Paso Intelligence Center (EPIC) in 1974. Today, EPIC is a successful fusion center, staffed by many other federal, state, local, and tribal organizations.

The following cabinet-level departments each have components with a specialized intelligence responsibility and represent them within the IC. The one exception is the DHS, which is represented in the IC by its *Office of Intelligence and Analysis* (OIA) and by *Coast Guard Intelligence*.

DHS

DHS is responsible for maintaining the domestic security of the United States. This includes preventing acts of terrorism and unifying America's response to all hazards, both natural and man made. The OIA is responsible for the analysis of multiple source information to identify threats against the homeland. When DHS was created, 22 entities merged into the new department.

DEPARTMENT OF ENERGY (DOE)

The *Office of Intelligence and Counterintelligence* (OIC) focuses on technological threats against the United States, with particular attention to nuclear terrorism and nuclear counterproliferation. DOE also manages the National Laboratory system.

DEPARTMENT OF STATE (DOS)

The *Bureau of Intelligence and Research* (INR) focuses on foreign all-source intelligence and analysis through the diplomatic and foreign service community; it provides timely global information relative to U.S. foreign policy and the IC needs.

DEPARTMENT OF THE TREASURY

In this department, the *Office of Intelligence and Analysis* is focused on financial intelligence issues, such as terrorist and insurgency financing.

DEPARTMENT OF DEFENSE (DOD)

The remaining members of the IC are all part of the DOD. Like the Department of Justice (DOJ), it is the DOD entities, both civilian and military, that represent the DOD within the IC.

DEFENSE INTELLIGENCE AGENCY (DIA)

DIA was created in 1961. It became the lead agency within the DOD for the collection and management of foreign intelligence for the military, and it is a key partner in the IC. It provides all-source military intelligence information, and its director is the key advisor to the secretary of defense and the Joint Chiefs of Staff. The DIA director is also chair of the Military Intelligence Board, the program manager for the DOD Foreign Counterintelligence Program, General Defense Intelligence Program, and the leader of the Defense Intelligence Operations Coordination Center. Other entities within the DIA are the Defense Counterintelligence and HUMINT Center, Directorate for Human Intelligence, Joint Intelligence Task Force for Combating Terrorism, Missile and Space Intelligence Center, National Center for Medical Intelligence, and the National Defense Industrial College.

NATIONAL GEOSPATIAL-INTELLIGENCE AGENCY (NGA)

Over the years, the NGA has evolved from a mapping agency to an integral part of the IC. It can provide electronic imagery and geospatial information to support military missions and political decisions. Three key elements of the agency are the Analysis and Protection Directorate, Source Operations and Management Directorate, and the Office of the NGA Command Center. In general terms, it is Google Earth with much, much more.

NATIONAL RECONNAISSANCE OFFICE (NRO) –

The NRO is called the nation's eyes and ears as its mission involves the collection of intelligence using satellites. The NRO operated as a classified agency for about 30 years before coming out into the public arena.

NSA

NSA has long been known as the nation's cryptographic agency. It is the primary agency involved with the collection, analysis, and distribution of signals intelligence (SIGINT). In addition to the SIGINT Directorate, its other elements include an Information Assurance Directorate; a Research Directorate; a Central Security Service; and two Operations Centers, one responsible for identifying global-network-based threats and the other involved in national security information needs.

MILITARY SERVICES

There are also five armed service organizations that are part of the IC. Four of these are the primary military organizations, representing the air force, army, navy, and Marine Corps, and the fifth organization, the coast guard, wears two hats, as it is considered to be both part of the DHS and the military.

The coast guard's *Intelligence Program* includes a Counter Intelligence Service, an Intelligence Coordination Center, and the Cryptographic Group. It also participates in Maritime Intelligence Fusion Centers and has Field Intelligence Support Teams. When the DHS was created, the coast guard was transferred from the Department of Transportation to DHS.

The air force's *Office of Intelligence, Surveillance and Reconnaissance*; the army's *Military Intelligence Branch*; the navy's *Office of Naval Intelligence*; and the Marine Corps' *Intelligence Activity* each provide representatives to the IC and conduct intelligence activities to support their service's missions.

OVERSIGHT

The NSC, HSC, the President's Intelligence Advisory Board, and Intelligence Oversight Board provide executive oversight of the IC. Legislative oversight comes primarily from the House Permanent Select Committee on Intelligence and the Senate Select Committee on Intelligence; there is also additional oversight from the appropriate defense committees, appropriations committees, and subcommittees with the respective legislative bodies. (See chapter 11 for more information on congressional oversight.) Judicial oversight, the last resort in the balance of power, is found in the Foreign Intelligence Surveillance Act (FISA) courts, state supreme courts, and the U.S. Supreme Court. While FISA courts and state courts have specific jurisdiction, the U.S. Supreme Court will always make the final determination based on federal laws and the Constitution.

THE NEXT STEP

As you see from this first look at the IC, it is a matrix structure of agencies, all of which have the safety and security of the United States as the primary mission. And unlike the UK and its MI5, the United States does not have a domestic intelligence agency, although there are those that would argue that DHS was created for that purpose. The chapters that follow will provide more detail about the history, structure, and functions of the IC. The chapters will also challenge the new IC, questioning whether it solved the problems that existed on 9/11 or whether there is a better way to conduct homeland security and intelligence.

NOTES

1. *An Overview of the United States Intelligence Community for the 111th Congress* (2009), http://www.dni.gov/overview.pdf.

2. U.S. National Commission on Terrorist Attacks Upon the United States, *The 9/11 Commission Report* (Washington, D.C.: GPO, 2004), pp. 399, 411.

3. Intelligence Authorization Act for Fiscal Year 2003, Public Law 107–306, 107th Congress (November 27, 2002).

4. Richard F. Grimmett, "9/11 Commission Recommendations: Implementation Status," *Congressional Research Report for Congress* (CRS Order Code RL33742), December 4, 2006.

5. Remarks by the Director of the National Counterproliferation Center (NCPC), Ambassador Kenneth C. Brill, at the NCPC Open Source Center Conference, May 28, 2009, http://www.dni.gov/speeches/20090528_speech.pdf.

6. Ibid.

7. *An Overview of the United States Intelligence Community for the 111th Congress.*

Intelligence Fundamentals

David M. Keithly

No other nation has a more comprehensive information system than the United States. Both public- and private-sector information and research industries are international in scope and enormous in scale. The government has a massive investment in collecting and analyzing data and in disseminating information, some of it produced by the various agencies of the intelligence community (IC). Information processed by the United States is doubtless one of the country's most valuable products, but at the same time, it represents a significant liability. As one observer put it, "While technology proliferation has made more information more available, it has also made information more vulnerable."[1] Numerous foreign governments, international businesses, criminal cartels, and terrorist organizations have within their grasp sophisticated tools for manipulating federal and private-sector databases.

Intelligence is customarily defined as the product resulting from the collection, evaluation, analysis, integration, and interpretation of all information that concerns one or more aspects of foreign countries or areas, immediately or potentially significant for the development or execution of plans, policies, and operations.[2] The popular concept of intelligence as a mysterious and hazardous activity has, in part, been derived from fictional accounts of international intrigue or from cloak-and-dagger exploits, both truth and fiction. Although mystery and hazard are inherent to some degree in the work of intelligence organizations, the aura of mystery is caused in greater part by the fact that the nature and purpose of intelligence activity are always guarded from public scrutiny by stringent security measures.

Because of the essential security of its operation, intelligence has sometimes been considered an activity foreign to American custom and procedure. Not until World War II did a genuine national interest in intelligence and a universal appreciation of its functions in civilian leadership and military command emerge. Complete, general agreement on what it should or can do has always been elusive. When properly utilized, intelligence can be a potent weapon, and its efficient use is based on certain indispensable principles and procedures.

The events of the last decades have made America intelligence conscious. Terrorism and war have demonstrated that intelligence is essential, not only to military commanders but also to the government of any country with global interests. The new appreciation and support of its endeavors have afforded the intelligence profession more stature. Increased use of its products has enhanced problem solving at various levels. Many qualified persons, both civilian and military, seem eager to make this profession their career.

The scope of American national intelligence is intrinsically broad because the United States is, for its own well-being and that of its allies, required to know a great deal about the attitudes, activities, interests, and long-range plans of all other states and many nonstate actors in the world. Focus of interest depends upon the conditions of international relations at the time. Because it is impossible for any nation to procure all pertinent knowledge about all potential enemies, substantial gaps will exist. Hence, intelligence resembles a vast collection of jigsaw puzzle pieces. Some pieces belong to different puzzles, some will not fit any apparent gap in the picture, and some obviously belong but require considerable work to decide where. For our purposes here, intelligence is of three types:

- Basic intelligence, which is concerned with the past and is relatively permanent
- Current intelligence, which deals with the present
- Intelligence estimates, which concern the future or the unknown but possible present

THE PROCESS

Intelligence products usually result from a series of interrelated activities termed the *intelligence cycle*. The process generally divides intelligence efforts into six phases: (1) direction and planning, (2) collection, (3) processing and exploitation, (4) production, (5) dissemination and integration, and (6) continuous evaluation. The phases, while part of a cycle, do not necessarily occur sequentially. For example, in the direction and planning phase, the necessity, management, and disposition of current and future efforts are determined and reevaluated.[3] The collection phase provides information, which is the input to the intelligence process. The information can include a variety of types, such as reports, observations, rumors, and documents obtained through official and unofficial channels. Raw information is converted to forms that can be readily used by intelligence analysts in the processing and exploitation phase. This processing results in the transformation into intelligence. Such intelligence, in the form of operational reports or strategic estimates and studies, is then disseminated to the appropriate agencies, military commanders, and additional lower echelons. During the evaluation phase, intelligence personnel at all levels assess the effectiveness of each phase of the intelligence cycle and search for solutions when deficiencies are discovered.

Direction and planning are chiefly managerial functions that apply to all phases of the intelligence cycle. Direction and planning should provide guidance and the continuous monitoring of the process to ensure that intelligence requirements are satisfied. These requirements are features of the needs of policy makers and military commanders. In the direction and planning phase, intelligence managers determine how the information required for the production of intelligence is collected. Such a determination includes notifying the appropriate intelligence organization that a certain kind of information is necessary to support national security and national military strategies. During this process, requirements are prioritized to ensure that finite collection assets are properly apportioned.

At the national level, a policy maker may request information, for example.[4] An intelligence collection manager supporting the policy maker researches the intelligence database to see if the information already exists. If it does, collection is unnecessary. If the data do not exist, the collection manager determines which disciplines should be used to collect the information and submits the requirements to the appropriate lead intelligence organization.

Intelligence sources can be used to observe and record the location, size, condition, or activity of a geographical area, an organization, a process, or an individual. Intelligence sources, consisting of people, documents, or mechanical sensors, are customarily grouped into five intelligence disciplines: geospatial intelligence (GEOINT), human intelligence (HUMINT), signals intelligence (SIGINT), measurement and signature intelligence (MASINT), and open source intelligence (OSINT). Analysts should seek information from the widest possible range of these sources to avoid bias and improve accuracy and completeness. The collection of information from multiple sources is also helpful in defeating an adversary's operational security and deception operations. The operation of all collection sources should be synchronized and coordinated to allow cross cueing and tip-offs to maximize collection opportunities.

Processing and exploitation include initial imagery interpretation, data conversion and correlation, document transmission, and decryption. Processing and exploitation may be performed by the same element that collected the information. Other units to which the raw information is disseminated may independently process and exploit it, possibly drawing different conclusions. A SIGINT example of processing is the association of a signal to a location, weapon system, or organization. Different types of information require different degrees of processing before they can be used.

Once the required information is collected and disseminated to the intelligence analyst, the production process commences. This is often the most critical phase of the intelligence cycle. During the production phase, new information is first evaluated to determine if the source of the information is credible. Then, evidence is analyzed to form hypotheses that may provide answers to critical questions. In complex situations involving numerous pieces of evidence and many hypotheses, various methods are employed to ensure that nothing is overlooked. These methods include, but are not limited to, various computer programs, analysis of competing hypotheses, causal linking, or matrix and link analysis. With these methods, or in simpler situations using deductive reasoning, evidence is integrated, comparisons made, and conflicts reconciled. Tentative conclusions are drawn, and the meaning and significance determined to form the final product: an intelligence estimate. This process may be accomplished in a matter of minutes, months, or even years, and any part may be reviewed, scrapped, and redone at any time.

The production phase consists of four steps: evaluation, analysis, integration, and interpretation. All four steps are necessary for transforming information into intelligence. These steps are actually mental processes that can occur simultaneously or in various sequences, depending on the specific issue, the evidence or data, and the analyst.[5] During the first step—evaluation—collected information is appraised as a contribution to a specific goal, its credibility, reliability, relevance, accuracy, or usefulness. If an analyst receives a memorandum from a source whose reports over time have consistently proved accurate, the source is judged reliable. If the analyst finds that the information in the report is inconsistent and lacks important detail, the report may not be considered credible but should not be forgotten in case later evidence corroborates it.

In the cases of SIGINT and GEOINT, evaluating the credibility of the source is not required in the same manner or degree, since this type of intelligence information does not rely on the human source providing testimony. HUMINT, OSINT, and occasionally MASINT, however, where human sources are reporting, require the analyst to determine to what degree the sources' statements are believable. Special care should be taken whenever considering open sources that are state-controlled or influenced by radical organizations, as many are organs of propaganda or disinformation, and as such, their credibility is suspect. Imagery interpreters and signals technicians also occasionally make mistakes. If their evidence does not fit the picture, its credibility should be reevaluated.

The second step in the production phase is analysis. Analysis is similar to evaluation in the sense that an attempt is made to determine the veracity of the facts in the report. During analysis, the intelligence analyst tries to

relate significant facts in the report to information in other reports. Therefore, analysis includes carefully examining related information, identifying
significant facts, and determining the relationship of the facts.

Analysis often has three key ingredients: hypotheses, evidence, and
assumptions. Advancing a hypothesis entails the development of a plausible explanation concerning the information. The testing of hypotheses,
a deductive method, underlies the accumulation of information. By comparing propositions and theories with actual observations, one confirms
or rejects generalizations or principles. Evidence involves data that are
relevant to the hypotheses being considered.[6] Finally, assumptions are the
theories that the analyst creates to fill the gaps left by missing information or
evidence. It is crucial to consider a range of hypotheses, not just the favored
one. The analyst will continue to research, gather reports, and relate pieces
of evidence, always challenging the hypotheses and assumptions.

During integration, the third step, the analyst assembles the facts and
relationships identified during the analysis step into a unified whole. The
analyst tries to ascertain a pattern to a larger subject by selecting and combining analyzed information. For example, an analyst might select and
combine information from various intelligence reports and discern a possible changing political pattern. This information can then be compared
to other various hypotheses. When several reports concur, hypotheses
supported by the data are substantiated. When reports contradict one
another, the hypotheses supported by them will be weakened. By this
process of refining the hypotheses, considering new hypotheses, challenging the assumptions, and comparing and contrasting evidence, the analyst
can decide which hypotheses are supported and which are weak.[7] The
integration step focuses on developing these patterns.

Once analysts have decided which information reports are significant
and support the primary hypotheses, they should determine why they
are important. Interpretation of processed information is the final step
of the production phase. During the interpretation step, the last step, the
meaning or significance of the new intelligence pattern is determined by
viewing all the processed information in the perspective of an overall
intelligence appraisal. For example, if a state's political patterns indicate
a shift away from radical political philosophies, the potential significance
is conspicuous. During interpretation, the analyst addresses the question,
why is this important? Without this step, the analyst is merely reporting
facts, and no analysis presents itself.[8] At this stage, one should resist the
temptation to achieve a scoop. The production phase ultimately involves
the conversion of information into a finished intelligence product to satisfy a customer. Completion entails meticulous evaluation of sources
and evidence, analysis, and the integration of various parts into a new
conclusion to the original requirement.

Once an analyst finishes an intelligence product, it must be made available to the appropriate consumers and policy makers who initiated the

requirements. Dissemination is the penultimate phase, and a crucial one. If it is left to chance, an analyst's or an entire intelligence center's work may be for naught, and an operation possibly jeopardized. Dissemination requires the timely distribution of the intelligence product in the correct format.

The final intelligence product needs to be packaged as required by the customer. Products may be packaged in a variety of methods depending upon the customer's needs. Some intelligence consumers may require the finished product in the form of slides. Others may require special charts, maps, or other graphics. The intelligence may be presented through a video display or data stored on a file server or other digital storage media. Once the product is packaged, it must be distributed to the various customers. Distribution methods should depend primarily on the urgency of the customer's need and, secondly, on the availability of systems, product format, and time constraints.

During evaluation, the last phase, intelligence personnel at all levels should assess whether each phase of the intelligence cycle is being accomplished appropriately. When areas for improvement are identified, the necessary changes are made. Evaluation is continuously performed during each phase of the intelligence cycle. Personnel involved in different phases coordinate and cooperate to determine whether transitions from one phase to another require improvement. Consumers should impart comments and suggestions. Individual intelligence professionals seek to improve their own performance and the performance of the processes in which they participate. As paradigms shift, analysts must adapt quickly and develop new ways of doing business.

The IC deals with both classified and unclassified information on foreign developments. Its analysts produce finished intelligence by analyzing, evaluating, interpreting, and integrating various pieces of information. The intelligence process also involves production of intelligence assessments and their timely dissemination to consumers. The IC offers the intelligence consumer a broad range of products through a variety of media:

- Daily publications and bulletins or briefings about current developments
- Biographical reports and psychological studies
- Assessments, briefs, and memorandums on specific subjects
- Technical analyses of weapons and weapon systems
- Formal estimates that analyze specific international situations
- Daily video reports
- Comprehensive research studies
- Serial publications and situation reports addressing specialized topics, key countries, or important foreign policy issues[9]

COMPONENTS AND METHODS

HUMINT is the collection discipline where humans are both the collector and the collection platform. Such nontechnical intelligence collection deteriorated during the 1970s in the United States following scandals related to HUMINT, and the subsequent investigations of these by congressional committees and other organizations. Certain policy changes in 1990s resulted in heavy-handed guidelines that governed the recruitment of assets with any kind of criminal background, further restricting HUMINT collection. While the policy was intended to cut America's ties to less desirable international people and groups, it tended to have a deleterious effect on the level of preparedness in dealing with terrorist threats. The FBI, for example, faced tight restrictions because it was required to seek prior approval for all interaction with individuals who were involved in unlawful activities. Hence, the fundamental question arises, how does ethics relate to the intelligence profession? The IC has an ethically responsible task. Yet, the business of intelligence is shrouded by secrecy, need to know, distrust, and deception.

The belief that the technical collection disciplines might for the most part fill the gap expanded this trend of HUMINT downgrading. Disclosures of several treasonous individuals continued to damage the U.S. HUMINT program from the late 1980s to at least the year 2000. Reassessment of HUMINT has since commenced, and attempts to restore HUMINT capability are in train.[10] Most observers now agree that HUMINT collection operations have considerable value in the 21st century, especially in technologically backward societies. HUMINT has the potential to counterbalance the asymmetrical dynamic between a major power and less sophisticated foes.[11] For example, when terrorist groups became aware of the capability to tap their communications via satellite telephones, they countered these efforts by relying on nontechnical communication methods. Once terrorists learn that their communications systems, including telephones and the Internet, have been compromised, they often revert to face-to-face communication via trusted operatives within their organization. Collection is difficult under such circumstances because of the small inner circles of trust and the compartmentalization of information within terrorist organizations.

HUMINT alone is seldom capable of producing sufficient information for accurate decision making. When used in conjunction with other collection methods, though, it can provide key pieces of the puzzle to aid in strategic considerations. If imagery seems to indicate that an enemy force is mobilizing, for instance, HUMINT sources can reflect on the images with visual verification. At the same time, SIGINT may detect increased radio communications and radar signatures from the mobilizing group.

SIGINT is intelligence derived from the interception and exploitation of foreign electromagnetic emissions. The type of information produced from SIGINT may consist of the numbers and disposition of military hardware, troops, locations and movements, plans, and capabilities. Since SIGINT collection requires an active target, it is susceptible to enemy deception in the form of counterfeit messages, phony radio networks, and other deceptive measures.

SIGINT in turn has three elements: communications intelligence (COMINT), electronic intelligence (ELINT), and foreign instrumentation signals intelligence (FISINT). COMINT is understood as intelligence derived from foreign communications systems by other than the intended recipients. Military intelligence organizations focus considerable efforts on COMINT, the passive monitoring of enemy transmissions. Intercepts are usually immediately followed by tactical analysis that allows a commander to take appropriate action to carry out the mission. Instead of disrupting enemy transmissions, it is often more beneficial to leave the communications networks operating so that the signals can be monitored to provide additional intelligence.

The most common kind of enemy communications the United States monitors is voice. Voice communications are a rapid means of passing orders, reports, and other information and are found at the lowest echelons of adversary organizations. Voice communications can provide substantial information, particularly in the heat of battle when immediate safety or experience takes precedence over security, and otherwise closely guarded secrets may be revealed. Voice systems at lower echelons are usually low power and short range. Exploitation requires close proximity to the battle area or flights within the line of sight of the transmitter. Trained linguists may be required for translation.

Morse code is another type of common signal. Some foreign militaries still make extensive use of Morse code. It is simple, reliable, and has a high degree of resistance to interference and jamming. The major drawback is its relatively slow speed. Usually, a Morse code communications system has a greater range than voice and as a result can be intercepted from friendly territory. Operators must be skilled in using and interpreting Morse code.

Radioteletype (RATT), another type of signal, is usually found at higher echelons and generally involves long-distance communications. Like Morse code, it can usually be intercepted a long distance from its point of origin. The wide variety of RATT systems means that exploitation requires a compatible receiver and deciphering equipment. Multichannel, another type of signal, can carry several channels of communications simultaneously. These can be mixed, with one channel transmitting voice and another transmitting teletype. Multichannel is usually a line-of-sight transmission and must be intercepted from a point near the battle space or while airborne. Tactical units also use landline, another method of transmitting communications that carry voice, teletype, and other signals. Unless the system has a radio link, intercept of landlines requires physical access to the transmission cable. Because of this limitation, landlines offer a high degree of security and resistance to disruption. By definition, exploitation of landline communications is COMINT.

The second element of SIGINT is ELINT, which is intelligence derived from foreign, noncommunications, electromagnetic radiation emanating from other than nuclear detonations or radioactive sources. There are in turn two forms of ELINT: operational ELINT and technical ELINT.[12]

Operational ELINT (OPELINT) refers to the introduction, disposition, movement, utilization, and tactics of known foreign noncommunications emitters and their associated systems. OPELINT is concerned with how the system is employed, and it is often useful in providing indications and warning of impending activity. Technical ELINT (TECHELINT) is the process by which intercepted data are analyzed to determine any emitter's function, capability, vulnerability, and technical characteristics. The remaining SIGINT element is foreign instrumentation signals, or FISINT. This involves intelligence derived from equipment parameters and performance monitoring and control systems such as telemetry, radio beacons, command links, and fuse arming signals.

Globalization and the latest incarnation of U.S. adversaries have significantly influenced the SIGINT mission. The technological advancements of today's information age and the speed and volume at which information flows have created a challenging SIGINT environment for the IC. SIGINT is now regarded as one of the most important intelligence disciplines in combating terror. Proper exploitation of terrorist communications can provide insight into the leadership, capabilities, and intentions of terrorist groups.

Radar beams, radio beacons, and other noncommunications signals differ from communications signals because they do not carry information in the conventional manner. Radar uses a receiver and viewing scope to disclose locational data of a reflected object. ELINT analysis requires that the signals be intercepted, recorded, and processed. Simultaneously, the signal sources can be located by direction finding. Recording may entail a written log sheet or transcription to magnetic tape or other means. During the processing phase, the signal is identified and correlated to a particular type of equipment. For example, a radar signal is detected and recorded, and the characteristics of the signal match those of a known air defense system. If one knows which units use this radar, the approximate location of a particular air defense unit can be determined.

Overhead collection systems fall into two broad categories: aerial and space. Each of these methods is capable of supporting multiple intelligence disciplines, such as GEOINT, SIGINT, and MASINT. GEOINT is an intelligence discipline that has evolved from the integration of imagery, imagery intelligence (IMINT), and geospatial information.[13] Aerial collection is constrained by mechanical failure, time, and above all, weather. A platform unable directly to engage the observation target cannot properly collect data. Space platforms, however, operate above the weather and are capable of collecting within a much larger area and across a greater range. Their orbit is the primary constraint. Orbits are routine, and the times during which overhead collection may occur are predictable. To counter the collection of intelligence from space, many countries calculate when satellites are over their territories and at those times curtail or enshroud activities they wish to hide.

Cameras aboard aircraft, drones, or satellites can collect information about areas that are otherwise inaccessible. These are also used to track storms at sea, map areas of drought or diseased crops, and determine likely sites for mineral exploitation. Imagery is a permanent record of the detail within the sensor field of view and provides an objective impression of the target to imagery interpreters. Imagery is nonjudgmental and reproducible; it can be studied and restudied for various purposes by different interpreters. It can be compared, detail by detail, with other imagery of the same area to provide comparative intelligence. Imagery may be used to chart an area's geographic and cultural detail, and to furnish coastal information including inshore bottom conditions. It can sometimes provide data on inshore water depth, but it cannot confirm offshore water depth, bottom contour, or composition. Imagery can provide much detailed ground force information, such as strength and disposition of troops and useful terrain features that help to determine its suitability for heavy vehicles and various tactics.

Imagery is not without limitations. Image interpreters cannot always see fine details, and sometimes they can only infer particulars through associated features. For example, certain geographic sizes may be estimated from a comparison of other objects visible in an image. Hence, imagery intelligence is often constrained by the ability and experience of the imagery interpreter. And imaging resources are finite and may not be focused on the particular area of interest.

The IC and the Department of Defense (DOD) are utilizing unmanned aerial vehicles (UAVs) for tactical and operational intelligence collection in growing measure. Some observers suggest that UAVs will largely replace manned aircraft for collection and reconnaissance purposes in the foreseeable future. UAVs and manned reconnaissance aircraft have individual capabilities and vulnerabilities, though, rendering it likely that both will maintain collection roles in the next decades. The U.S. government defines UAVs as "powered, aerial vehicles that do not carry a human operator, use aerodynamic forces to provide vehicle lift, can fly autonomously or be piloted remotely, can be expendable or recoverable, and can carry a lethal or nonlethal payload."[14] Many different types of UAVs are already in use, and technological advancement continues apace. UAVs can either be remotely piloted or self-piloted and can carry a wide range of geospatial and signals intelligence collection equipment, including cameras, sensors, and other sophisticated collection equipment.

Operation Desert Storm/Desert Shield in 1990–1991 brought extensive UAV utilization in combat zones for the first time. Pioneer UAVs were deployed to provide overhead imagery in many areas of the conflict. Procured initially in 1985 with imagery intelligence capabilities allowing commanders in the field to see to distances up to 185 kilometers, Pioneer UAVs facilitated intelligence collection on the enemy for tactical planning. UAVs were instrumental to intelligence collection in the Balkans in the

1990s, and the platforms continue to provide crucial intelligence in the Iraq and Afghanistan conflicts. Use of full motion video (FMV) during operations enhances situational awareness of the battles pace by furnishing near real-time (NRT) actionable intelligence. Different perspectives of the battle space are afforded by electro-optical (EO), infrared (IR), synthetic aperture radar (SAR), and moving target indicators (MTI). UAVs are also in use by U.S. Customs and Border Protection (CBP) for domestic border protection. UAVs provide border patrol agents with real-time imagery of borders where illegal crossings are frequent.

Finally, MASINT is technically derived intelligence that detects, locates, tracks, identifies, and describes the unique characteristics of fixed and dynamic target sources. MASINT includes the scientific and technical intelligence obtained by quantitative and qualitative analysis of angle, spatial, wavelength, time dependence modulation, plasma, and hydromagnetic data collected by MASINT sensors for the purpose of identifying distinctive signatures of a source. MASINT is predominately collected by dedicated technical sensors and processed by the MASINT production infrastructure.[15] MASINT is also derived from additional processing and exploitation of data collected by sensors of the other collection disciplines.

Measurement in MASINT refers to the data collected in order to obtain precise parameters, such as height, weight, distance, and depth. MASINT techniques can derive parameters that are not directly measurable by the sensor. *Signature* refers to data indicating the distinct characteristics of a particular event, piece of equipment, or object. Signatures can be used to recognize and quantify the event, equipment, or object. Some examples of signature data include the amplitude of radar returns over a period of time or the frequencies at which a target produces acoustic waves.

MASINT is composed of six subdisciplines: materials sampling, radar, radio frequency, geophysics (seismic, acoustic), electro-optical, and nuclear radiation. Electro-optical intelligence (MASINT EO) involves the collection, processing, exploitation, and analysis of emitted or reflected energy across the optical portion (ultraviolet, visible, near infrared, and infrared) of the electromagnetic spectrum. MASINT EO may provide detailed information on the radiant intensities, dynamic motion, spectral and spatial characteristics, and the materials composition of targeted objectives. EO data collection provides broad applications to a variety of military, civil, economic, and environmental issues. Data may be collected by optically sensitive devices, such as radiometers, spectrometers, nonliteral imaging systems, lasers, and laser radar (LADARS).[16]

MASINT is frequently used in the scientific and technical intelligence arena but has applications for many other areas of intelligence analysis. MASINT sensors provide important intelligence information in support of treaty monitoring; weapons characterization; materials production;

power supply characterization; and ship, aircraft, and ballistic missile signatures. The overall manager for the MASINT program is the Central MASINT Office (CMO) within the Defense Intelligence Agency.

OUTLOOK

Information is central to the conduct of both peace and war. Spectacular recent advances in how rapidly and inexpensively it can be generated, transmitted, and processed will alter both. These advances are exogenous phenomena to which all international actors must be prepared to adapt. Government policy decisions affect the precise direction in which information technologies advance, the channels through which they are allowed to flow, and the speed at which they spread from the technologically advanced countries to other societies.

Utilizable intelligence requires insights into the intentions of government and nongovernment leaders, for which the human collector is as critical as ever. On a high level of generalization, intelligence involves knowledge and foreknowledge of the world—the prelude to decision and action by policy makers. Intelligence organizations provide information in a manner that allows consumers to consider alternative options and outcomes. The analytical process must be rigorous, timely, and relevant to policy needs and concerns. The IC currently strives toward a more multidisciplined approach to intelligence gathering, largely as a result of the hard lessons learned from recent intelligence failures. Augmentation of HUMINT capabilities as a major collection asset will continue to be an IC priority. OSINT, publicly available information and other unclassified information that has limited public distribution or access, will be employed to complement the more sensitive collection disciplines.[17] OSINT results largely from the analysis of open source information and the comparison of it with other sources.[18] Particularly since the advent of the Internet, OSINT has been recognized as a crucial discipline in support of all-source intelligence.

A retrospective look at technological advancement in the 20th century indicates that the United States periodically faces determined and sophisticated enemies. At the same time, the last six decades also marked numerous groundbreaking innovations in U.S. intelligence-gathering technology. Such technological breakthroughs suggest that the United States has the capability to discover and counter contemporary enemy threats.

Modern technical intelligence disciplines, such MASINT, will help prepare the IC to deal with these threats. According to a study conducted by the House of Representatives Permanent Select Committee on Intelligence, "MASINT can provide specific weapon system identifications, chemical compositions and material content and a potential adversary's ability to employ these weapons."[19] MASINT is an esoteric intelligence collection method that can furnish the IC with a wide range of collection opportunities, and it is arguably still the most underutilized and perhaps undervalued intelligence discipline. Without adequate study of the advantages of MASINT and a grasp of the type of information that can be derived from its application, the IC will not be as capable of addressing collection problems as it should be. Emplacement of sources frequently requires considerable periods of time, and intelligence resources are notoriously insufficient to meet demand. Technology and automation can assist, of course, but trained, analytical expertise remains beyond the capacity of machines. Analysts have learned over the years not to be bound by rigid intelligence requirements, but to anticipate where resources must be applied to meet emerging intelligence needs.

TERMS AND DEFINITIONS[20]

Acoustic intelligence (ACINT): Intelligence derived from the collection and processing of acoustic phenomena.

All-source intelligence: Intelligence products and/or activities that incorporate all sources of information, including, most frequently, HUMINT, GEOINT, MASINT, SIGINT, and OSINT, in the production of finished intelligence.

Battle space: All aspects of air, surface, subsurface, land, space, and the electromagnetic spectrum that encompass the area of influence and area of interest.

Communications intelligence (COMINT): Technical and intelligence information derived from foreign communications by other than intended recipients.

Counterintelligence (CI): Information gathered and activities conducted to protect against espionage, other intelligence activities, sabotage, or assassinations conducted by or on behalf of foreign governments or elements thereof, foreign organizations, or foreign persons, or international terrorist activities.

Critical vulnerability: That element of military force that is vulnerable to attack and whose degradation or destruction will lead to defeating the enemy's center of gravity and, ultimately, his ability to resist.

Deception: Those measures designed to mislead the enemy by manipulation, distortion, or falsification of evidence to induce him to react in a manner prejudicial to his interests.

Electronics intelligence (ELINT): Technical and geolocation intelligence derived from foreign noncommunications electromagnetic radiations emanating from other than nuclear detonations or radioactive sources.

Electro-optical intelligence (ELECTRO-OPTINT): Intelligence other than signals intelligence derived from optical monitoring of the electromagnetic spectrum from ultraviolet through far infrared.

Foreign instrumentation signals intelligence (FISINT): Technical information and intelligence information derived from the intercept of foreign instrumentation signals by other than the intended recipients.

Fusion: In intelligence usage, the process of examining all sources of intelligence and information to derive a complete assessment of activity.

Fusion center: In intelligence usage, a physical location to accomplish fusion. It normally has sufficient intelligence automated data processing capability to assist in the process.

Geospatial intelligence (GEOINT): The exploitation and analysis of imagery and geospatial information to describe, assess, and visually depict physical features and geographically referenced activities on the earth.

Human intelligence (HUMINT): A category of intelligence derived from information collected and provided by human sources.

Imagery intelligence (IMINT): Intelligence derived from the exploitation of collection by visual photography, infrared sensors, lasers, electro-optics, and radar sensors such as synthetic aperture radar wherein images of objects are reproduced optically or electronically on film, electronic display devices, or other media.

Indications and warning (I&W): Those intelligence activities intended to detect and report time-sensitive intelligence information on foreign development that could involve a threat to the United States or allied military, political, or economic interests or to U.S. citizens abroad. It includes forewarning of enemy actions or intentions; the imminence of hostilities; insurgency; nuclear/nonnuclear attack on the United States, its overseas forces, or allied nations; hostile reactions to U.S. reconnaissance activities; terrorists' attack; and other similar events.

Infrared intelligence (IRINT): Intelligence derived from information collected by infrared sensors.

Intelligence estimate: The appraisal, expressed in writing or orally, of available intelligence relating to a specific situation or condition with a view to determining the courses of action open to the enemy or potential enemy and the order of probability of their adoption.

Intelligence requirement: Any subject, general or specific, upon which there is a need for the collection of information or the production of intelligence.

Joint Intelligence Center (JIC): The intelligence center of the joint forces headquarters. The JIC is responsible for providing and producing the intelligence required to support the joint forces commander and staff, components, task forces and elements, and the national IC.

Laser intelligence (LASINT): Technical and geolocation intelligence derived from laser systems, a subcategory of electro-optical intelligence.

Measurement and signature intelligence (MASINT): Scientific and technical intelligence obtained by quantitative and qualitative analysis of data (metric, angle, spatial, wavelength, time dependence, modulation, plasma, and hydromagnetic) derived from specific technical sensors for the purpose of identifying any distinctive features associated with the source, emitter, or sender and to facilitate subsequent identification and/or measurement of the same.

Medical intelligence (MEDINT): That category of intelligence resulting from collection, evaluation, analysis, and interpretation of foreign medical, bioscientific, and environmental information that is of interest to strategic planning and operations for the conservation of the fighting strength of friendly forces and the formation of assessments of foreign medical capabilities in both military and civilian sectors.

National intelligence support team (NIST): A nationally sourced team composed of intelligence and communications experts from either the Defense Intelligence Agency, Central Intelligence Agency, National Security Agency, or any combination of these agencies.

Nuclear intelligence (NUCINT): Intelligence derived from the collection and analysis of radiation and other effects resulting from radioactive sources.

Open source intelligence (OSINT): Information of potential intelligence value that is available to the general public.

Operational intelligence: Intelligence that is required for planning and conducting campaigns and major operations to accomplish strategic objectives within theaters or areas of operations.

Photographic intelligence (PHOTINT): The collected products of photographic interpretation, classified and evaluated for intelligence use.

Radar intelligence (RADINT): Intelligence derived from data collected by radar.

Scientific and technical intelligence (S&T): The product resulting from the collection, evaluation, analysis, and interpretation of foreign scientific and technical information that covers (a) foreign developments in basic and applied research and in applied engineering techniques and (b). scientific and technical characteristics, capabilities, and limitations of all foreign military systems, weapons, weapon systems, and matériel, the research and development related thereto, and the production methods employed for their manufacture.

Signals intelligence (SIGINT): A category of intelligence comprising either individually or in combination all communications intelligence, electronics intelligence, and foreign instrumentation signals intelligence, however transmitted.

Strategic intelligence: Intelligence that is required for the formulation of strategy, policy, and military plans and operations at national and theater levels.

Surveillance: The systematic observation of aerospace, surface or subsurface areas, places, persons, or things by visual, aural, electronic, photographic, or other means.

Tactical intelligence: Intelligence that is required for planning and conducting tactical operations.

Technical intelligence (TECHINT): Intelligence derived from exploitation of foreign material, produced for strategic-, operational-, and tactical-level commanders.

Telemetry intelligence (TELINT): Technical intelligence derived from the intercept, processing, and analysis of foreign telemetry. Telemetry intelligence is a category of foreign instrumentation signals intelligence.

Unintentional radiation intelligence (RINT): Intelligence derived from the collection and analysis of non-information-bearing elements extracted from the electromagnetic energy unintentionally emanated by foreign devices, equipment, and systems, excluding those generated by the detonation of nuclear weapons.

Validation: A process normally associated with the collection of intelligence that provides official status to an identified requirement and confirms that the requirement is appropriate for a given collector and has not been previously satisfied.

NOTES

1. Michelle K. Van Cleave, Assistant Director for National Security Affairs, Office of Science and Technology Policy, Executive Office of the President, remarks to the Information Security Seminar for Business and Government, New York, October 18, 1989.

2. Thomas F. Troy, "The 'Correct' Definition of Intelligence," *International Journal of Intelligence and Counterintelligence* 5, no. 4 (1991): 433–34.

3. Robert M. Clark, *Intelligence Analysis: A Target-Centric Approach*, 2nd ed. (Washington, D.C.: CQ Press, 2007), pp. 53–54.

4. Mark M. Lowenthal, *Intelligence: From Secrecy to Policy*, 2nd ed. (Washington, D.C.: CQ Press, 2003), pp. 142–43.

5. John A. Gentry, "Intelligence Analyst/Manager Relations at the CIA," in *Intelligence Analysis and Assessment*, ed. David A. Charters, A. Stuart Farson, and Glenn P. Hastedt (London: Frank Cass, 1996), pp. 135–36.

6. Morgan D. Jones, *The Thinker's Toolkit: 14 Powerful Techniques for Problem Solving* (New York: Three Rivers Press, 1998), pp. 179–80.

7. Alexander L. George and Andrew Bennett, *Case Studies and Theory Development in the Social Sciences* (Cambridge, Mass.: MIT Press, 2004), pp. 115–16.

8. See "Devil's Advocacy," in Jones, *The Thinker's Toolkit*, pp. 217–23.

9. *A Consumer's Guide to Intelligence* (Washington, D.C.: Central Intelligence Agency, 1995), p. vii.

10. Burton Gerber, "Managing HUMINT: The Need for a New Approach," in *Transforming U.S. Intelligence*, ed. Jennifer E. Sims and Burton Gerber (Washington, D.C.: Georgetown University Press, 2005), pp. 180–81.

11. See "Special Report: Seeking Spies," *U.S. News and World Report*, February 13, 2006, pp. 35–41.

12. Clark, *Intelligence Analysis*, pp. 104–5.

13. *National System for Geospatial Intelligence (GEOINT)*, Basic Doctrine Publication 1–0 (Washington, D.C.: National Geospatial Intelligence Agency, 2006), p. 5.

14. Elizabeth Bone and Christopher Bolkom, "Unmanned Aerial Vehicles: Background and Issues for Congress," *Report for Congress*, April 25, 2003, http//www.fas.org/irp/crs/RL31872.pdf (accessed August 2, 2009).

15. James Monnier Simon, Jr., "Managing Domestic, Military, and Foreign Policy Requirements: Correcting Frankenstein's Blunder," in *Transforming U.S. Intelligence*, ed. Sims and Gerber, p. 152.

16. *A Consumer's Guide to Intelligence*, p. 55.

17. Robert David Steele, "Private Enterprise Intelligence: Its Potential Contribution to National Security," in *Intelligence Analysis and Assessment*, ed. Charters, Farson, and Hastedt, pp. 213–14.

18. Amy Sands, "Integrating Open Sources into Transnational Threat Assessments," in *Transforming U.S. Intelligence*, ed. Sims and Gerber, pp. 64–65.

19. U.S. Congress, House of Representatives, Permanent Select Committee on Intelligence, *IC21: The Intelligence Community in the 21st Century*, Staff Study, 104th Cong., http//www.access.gpo.gov/congress/house/intel/ic21/ic21007.html (accessed August 2, 2009).

20. Courtesy of the Naval Doctrine Command, U.S. Department of the Navy.

Intelligence Analysis: A 9/11 Case Study

Michael W. Collier

Intelligence analysis is the pivotal activity in the intelligence process. The analyst must make sense of often incomplete and conflicting information and provide analytic products useful to decision makers. This requires the analyst to work closely with intelligence planners and collectors to identify intelligence requirements and task intelligence collectors to fill information gaps. Analysts must also be in continual contact with the consumers of intelligence, the decision makers, to make sure the analytic products meet consumer needs.

Perceived failures in intelligence analysis leading up to the September 11, 2001, terrorist attacks on the New York World Trade Center and Pentagon were part of the justification for the formation of the U.S. homeland security structure. Post-9/11 investigations criticized the U.S. intelligence community (IC) for its lack of imagination, failure of agencies to share information, and inability of analysts to connect-the-dots, implying the IC had significant responsibility for the attacks, which killed over 3,000 people.[1] Adding to criticism of the IC's analysis, the 2002 National Intelligence Estimate (NIE) on Iraqi weapons of mass destruction (WMD) came under media and congressional scrutiny with claims that analysts failed to properly assess available information and that the NIE was politicized to help justify the Bush administration's plan to invade Iraq.[2] Together, criticism of the IC's pre-9/11 performance and poor analysis in the Iraqi WMD NIE resulted in a number of IC reforms mandated in the 2004 Intelligence Reform and Terrorism Prevention Act (IRTPA).

This chapter focuses on the state of U.S. intelligence analysis both before and after 9/11 as it affects the counterterrorism mission of homeland security. First, the chapter surveys the general procedures used for intelligence analysis prior to 9/11. Second, it describes the IC shift after 9/11 to more robust critical thinking and structured analysis techniques. Finally, the chapter provides a short counterfactual case study of IC actions during the period just prior to 9/11, revealing what could have happened if the IC and U.S. national security decision makers had followed the critical thinking and structured analysis techniques now in use. The findings reveal a high probability that 9/11 could have been prevented.

ANALYSIS PROCEDURES PRIOR TO 9/11

A number of different analytic procedures are used in the IC. Those who work in scientific and technical fields utilize the latest scientific analysis procedures in their related fields. Economic intelligence analysis is based largely on the latest quantitative procedures in econometrics. Analysis in the political-military field, where terrorism analysis resides, is a mixture of *descriptive analysis,* meant to inform strategic and tactical decision makers, and *predictive analysis,* which attempts to forecast or estimate the behavior or decisions of adversaries. Political-military descriptive analysis products include order-of-battle studies (e.g., sizes, organization, capabilities, and locations of adversary forces), biographical reports of political and military leaders, transportation and industrial infrastructure reports, and a bevy of other reports and studies requested by national security and military decision makers. Predictive analysis is more challenging, as analysts often face incomplete information and must deal with both the complexities of the situation and the free will of adversaries to act or decide in ways that differ from their prior behavior.

Prior to 9/11, IC predictive analysis in the political-military field could be characterized as "unaided judgment."[3] These procedures include significant reliance on the inductive approach to reasoning (working from the data directly to the findings), which are based on procedures related to evidentiary reasoning, historical method, reasoning by analogy, case-study method, and basic critical-thinking skills.[4] There are a number of problems with reliance on unaided judgment for intelligence analysis. First, the approach stresses individual and not group analyses. Second, the analytic process occurs mainly in the head of the analyst and thus cannot be assessed for either reliability or validity, as little is written down except the findings. *Reliability* refers to the ability of a second analyst to use the same procedures as the first and obtain the same results; this is difficult where there is little documentation of the analytic procedures. *Validity* refers to the accuracy in conceptualizing and modeling the behavior under study. As with reliability, it is impossible to assess validity without detailed documentation of the analytic procedures. Lacking both reliability and validity, political-military intelligence reports prior to 9/11 were based more on opinion than scientific analysis. While the experience of the analyst may make such intelligence reporting well-informed opinion, it is still opinion, as might be found in nonscholarly periodicals such as *The Economist* or *Foreign Policy.*

Use of unaided judgment for analysis has strong roots in the IC. Many of the original IC analysts were historians who were educated or taught in elite U.S. northeastern colleges and universities. For example, Sherman Kent, a Yale University history professor, headed the Central Intelligence Agency's (CIA) Office of National Estimates from 1952 to 1967.[5] Somehow, social science advances in behavioralism beginning in the 1960s bypassed the IC. During the last five decades, *behavioralism*, the application of scientific principles to the study of human behavior, human decision making, and human conditions, replaced historicism as the main academic analytic approach toward social issues. While many new IC analysts were trained in the methods of behavioralism, and a number of analysts advanced their use, the IC continued its traditional use of unaided judgment as the main basis for their analysis.[6]

The attacks on 9/11 and the Iraqi WMD NIE brought the use of unaided judgment as the primary means of IC analysis under close scrutiny. As a result, the 2004 IRTPA not only created the new position of director of national intelligence (DNI) to better coordinate and oversee the IC, but also directed the new DNI to "establish a process and assign an individual or entity the responsibility for ensuring that, as appropriate, elements of the intelligence community conduct alternative analysis . . . of the information and conclusions in intelligence products."[7] Some components of the IC had begun experimenting with alternative analysis techniques soon after 9/11. In 2008, the Office of the Director of National Intelligence (ODNI) formalized their use in the *Analytic Transformations* initiative directed at improving U.S. intelligence analysis. The ODNI program entitled "Tradecraft Training in Critical Thinking and Structured Analysis" in this initiative was designed to replace unaided judgment as the main basis for IC analysis.[8]

CRITICAL THINKING AND STRUCTURED ANALYSIS TECHNIQUES

Critical thinking and structured analysis techniques are not new to the IC. Morgan Jones's *The Thinker's Toolkit: 14 Powerful Techniques for Problem Solving* (1995) and Richards Heuer's *Psychology of Intelligence Analysis* (1999) were widely available before 9/11.[9] Jones and Heuer were both CIA analysts. Prior to 9/11, the strong reliance on unaided judgment resulted in little IC interest shown in these books. After the 9/11 terrorist attacks, the demand for these two books skyrocketed as they became must-haves on the desks of IC analysts. Both Jones and Heuer start their books with discussions of the cognitive limitations of human reasoning and then provide recommended analytic procedures to help overcome these limitations. Jones provides 14 different tools, grounded in critical thinking and rational choice theories. Heuer's most significant analytic contribution is his development of the structured analysis technique *Analysis of Competing Hypotheses* (*ACH*).[10] Heuer worked hard to promote the *ACH* procedures while still a CIA analyst, but they only received widespread notice after 9/11. Jones and Heuer's works became the basis for expansion of structured analysis techniques now taught both within the IC and in emerging academic programs in intelligence analysis.

Critical thinking has been a topic of study in both the business and management world and in academia for several decades. Building on this previous work, the IC now considers critical thinking as the basic intellectual procedures or standards that must be applied to any analysis, whether descriptive or predictive. Linda Elder and Richard Paul provide the model of critical thinking now widely accepted as the IC standard.[11] Critical thinking can be simply defined as "thinking about our thinking." In other words, in critical thinking "a person reflects on the quality of the reasoning process simultaneously while reasoning to a conclusion."[12] Elder and Paul offer a framework to guide the critical-thinking process, allowing analysts to improve their reasoning abilities and lead them to a best solution. It is now assumed that IC analysts use critical-thinking skills at every step of the analytic process.

Structured analysis techniques serve a number of purposes. First, they "mitigate the adverse impact on our analysis of known cognitive limitations and pitfalls" in our reasoning and decision making.[13] Second, the procedures are designed to guide us through the step-by-step analysis of any behavior. The specific structured analysis techniques used depend on the behavior under study. Third, these techniques help us create models of the behavior under study that coincide with the deductive or scientific approach to analysis. Fourth, these techniques can be used for either qualitative or quantitative analyses. In fact, they take qualitative analysis to a higher level than is normally taught in most U.S. social science graduate programs. Fifth, most of the structured analysis techniques can be used by either individual analysts or, more appropriately, used by teams of analysts assigned to the same study. Finally, these techniques allow detailed documentation of the analysis process such that other analysts or teams of analysts can check the work for reliability and validity.

Structured analysis techniques include a toolbox of supporting procedures and techniques analysts can select from, depending on the purpose of their assigned study. As the following case study will show, most studies start with structured analysis techniques that first frame the study of interest. There are also techniques for assessing the quality of information and assumptions used in the study. For predictive studies, tools are provided to test hypotheses and generate probabilities of future events. Predictive analyses include techniques for creating indicators that allow analysts to refine their estimates and point to which of the predicted outcomes is developing. An important step in IC analysis is the use of challenge analysis techniques, which allow other analysts to critique the procedures and findings of the completed analysis. When conducting predictive analysis of human behavior or decisions, the proper use of structured analysis techniques ensures the findings are as close to the truth as possible and should prevent future strategic surprises such as the 1941 Pearl Harbor attacks, the 1950 North Korean invasion of South Korea, and terrorist attacks similar to 9/11.

THE 9/11 CASE STUDY

A short counterfactual case study of 9/11 demonstrates how critical thinking and structured analysis techniques could have prevented the catastrophic terrorist attacks on the United States. Counterfactual analyses look at "what-might-have-been," with a goal of uncovering cause-and-effect relationships or other insights about the case under study.[14] In this case study, I will first conduct the counterfactual analysis, assuming the IC was using current (2009) critical thinking and structured analyses techniques. Then, I will take facts of the actual case and compare them to the counterfactual analysis to gain insight. This reveals that if the latest analytic procedures were used, and if U.S. decision makers had acted on the results of this analysis, 9/11 was likely preventable.

The Counterfactual Analysis

In the lead up to 9/11, a key point on the case timeline was late June 2001. At that point, there was enough information obtained through communications intercepts by the National Security Agency (NSA), anonymous tips and walk-in information, and public statements by al-Qaeda leadership to indicate that an al-Qaeda attack on U.S. interests was imminent. The problem with this information was that none of it was specific enough to indicate what type of attack would be attempted or where such an attack would take place. CIA Director George Tenet characterized the situation by late June 2001 as "blinking red," indicating a high probability of a spectacular al-Qaeda attack.[15]

The CIA Counterterrorism Center (CTC) had been watching al-Qaeda for several years. After the October 2000 attack on the USS *Cole* in Yemen by an al-Qaeda suicide boat loaded with explosives, the CTC focused their intelligence collection and analysis on al-Qaeda even closer in the later months of 2000 and the first half of 2001. Even before 9/11, the CTC was involved in a structured analysis technique of *High-Impact/Low Probability Analysis*, meaning that although there was a low probability of a terrorist attack on any particular U.S. target, the impact of such an attack in terms of personnel casualties, property damage, and interruption of U.S. infrastructure was so high that such an unexpected event must be brought to the attention of senior national security decision makers.[16] CTC data collection on al-Qaeda was constrained, however, due to the lack of human intelligence (HUMINT) sources that could penetrate al-Qaeda's inner circle and report on the plans or intentions of the al-Qaeda leadership. This lack of HUMINT resources was a result of CIA budget cuts in the 1990s after the cold war. Tenet reported that by the late 1990s, the CIA was in the equivalent of "Chapter 11 [bankruptcy], and neither the Congress or the executive branch did much about it."[17] NSA was in a similar degraded condition as its aging technology used against cold war adversaries was not able to keep up with advancing communications methods, and it would later need more than $1 billion in additional funding to modernize its signals intelligence (SIGINT) capabilities.[18]

In late June 2001, with the system "blinking red" and no specific details on a pending al-Qaeda attack, I begin the counterfactual analysis. Critical thinking and structured analysis techniques begin by asking the right questions. The right questions in this case included: Will al-Qaeda likely attack the United States? If a U.S. attack is likely, what is the most likely type of attack (explosives, WMDs, etc.)? What are the most likely targets? Both the CIA's CTC and the FBI should have been asking these questions. Here I will assume that CTC and FBI did ask the right first question and determined that a domestic attack on the United States was a likely scenario. Thus, the focus of the analysis then shifts to the second question on what is the most likely type of attack. To answer this second question, the *ACH* technique is appropriate.

The structured analysis technique of *ACH* employs a matrix analysis with the competing hypotheses placed along the top axis of the matrix and evidence supporting the hypotheses listed down the left axis. The competing hypotheses and the evidence list can be developed through a combination of structured *Brainstorming* (group brainstorming is recommended) and the use of causal or process models that pertain to the question under study. In the evidence column, analysts should list information or data that is known and assumptions (what is usually not known) that are needed to make the hypotheses plausible. The *ACH* technique then has the analyst determine which evidence is consistent (C), very consistent (CC), inconsistent (I), or very inconsistent (II) with each competing hypothesis. The objective is to determine which hypotheses have the least-inconsistent evidence—based on assigning 1 point for an inconsistent rating and 2 points for a very inconsistent rating. The hypothesis(es) with the lowest score(s) is/are considered to have the highest relative probability(ies) of occurring. Table 4.1 provides a potential *ACH* matrix for the question, if a U.S. attack is likely, what is the most likely type of attack (explosives, WMD, etc.)? Four competing hypotheses are addressed in Table 4.1 concerning the type of attack al-Qaeda would likely attempt on the United States (explosives, aircraft hijacking, nuclear, or biological/chemical). The analysis assesses five key evidence factors. First, would a U.S. attack meet al-Qaeda's goals to attack U.S. interests? Second, does al-Qaeda have the weapons capabilities to carry out the attack? Third, does al-Qaeda have an information structure that allows them the latest data on the intended targets (via surveillance, etc.) and to be able to provide command and control to such an attack? Fourth, is the risk to al-Qaeda's personnel conducting the attack acceptable to their organization? Finally, are the reactions of the United States or other nations to each type of attack acceptable to al-Qaeda?

Table 4.1 provides the *ACH* evaluation of individual evidence factors as they relate to each competing hypothesis with what was known in late June 2001. It reveals that the most likely types of attack within the United States (the hypotheses with the least inconsistencies) would be an explosives attack or an aircraft hijacking. Previously, al-Qaeda conducted several explosives bombing attacks on U.S. interests (the World Trade Center in 1993, Khobar Towers in Saudi Arabia in 1996, the 1998 U.S. Embassy bombings in Africa, and the 2000 USS *Cole* attack). Al-Qaeda is thus well versed in explosives attacks. Information that al-Qaeda may attempt an aircraft hijacking had been received, and the Federal Aviation Administration (FAA) had warned the airline industry at least 15 times in the first six months of 2001 to increase aviation security measures.[19] At this point in the counterfactual analysis, it would be safe to say that an aircraft hijacking could be used for ransom or other demands (e.g., release of the convicted 1993 World Trade Center bombers), to kill the passengers onboard, or as an ad hoc missile crashed into a target important to U.S. interests. The nature of the aircraft hijacking was not what was important at this point, as simply taking action that would prevent any hijacking from occurring should have been the U.S. objective.

Two additional structured analysis techniques are included in Table 4.1: *Quality of Information Checks* and *Assumption Checks*. These are two techniques that must be continually addressed and updated during any type of analysis. Including the evidence source type, credibility, and relevance in the *ACH* matrix allows analysts to continually assess their information and assumptions as they complete their analysis. The accuracy of information plays a major role in assessing the validity of any analysis. By listing our assumptions, we can identify information that would demand our rethinking them. Another important structured analysis technique that must be considered is *Deception Detection*—meaning whether the adversary would take purposive actions to influence the perceptions, decisions, or actions of the United States. In evidence known by late June 2001, the National Security Agency and the CIA director both considered that there were no deceptive actions taking place by al-Qaeda.[20]

With the above *ACH* findings in hand (explosives attack or aircraft hijacking as the most likely types of attack), we must then assess the third question: What are the most likely targets? To date, al-Qaeda had limited itself to attacks on U.S. military units, diplomatic targets, and financial targets—all

Table 4.1 *ACH* Matrix for 9/11 Competing Hypotheses

Evidence	Source/Type	Credibility	Relevance	1. Explosives	2. Aircraft Hijacking	3. Nuclear	4. Biological/Chemical
Al Qaeda Goals	Al-Qaeda public statements	High	High	C	C	CC	CC
Weapons Capabilities	Intel Reporting	Medium	High	CC	C	II	I
Information Structure: command and control, surveillance, etc.	Assumption (based on previous attacks)	Medium	High	C	C	I	C
Risk Aversion to own Forces	Assumption (past suicide attacks)	High	High	C	C	C	C
Unintended Consequences, i.e., reactions from U.S. or other states	Assumption (e.g., no U.S. reaction after USS Cole attack)	Low	Low	C	C	II	I
Total Score				0	0	5	2

C = consistent; CC = very consistent; I = inconsistent, 1 point; II = very inconsistent, 2 points.
Table format and scoring modified from example in Richards J. Heuer, Jr., "Computer-Aided Analysis of Competing Hypotheses," in *Analyzing Intelligence, Origins, Obstacles, and Innovations*, ed. Roger Z. George and James B. Bruce (Washington, D.C.: Georgetown University Press, 2008), 254–55.

of which could be considered icons of U.S. military and financial power. Measures were taken to increase security on such targets overseas in summer 2001. However, there are thousands of such targets within the United States. Thus, attempting to determine which targets al-Qaeda might attack inside the United States is akin to the search for the needle in the haystack. More detailed and specific information was needed on the probable al-Qaeda attack to both determine the exact type of attack being planned and where the attack would be located. The intelligence community handles this data collection contingency through the structured analysis technique of *Indicators Analysis*.

An *Indicators Analysis* allows the analyst to determine information needed to support one or more hypotheses (i.e., type of attack and location in this case study). When included in intelligence products, an indicators list allows decision makers to watch a developing scenario and place more confidence in the analytic judgments.[21] A good indicators list will include items particular to all likely scenarios. Knowing from Table 4.1 that the most likely al-Qaeda attacks would be either explosives or aircraft hijackings does not mean that a nuclear or biological/chemical attack could be totally discounted. The indicators list must account for all these scenarios. Once developed, the indicators list is tasked to the appropriate intelligence collectors.

An indicators list developed to support the Table 4.1 findings would include information about the following:

- Recent entry or attempted entry of potential al-Qaeda operatives into the United States
- Identification and location of potential al-Qaeda operatives residing in the United States
- Travel of potential al-Qaeda operatives inside the United States and overseas
- Personal contacts by al-Qaeda operatives residing in the United States
- Financial transactions of potential al-Qaeda operatives inside the United States (bank accounts, credit cards, leases, Social Security numbers, etc.)
- Other transactions of potential al-Qaeda operatives inside the United States (drivers licenses, pilot licenses, education, religious affiliations, etc.)
- Interest of potential al-Qaeda operatives in aviation security or other aviation-related activities
- Evidence of potential al-Qaeda operatives smuggling into the United States, or procuring in the United States, arms and ammunition, explosives, nuclear materials, or biological/chemical materials

Once the Indicators Analysis is completed, the entire analytic effort (above) would be sent to a second analyst or group of analysts to undergo challenge analysis. Techniques such as *Devil's Advocacy*, *"What If" Analysis*, and *Red Team Analysis* are used to challenge the findings of other analyses.[22] Challenge analysis helps ensure reliability and validity in the original findings. Once the challenge analysis was complete, the

U.S. government would be ready to begin an aggressive investigation of al-Qaeda based on the above indicators list. In the real case, that is not what happened.

What Really Happened on 9/11

The following is a summary of what really happened on 9/11 with corresponding insights related to the above counterfactual analysis. Procedures whereby agencies asked the right questions, used *ACH* to determine the most likely types of attack, developed the indicators list to fill data gaps, submitted their findings to challenge analysis, and then took aggressive action to collect information on the indicators list simply did not happen. The CIA and the CTC mounted an effort to warn U.S. national security decision makers of a pending al-Qaeda attack. National Security Advisor for Counterterrorism (NSAC) Richard Clarke worked closely with Tenet and attempted to keep the al-Qaeda threat in front of decision makers. However, despite the CIA and Clarke's efforts, the FBI and national decision makers gave little credence to the al-Qaeda threat, which largely explains why the 9/11 attacks were successful.

Why no one was asking the right questions in late June 2001, as the system was "blinking red," can best be explained by organizational behavior theory. Allison and Zelikow (1999) developed, through a case study of the 1962 Cuban missile crisis, how government organizations are limited in their range of behavior in a particular situation by a well-defined set of rules, routines, and repertoires (i.e., standard operating procedures) that are developed within the organization over time.[23] Al-Qaeda, probably unknowingly, found a seam to exploit in how U.S. foreign and domestic intelligence standard operating procedures were in conflict. The rules, routines, and repertoires of the CIA, responsible for U.S. foreign intelligence, and the FBI, responsible for U.S. domestic intelligence, created almost impenetrable walls between U.S. foreign and domestic intelligence over the 50-plus-year history of the IC. While there was limited cooperation between the CIA and FBI prior to 9/11, this foreign-domestic intelligence wall precluded significant amounts of information sharing.

The CIA focused its collection, analysis, and covert action activities outside the United States. It never recommends policy, but has a primary responsibility for informing and alerting U.S. senior decision makers on foreign matters. It informs them through recurring and incident-specific reporting. It also alerts decision makers to opportunities to advance or protect U.S. interests overseas. Part of this alerting function is to warn decision makers of threats to U.S. interests. The CIA works from what is known as the national security intelligence model, which follows the intelligence cycle. As should be expected through the rules, routines, and repertoires existing in the CIA, the CTC and its al-Qaeda research was focused on an overseas attack. In late June 2001, the CTC estimated that

U.S. interests in either Israel or Saudi Arabia would be al-Qaeda's next target.

As a federal law enforcement agency, the FBI's intelligence functions prior to 9/11 focused on investigating crimes, apprehending criminals, and obtaining convictions. While counterterrorism was an FBI mission prior to 9/11, few resources were dedicated to this mission in the Clinton and early Bush administrations.[24] The FBI rules, routines, and repertoires bounded its actions into a criminal case file mentality (i.e., resources were not dedicated to cases where a federal crime had not been committed and lacked a good chance of an eventual conviction). Without any hard evidence that al-Qaeda was about to strike the United States in the summer of 2001, the FBI showed little interest in investigating that possibility. The head of FBI counterterrorism later said he felt something was going to happen, but the information was nebulous. He also reported he wished he had 500 analysts working on the al-Qaeda threat, instead of 2.[25] The FBI's lack of interest in counterterrorism was also affected by the priorities of Attorney General John Ashcroft. The feeling was that he wanted the FBI to get back to its "investigative basics: guns, drugs, and civil rights."[26]

In late June 2001, the CIA was focused on threats to U.S. interests overseas, and the FBI was bounded by its criminal case file mentality, giving little attention to preventing terrorist attacks. Al-Qaeda was about to conduct a U.S. domestic terrorist attack using operatives from outside the United States, a situation that fell through the cracks in the wall created between U.S. foreign and domestic intelligence.

In the months leading up to late June 2001, the CTC, CIA Director Tenet, and NSAC Clarke and his staff kept in frequent contact as they followed the developing al-Qaeda intelligence. The CIA was working hard to develop more information on a potential attack from sources overseas—something made more difficult by the gutting of U.S. HUMINT resources in the 1990s and the fact that the CIA had no sources in Afghanistan with access to information on al-Qaeda intentions. Clarke decided to take action.

During the first week of July [2001], I (Clarke) convened the CSG (Counterterrorism Security Group) and asked each agency to consider itself on full alert. I asked the CSG agencies to cancel summer vacations and official travel for the counterterrorism response staffs. Each agency should report anything unusual. . . . I asked FBI to send another warning to the 18,000 [U.S.] police departments, State to alert the embassies, and Defense Department to go to Threat Condition Delta . . . s.[July 5] I asked the senior security officials at FAA, Immigration, Secret Service, Coast Guard, and Customs and the Federal Protective Service to meet at the White House. I asked the FAA to send another security warning to the airlines and airports and requested special scrutiny at the ports of entry.[27]

On July 5, CTC officials also briefed Ashcroft on the potential for an al-Qaeda threat. Their message conveyed how preparations for an attack were in their last stages and that a significant attack was imminent.

However, CTC officials also told the attorney general that they believed an attack was more likely overseas.[28] It was not until late July that the CTC changed its assessment to show a U.S. domestic attack was likely.[29]

Clarke's actions in the first week of July did not mobilize the U.S. government to any great length. The FBI did notify law enforcement agencies of possible al-Qaeda strikes overseas. The report included the statement: "The FBI has no information indicating a credible threat of terrorist attack in the United States."[30] It added that domestic strikes could not be ruled out.[31] Participants in the July 5 meeting at the White House with Clarke reported they were asked to take the information back to their home agencies and "do what you can" with it.[32] An Immigration representative at the meeting asked for a summary of the information that could be shared with Immigration and Naturalization Service (INS) field offices, but the summary was never provided.[33] Although Clarke made an attempt to mobilize the U.S. government for a potential attack, it was not successful domestically. Overseas it worked as CIA information collection and security at U.S. embassies and military sites did increase. It did not work for a potential U.S. domestic attack as the National Security Council directions provided by Clarke gave few specifics and did not convince agencies to change much in the way of their data collection and security status.

A real mobilization of U.S. government agencies in early July 2001 would have resulted in a high likelihood of stopping the 9/11 attacks. Such a mobilization would have started with an aggressive data collection plan based on the previous counterfactual study's indicators list. This data collection should have started with locating Khalid al-Midhar and Nawaf al-Hazmi, two known al-Qaeda operatives and later 9/11 hijackers that arrived in Los Angeles in January 2000. Al-Hazmi remained in the United States through the 9/11 attacks. Al-Midhar departed the United States in June 2000 and returned on July 4, 2001, after recruiting other hijackers. Al-Midhar and al-Hazmi traveled and made financial and other transactions in their own names while in the United States.[34] Both the CIA and FBI had information on al-Midhar and al-Hazmi's entry into the United States in January 2000, including a possible connection with al-Qaeda.[35]

The now infamous FBI Phoenix memo would have correlated with the above indicators analysis, if such analysis had existed. The Phoenix memo, written by an FBI agent in Phoenix on July 9, 2001, reported how eight Arab men who studied in Arizona flight schools might be related to terror activities against civil aviation targets.[36] The Phoenix memo requested FBI headquarters to develop a list of civil aviation teaching facilities and have FBI offices liaise with them to determine if there were other instances of Arabs raising suspicion in these facilities. With no indicators analysis to document a need for information on aviation anomalies, the Phoenix memo ended up all but ignored at both FBI headquarters and in the FBI New York field office, the FBI's lead office for investigating al-Qaeda.[37]

Finally, on August 15, 2001, INS arrested Zacarias Moussaoui in Minnesota on a visa violation after he raised suspicion by his statements and behavior at a local flight school. The flight school notified the FBI's Minneapolis office, whose investigation led to the INS arrest. The FBI Minneapolis office made a Foreign Intelligence Surveillance Act (FISA) request to search Moussaoui's personal belongings, but it was denied. A search of Moussaoui's personal belongings would have linked him to al-Midhar and al-Hazmi. We will probably never know for sure, but it appears that Moussaoui was to be either the 20th 9/11 hijacker or was in training as a backup 9/11 pilot in case one of the other four pilots suddenly became unavailable. By not following up on the FISA request from Minneapolis, another opportunity to investigate leads that could have led to the 9/11 plot was lost. Senator Bob Graham, chairman of the Senate Select Committee on Intelligence and co-chair of the House-Senate Joint Inquiry into 9/11, counted a total of 12 lost opportunities by U.S. government agencies where aggressive follow-up on a lead could have uncovered the 9/11 plot.[38]

CONCLUSION

The findings in this chapter's counterfactual case study of 9/11 are not new. Most of the official inquiries, journalistic reporting, and personal memoirs of senior officials cited in the endnotes section of this chapter offer similar findings. The main contribution of this chapter is to demonstrate how if current (2009) IC analysis procedures had been used prior to 9/11, there would have been a high probability that 9/11 could have been prevented. I hope this is the case in the future.

The 9/11 and Iraqi WMD NIE cases did lead to a number of U.S. government changes. The post-9/11 formation of the National Counterterrorism Center (NCTC), an expanded FBI National Security Branch, and the creation of the Department of Homeland Security now provide vastly increased resources for intelligence data collection and analysis against the terrorist threat. Actions such as the USA PATRIOT Act, the 2004 IRTPA, and the ODNI Information Sharing Environment program are meant to tear down the wall that existed between national security and law enforcement intelligence. Although it took seven years to formalize, the ODNI *Analytic Transformations* initiative provides the framework for improved intelligence analysis through the implementation of critical-thinking skills and structured analysis techniques. While no intelligence system is perfect, these post-9/11 actions are a good starting point to detect and prevent future terrorist attacks.

The post-9/11 years have seen a revolution in IC analysis procedures. There no doubt will be significant resistance to the new critical thinking and structured analysis techniques being implemented across the IC. Fifty years of using unaided judgment as a primary analysis procedure will be hard to change. Advances in computer software programs related to data mining, qualitative and quantitative analysis, and geographic information systems all show potential for further improving intelligence analysis. Most of the structured analysis techniques in use today use manual procedures; it should only be a matter of time until they too become computer assisted. Even with the increased use of computers in intelligence analysis, the human analyst remains the key linchpin in the system. The IC faces a huge education and training challenge in implementing advanced analysis technology and improving structured analysis techniques. The next generation of IC analysts will rise to these challenges.

NOTES

1. See Senate Select Committee on Intelligence and House Permanent Select Committee on Intelligence, *Joint Inquiry into Intelligence Community Activities Before and After the Terrorist Attacks of September 11, 2001*, 107th Cong., 2nd Sess., 2002, S. Rep. 351, H. Rep. 792; and 9/11 Commission, *The 9/11 Commission Report, Final Report of the National Commission on Terrorist Attacks Upon the United States* (New York: W.W. Norton & Company, 2004), 339–44, 407–19.

2. See Senate Select Committee on Intelligence, *Report on the U.S. Intelligence Community's Prewar Intelligence Assessments on Iraq*, 108th Cong., July 7, 2004.

3. Richards J. Heuer, Jr., "Taxonomy of Structured Analytic Techniques" (paper presented at the annual meeting of the International Studies Association, San Francisco, CA, March 26–29, 2008), http://www.pherson.org/Library/H12.pdf (accessed July 17, 2009).

4. Ibid., 3–4.

5. Donald P. Steury, ed., *Sherman Kent and the Board of National Estimates. Collected Essays* (Washington, D.C.: Center for the Study of Intelligence, Central Intelligence Agency, 1994).

6. Richards J. Heuer, Jr., ed., *Quantitative Approaches to Political Intelligence: the CIA Experience* (Boulder, Colo.: Westview Press, 1978).

7. *Intelligence Reform and Terrorism Prevention Act of 2004*, Public Law 458, 108th Cong. (December 17, 2004) § 1017.

8. Office of the Director of National Intelligence, *Analytic Transformation, Unleashing the Potential of a Community of Analysts* (Washington, D.C.: Office of the Director of National Intelligence, 2008), http://www.dni.gov/content/AT_Digital%2020080923.pdf (accessed July 17, 2009).

9. Morgan D. Jones, *The Thinker's Toolkit: 14 Powerful Techniques for Problem Solving* (New York: Three Rivers Press, 1995); Richards J. Heuer, Jr., *Psychology of Intelligence Analysis* (Washington, D.C.: Center for the Study of Intelligence, Central Intelligence Agency, 1999).

10. Specific structured analysis techniques will be indicated by italics.

11. Linda Elder and Richard Paul, *Analytic Thinking, How to Take Thinking Apart and What to Look For When You Do* (Dillon Beach, Calif.: Foundation for Critical Thinking, 2007).

12. David T. Moore, *Critical Thinking and Intelligence Analysis* (Washington, D.C.: National Military Intelligence College Press, 2006), 8.

13. Heuer, "Taxonomy of Structured Analytic Techniques," 4.

14. Philip E. Tetlock and Aaron Belkin, eds., *Counterfactual Thought Experiments in World Politics. Logical, Methodological, and Psychological Perspectives* (Princeton, N.J.: Princeton University Press, 1996).

15. 9/11 Commission. *The 9/11 Commission Report*, 259.

16. Sherman Kent School, *A Tradecraft Primer, Structured Analytic Techniques for Improving Intelligence Analysis*, 22–23.

17. George Tenet, *At the Center of the Storm, My Years at the CIA*, with Bill Harlow (New York: HarperCollins Publishers, 2007), 108.

18. Senator Bob Graham, *Intelligence Matters, The CIA, the FBI, Saudi Arabia, and the Failure of America's War on Terror*, with Jeff Nussbaum (New York: Random House, 2004), 71.

19. Peter Lance, *1000 Years for Revenge, International Terrorism and the FBI—The Untold Story* (New York: HarperCollins Publishers, 2003), 400–401.

20. Tenet, *At the Center of the Storm, My Years at the CIA*, 154.

21. Sherman Kent School, *A Tradecraft Primer, Structured Analytic Techniques for Improving Intelligence Analysis*, 12–13.

22. Sherman Kent School, *A Tradecraft Primer, Structured Analytic Techniques for Improving Intelligence Analysis*.

23. Graham Allison and Philip Zelikow, *Essence of Decision, Explaining the Cuban Missile Crisis*, 2nd ed. (New York: Longman, 1999).

24. Bill Gertz, *Breakdown, How America's Intelligence Failures Led to September 11* (Washington, D.C.: Regnery Publishing, 2002), 83–104.

25. 9/11 Commission. *The 9/11 Commission Report*, 265.

26. Ibid., 209.

27. Richard A. Clarke, *Against All Enemies, Inside America's War on Terror* (New York, Free Press, 2004), 236.

28. Tenet, *At the Center of the Storm, My Years at the CIA*, 150.

29. Ibid., 158.

30. 9/11 Commission. *The 9/11 Commission Report*, 258.

31. Lance, *1000 Years for Revenge, International Terrorism and the FBI—The Untold Story*, 405.

32. 9/11 Commission. *The 9/11 Commission Report*, 258.

33. Ibid.

34. Ibid., 215–23.

35. Tenet, *At the Center of the Storm, My Years at the CIA*, 197–99.

36. Graham, *Intelligence Matters, The CIA, the FBI, Saudi Arabia, and the Failure of America's War on Terror*, 45.

37. Lance, *1000 Years for Revenge, International Terrorism and the FBI—The Untold Story*, 406.

38. Graham, *Intelligence Matters, The CIA, the FBI, Saudi Arabia, and the Failure of America's War on Terror*, 75.

PART II

The Post-9/11 Intelligence Community

The post-9/11 intelligence community (IC) contains several new players. It reflects the largest reorganization of the federal government in history, with the creation of the Department of Homeland Security (DHS), incorporating 22 entities under one department to enhance communication and function in intelligence and security. The authors in this part build on the discussion of the basic IC structure; not only does the reader gain a better understanding of the IC, but several of the authors provide insight into some of the problems that have arisen with the new organization. There are also presentations regarding the roles of law enforcement and private security. One key element that appears in several chapters is the role of the fusion centers. In the last chapter, the author has the reader take a step back and consider another perspective to security, the Israeli perspective.

CHAPTER 5: THE DEPARTMENT OF HOMELAND SECURITY AND INTELLIGENCE—PAST, PRESENT, AND FUTURE

In this chapter, the author discusses the role that intelligence plays within the DHS. It begins by describing the initial challenges that intelligence played in defining DHS's overall mission and how DHS overcame those obstacles. The crux of the chapter focuses on two significant DHS programs that focus on intelligence sharing: the State and Local Fusion Centers, whose goal is to fuse and share information at the federal, state, and local levels and the Interagency Threat Assessment Coordination Group (ITACG), whose purpose is to involve the state and local governments in creating federally coordinated intelligence that is available and relevant to domestic law enforcement. Both of these initiatives have involved their share of controversy and initial growing pains. Nonetheless, while their future may be uncertain, they have enormous potential for reshaping and expanding the role of homeland security intelligence. As Secretary Napolitano takes the reigns, the final section concludes with thoughts for the future and how her priorities may affect the overall role of intelligence within DHS.

CHAPTER 6: MILITARY INTELLIGENCE

The author provides an overview of military intelligence for those new to the field who want a basic understanding of the modern (post–World War II) U.S. military intelligence community. Starting with its antecedents between the two great world wars, the author provides an overview of the legal underpinnings of the fundamental reorganization of the U.S. military intelligence structure in the immediate aftermath of World War II. He provides a working definition of strategic and tactical intelligence, as those terms apply to the larger field of military intelligence. The author identifies some of the pitfalls that were encountered with the development of the military intelligence community and provides the reader with an outline of the U.S. military intelligence community in the post-9/11 era.

CHAPTER 7: CONNECTING POLICE INTELLIGENCE WITH MILITARY AND NATIONAL INTELLIGENCE

In this chapter, the authors discuss the key role played by the police in collecting and sharing terrorism-related information and intelligence. Prior to 9/11, few would have seen much common ground between police intelligence and either military intelligence or national intelligence. Today, the reality of international terrorism has shifted the terrain substantially. At the federal level, new information-sharing strategies and the new architecture of the ODNI, National Counterterrorism Center (NCTC), and Information Sharing Environment (ISE) hold great promise, if traditional interagency competition can be overcome. At the state level, fusion centers have been created and are beginning to operate as the linking pin with federal agencies and networks. It is the local level that presents the greatest challenges. U.S. policing is mainly local and extremely fragmented, and local police relations with state and federal agencies have always been tenuous. In addition, police work has not traditionally emphasized intelligence gathering and sharing. The reactive nature of most police work, the principal strategies of modern policing, and the dominant values of the police culture all tend to support enforcement and investigation rather than intelligence. Local police are ready to be first responders to terrorism and are learning that they should also be first preventers.

CHAPTER 8: PRIVATE SECURITY INTELLIGENCE AND HOMELAND SECURITY

The tragedies of 9/11 signified a mandate for change. The authors point to the inability of the U.S. IC to "connect the dots" due to a lack of efficient information-sharing mechanisms (National Commission on Terrorist Attacks upon the United States, 2003). They point to a series of subsequent changes in an attempt at improving the nation's intelligence system. The most significant changes were the creation of several national organizations and changes in the FBI's efforts to restructure and upgrade its intelligence support. They remind us that the protection of critical infrastructure, as well as the response to an initial attack, is largely the responsibility of state, local, and private entities. Because most of the critical infrastructure of the United States is privately owned, it is essential to ensure that the private sector is a true partner in all aspects of prevention, mitigation, and response.

CHAPTER 9: FOREIGN INTELLIGENCE AND COUNTERTERRORISM—AN ISRAELI PERSPECTIVE

After the reader has had an opportunity to view the U.S. response in the preceding chapters, the author presents a different perspective. This chapter deals with Israel's counterterrorism intelligence and policies. It begins with a survey of the types of terrorism threats Israel faces and then moves to a discussion of the nature of Israeli counterterrorism legislation. There is also an analysis of the role of Israel's law enforcement, counterterrorism, and intelligence agencies, as well as the role of the cabinet-level decision makers. There is a discussion of Israel's counterterrorism strategy, which is based on five elements: deterrence, intelligence, prevention, arrests/executive action, and public cooperation. This strategy is designed to reduce the number and scope of terrorist attacks rather than ending them completely. The author will argue that a consistent and intensive policy (based on intensive HUMINT collection and rapid sharing of intelligence information) of disruption of terrorist planning and operations leads to a significant reduction in both the frequency and scope of attacks.

The Department of Homeland Security and Intelligence: Past, Present, and Future

Stephanie Cooper Blum

[I]ntelligence analysis lies at the heart of everything we do.
　　—Michael Chertoff, former secretary of homeland security

After September 11, 2001, as the government searched for how such a calamity occurred and who to blame, one reemerging theme prominently stood out: the inability to "connect the dots" caused by a lack of intelligence sharing among various governmental agencies.[1] Whether true or not, at its heart, 9/11 was seen as an intelligence failure.[2] Congressional testimony revealed that critical pieces of information were in intelligence and law enforcement agencies but were not shared with each other or other agencies.[3]

In June 2002, the former director of central intelligence (DCI) George Tenet testified before the Government Affairs Subcommittee that while we have a foreign intelligence community and law enforcement agencies, "we have not had a cohesive body responsible for homeland security."[4] In discussing the eventual creation of the Department of Homeland Security (DHS), Tenet testified that DHS would not duplicate the roles of foreign intelligence or law enforcement but would rather "merge under one roof the capability to assess threats to the homeland, map those threats against our vulnerabilities, and take action to protect America's key assets and critical infrastructure."[5] Significantly, he stated that DHS would review intelligence and "provide and develop an action plan to counter the threat." He explained that, by making security enhancements to infrastructure, the costs and risks for terrorists to operate in the United States would increase. He further elaborated that the Central Intelligence

Agency's (CIA) counterterrorism mission for years had "been to understand and reduce the *threat.*" DHS's new mission, in contrast, would be to" understand and reduce the nation's domestic *vulnerability.*"[6] Almost as if a harbinger for future problems that would plague DHS's mission, he emphasized that the CIA pledged "support not as a change of mission, but as an expansion of our mission" and that the intelligence community (IC) would not merely treat DHS "as an important customer" but would treat it as a genuine partner.[7]

Against this ambitious backdrop, on November 25, 2002, Congress passed the Homeland Security Act of 2002 (HSA),[8] which created DHS by bringing together 22 governmental agencies. The White House described DHS as "the most significant transition of the U.S. government in over half-century by largely transforming and realigning the current confusing patchwork of government activities into a single department whose primary mission is to protect our homeland."[9] DHS's primary statutory mission is to "(A) prevent terrorist attacks within the United States; (B) reduce vulnerability of the United States to terrorism; and (C) minimize the damage, and assist in the recovery, from terrorist attacks that do occur within the United States."[10]

Because the crux of DHS's goal was, and to a large extent still is, the prevention of terrorist attacks within the homeland,[11] one of DHS's key missions is to collect, analyze, and disseminate available intelligence that contributes to an understanding of the nature and scope of the terrorist threat to the homeland and share that information with the federal government as well as nontraditional partners, such as state and local governments and the private sector. While DHS has many responsibilities and initiatives, the purpose of this chapter is to generally discuss the role that intelligence plays within DHS and focus on some particular initiatives. The role of intelligence within DHS has evolved along with DHS's more general challenges of defining its mission. While the HSA made DHS's Directorate for Intelligence Analysis and Infrastructure Protection (IAIP) the 16th member of the IC, thus giving DHS a formal role when the IC set priorities for collection and analyses, the early creation of the Terrorist Threat Integration Center (TTIC), whose purpose was to integrate and fuse terrorist-related information, challenged and confused the role of intelligence within DHS, causing some to believe the TTIC was encroaching on IAIP's statutory mandate.[12] Nonetheless, through the Intelligence Reform and Terrorism Prevention Act of 2004 (IRTPA), which created the Information Sharing Environment (ISE), the Implementing Recommendations of the 9/11 Commission Act of 2007 (9/11 Act), the replacement of the IAIP with the Office of Intelligence and Analysis (I&A), and subsequent initiatives such as the State and Local Fusion Centers and the Interagency Threat Assessment Coordination Group (ITACG), the role of intelligence, especially intelligence sharing, within DHS has become paramount and only seems to be growing. In fact, the new Secretary of Homeland Security

Janet Napolitano has made information sharing a top priority by issuing on her very first day in office an "evaluation of which activities hold the most promise for achieving the smooth flow of information on a real-time basis."[13]

This chapter first describes the initial challenges that intelligence played in defining DHS's overall mission and how DHS overcame those obstacles. The second section discusses two significant DHS programs that focus on intelligence: the State and Local Fusion Centers and the ITACG. As Secretary Napolitano takes the reigns, the final section concludes with thoughts for the future and how her priorities may affect the overall role of intelligence within DHS.

THE ROLE OF INTELLIGENCE DURING DHS's EVOLUTION

The creation of DHS was a monumental effort. DHS has been described as the "most significant change in the Federal government since the creation of the Department of Defense (DOD) and the National Security Counsel following the Second World War."[14] It has more than 200,000 employees and is the third largest cabinet department.[15] In 2009—seven years after its creation—it appears that DHS is a permanent part of our government (although there is still conjecture about reorganization such as removing the Federal Emergency Management Agency from DHS).[16] In the early years of its formation, however, its future was not so certain as it was plagued by three problems: (1) lack of respect and resources, (2) a decision not to give DHS access to raw intelligence, and (3) competition and potential overlap in mission with the TTIC. As will be shown, DHS has largely overcome all three obstacles.

Lack of Respect and Resources

It was hard to establish a full-fledged equal member of the IC from scratch. Four months after DHS's creation, according to some members of Congress and national security experts, the IAIP—the intelligence unit of DHS—was "understaffed, unorganized and weak-willed in bureaucratic struggles with other government agencies"[17] Paul Redmond, a 33-year veteran of the CIA, and the then head of the IAIP, testified before Congress in June 2003 that his office only had 26 analysts and lacked secure communications lines required to access classified CIA and FBI reports.[18] Rep. Jim Turner (D-TX) wrote President Bush a letter in June 2003 stating that "a disturbing hearing . . . revealed that there are serious problems" with DHS's intelligence unit. He wrote that the department "is not remotely close to having the tools it needs to meet its critical mandate." Redmond, citing health reasons, resigned three weeks after the hearing.[19]

By July 2003, under the new head of IAIP, retired U.S. Marine Lt. Gen. Frank Libutti, DHS had 53 analysts with plans to increase to 150. Yet, by contrast, the TTIC (discussed below) had 100 analysts in July 2003 with plans to increase to 300 by May 2004.[20] Although members of Congress became frustrated because they thought DHS would have had hundreds of analysts like the CIA and FBI, former secretary of homeland security Tom Ridge had a difficult time recruiting people for intelligence jobs. For instance, retired U.S. Air Force Lt. Gen. James R. Clapper, Jr., who ran the U.S. National Imagery and Mapping Agency, initially agreed to be undersecretary for intelligence but changed his mind stating that the job lacked clout and resources. Moreover, DHS was competing for intelligence professionals with the higher-profile FBI, CIA, and TTIC.[21]

Access to Raw Intelligence

When Congress created DHS in 2002, it did not transfer to the new agency existing government intelligence and law enforcement agencies. Rather, Congress sought an analytical office that would use the products from other agencies such as the FBI and CIA to provide necessary warning of terrorist attacks; conduct vulnerability assessments of key resources and infrastructure; and make recommendations for remedial actions at the federal, state, and local levels as well as to the private sector. Yet, concerns that DHS was a "new and untested agency" tasked with producing all-source intelligence led to the Bush administration deciding that DHS would not be given raw intelligence from the CIA and the FBI.[22] Rather, DHS would obtain its intelligence reports from the CIA, FBI, and TTIC and then analyze them and decide what warnings needed to be provided to the federal, state, and local levels as well as the private sector.

Richard A. Clarke, former top White House counterterrorism official in the Clinton and Bush administrations, observed early on in 2003 that "the department is damned if it does and damned if it doesn't" arguing that the "people in Congress who wrote the legislation creating the department wanted a 'Team B' analytical capability" that would scrutinize and review every piece of terrorism intelligence assembled by CIA and FBI. However, because the White House agreed that DHS should not get the raw intelligence, the "department is going to get squeezed and victimized."[23] It appears Clarke was concerned that DHS would not have the tools it needed to produce actionable intelligence. His concern became further justified when President Bush announced the creation of the TTIC during his January 2003 State of the Union address. As addressed in more detail below, TTIC's purpose was to "integrate terrorist-related information collected domestically and abroad" and to provide "terrorist threat assessments for our national leadership."[24] Because TTIC's mandate seemed to overlap with the purpose of DHS's IAIP, DHS again appeared to be marginalized.

TTIC

The TTIC (which the National Counterterrorism Center [NCTC] superseded in December 2004) became operational in May 2003. It was a multiagency entity with "access to information systems and databases spanning the intelligence, law enforcement, homeland security, diplomatic, and military communities that contain information related to the threat of international terrorism."[25] As former director John Brennan testified, the TTIC's "unprecedented access to information allows us to gain a comprehensive understanding of terrorist threats to U.S. interests at home and abroad and, most importantly, to provide this information and related analysis to those responsible for detecting, disrupting, deterring, and defending against terrorist attacks."[26] Because TTIC's purpose of fusing intelligence appeared to overlap with many of the tasks that DHS's newly created IAIP was supposed to undertake, some members of Congress thought TTIC was encroaching on IAIP's statutory mandate and that the IAIP was being set up to fail.[27]

Based on these concerns, in April 2004, the FBI, TTIC, IAIP, and CIA wrote a letter to Senator Susan Collins and Senator Carl Levin explaining how the responsibilities of the TTIC and IAIP were different.[28] While the TTIC had the primary responsibility for terrorism analyses (unless solely domestic), the IAIP had primary responsibility for "matching the assessment of the risk posed by identified threats and terrorist capabilities to our Nation's vulnerabilities."[29] Furthermore, the IAIP, along with the FBI, had significant responsibilities for purely domestic terrorism. The letter noted that the IAIP was responsible for the "full-range of intelligence support—briefings, analytic products, including competitive analysis, 'red teaming,' and tailored analysis responding to specific inquiries" to DHS leadership. The letter concluded by emphasizing that collection and analysis of terrorism-related information is a shared responsibility.[30]

Nonetheless, in May 2004, homeland security expert James Carafano from the Heritage Foundation argued that the TTIC and the Terrorist Screening Center (TSC)[31] should be consolidated with the IAIP to create a single interagency staff under the supervision of DHS.[32] He further advocated that Congress allow DHS to exercise meaningful budget oversight for intelligence integration. According to Carafano, the HSA gave DHS—not TTIC—the responsibility for intelligence integration. Carafano concluded that the "[c]urrent arrangement leaves no one person or agency in charge of all these related activities, and it makes the DHS little more than an end-user—competing with other agencies for intelligence support."[33] Ultimately, Carafano's suggestions became a moot point as the IRTPA in 2004 required additional reorganization of the IC by creating the Director of National Intelligence (DNI) and placing the NCTC (which replaced the TTIC) under its mandate.

While there was confusion at the outset, it appears that TTIC had more of a global focus, while the DHS IAIP focused more on the protection of the homeland from attack and conducting vulnerability and risk assessments of infrastructure. Significantly, the TTIC had no operational authority; it had to task collect from other IC agencies such as the FBI and DHS. By comparison, DHS tasks its own components for intelligence collection (e.g. coast guard, Secret Service, Transportation Security Information [TSA], Immigration Customs Enforcement [ICE], and Customs Border Protection [CBP]) and turns a voluminous amount of information into usable actionable intelligence that is then shared with federal, state, and locals as well as the private sector.[34]

Overcoming Challenges

In early 2005, former secretary Chertoff commissioned a Second Stage Review to identify issues and opportunities for improvement. His review found that intelligence components were not integrated: there were "multiple points of collection without coordination of intelligence and information sharing standards or processes."[35] In essence, DHS was not meeting the needs of its stakeholders to include DHS components, the IC at large as well as state and local governments and the private sector. Furthermore, a 2005 report by the Commission on Intelligence Capabilities of the United States Regarding Weapons of Mass Destruction (WMD Commission) found that DHS "faces challenges in all four roles it plays in the Intelligence Community—as collector, analyst, disseminator, and customer."[36] The WMD Commission recommended that DHS strengthen its relationships with the IC.

In response to the review and the WMD Commission's report, Chertoff reorganized the department-level intelligence components by creating the Office of Intelligence and Analysis (I&A) to replace the heavily criticized IAIP. The I&A, which exists today, reports directly to the secretary and runs the intelligence component of DHS. Its mission is to "ensure that intelligence is coordinated, fused and analyzed within the Department so that we have a common operational picture."[37] By receiving and analyzing national intelligence, terrorism information, law enforcement information, domestic intelligence, and other information that is publicly available, I&A ensures that intelligence concerning protecting the homeland is collected from many sources, processed, analyzed, and disseminated to the relevant consumers inside DHS, as well as first-line responders at state, local, and tribal levels and the private sector. In essence, I&A manages the collection, analysis, and fusion of intelligence for DHS. It is led by the undersecretary for intelligence and analysis, also called the chief intelligence officer, with guidance from the Homeland Security Council[38] and Homeland Security Intelligence Council.

Charles Allen, a former CIA operative, became the department's first chief intelligence officer and assistant secretary for information analysis in August 2005.[39] Upon appointment, Allen stressed that his first priority would be intelligence gathering, noting that, for the first three years, DHS officials had struggled with obtaining information from other "turf-conscious" intelligence agencies like the FBI and CIA.[40] By 2007, he organized I&A into five groups focusing on particular threats: border, critical infrastructure, radicalization and extremism, particular groups entering the United States (demographic movements), and chemical, biological, radiological, and nuclear (CBRN) threats.[41] He also instituted several initiatives to improve I&A's ability to collect, analyze, and disseminate homeland security intelligence to its customers. While a discussion of all his initiatives is beyond the scope of this chapter, some significant ones are discussed below and in the section relating to the State and Local Fusion Centers and the ITACG.

Allen created the Homeland Security Intelligence Council composed of the heads of the intelligence components in DHS to ensure integration of intelligence activities. He also created the Homeland Security State and Local Intelligence Community of Interest (HS SLIC), which is a virtual network of federal, state, and local intelligence analysts that communicate and share best practices through a portal on the Homeland Security Information Network (HSIN). While in 2006 there were 6 state pilot programs, by 2008, the HS SLIC had grown to 45 states; Washington, D.C.; as well as seven federal agencies.[42]

Significantly, in January 2006, Allen enacted the DHS Intelligence Enterprise Strategic Plan, which contains long-term direction of DHS and is updated each year.

The plan defines the DHS intelligence enterprise to include "all component organizations within the department that have activities producing raw information, intelligence-related information or finished intelligence."[43] According to the plan, the mission of the DHS intelligence enterprise is to:

provide valuable, actionable intelligence and intelligence-related information for and among the National leadership, all components of DHS, our federal partners, state, local, territorial, tribal, and private sector customers. We ensure that information is gathered from all relevant DHS field operations and is fused with information from other members of the Intelligence Community to produce accurate, timely, and actionable intelligence products and services. We independently collate, analyze, coordinate, disseminate, and manage threat information affecting the homeland.[44]

In 2007, DHS developed its first annual DHS integrated research plan called the Homeland Security Threat Assessment, which provides DHS with an analytic framework to identify and prioritize gaps in knowledge and understanding of threats. It projects threats out to 2010 and is updated annually.[45]

While DHS's role in the IC began with challenges, mainly caused by lack of resources and respect, as well as by competition and potential overlap in mission with other entities, by 2008, DHS's I&A had largely overcome these initial growing pains. As Allen testified in May 2008:

[W]e are building a departmental intelligence organization out of nothing. We have had to recruit and train new cadres of intelligence officers, integrate existing intelligence functions, bring others up to standards recognized by the Intelligence Community, and fundamentally define the new realm of Homeland Security Intelligence.[46]

DHS has made obvious and substantial progress since its inception in 2002. The next section discusses two key DHS initiatives that have the potential to truly transform the creation and dissemination of homeland security intelligence.

KEY DHS INITIATIVES THAT FOCUS ON INTELLIGENCE

Since DHS's creation in 2002, many initiatives have focused on intelligence. Although this chapter cannot address all of DHS's initiatives, this section serves to highlight two that have vast potential: (1) the State and Local Fusion Centers, whose goal is to fuse and share information at the federal, state, and locals levels; and (2) the ITACG, whose purpose is to involve the state and local governments in creating federally coordinated intelligence that is available and relevant to domestic law enforcement. Both of these initiatives have involved their share of controversy and initial growing pains. Nonetheless, while their future may be uncertain, they have enormous potential for reshaping and expanding the role of homeland security intelligence. As DHS continues to evolve under Secretary Napolitano's leadership, these particular initiatives should be watched to see if they contribute to the effective creation and dissemination of homeland security intelligence or whether they serve as distractions to the new administration.

State and Local Fusion Centers

Fusion centers, recommended by the 9/11 Act, are facilities owned by state and local governments where federal, state, local, tribal, and territorial governments as well as the owners of critical infrastructure come to share information about terrorists threats, criminal activities, and other hazards. The goal is to fuse together lots of information into intelligence products that are useful to customer needs both at the federal and state/local levels.

The Bush administration viewed the fusion centers as critical to information sharing, and they were a central component in the *National Strategy for Information Sharing*. The *Strategy* considers fusion centers to be "vital assets" that provide the federal government with critical information about state and local governments, while the state and local governments obtain information about terrorist-related threats.[47] The *Strategy* states that "a sustained Federal partnership with State and major urban area fusion centers is critical to the safety of our Nation, and therefore a national priority."[48]

The federal government provides personnel as well as financial and technical support to the fusion centers. Congress designated DHS as the lead federal agency in charge of coordinating the effort. Fusion centers are financed by a mix of state and local budgets as well federal grants. During fiscal years 2004–2008, DHS spent more than $327 million on the fusion centers through its grant program.[49] As of March 2009, there were approximately 70 fusion centers across the country—one in every state and large city.[50] As of April 2009, 34 DHS intelligence operations specialists were deployed to the fusion centers to serve as a "critical link" between DHS and the fusion centers and "augment the analytical capabilities of the fusion centers."[51] According to Director of the State and Local Program Office Robert Riegle, he hopes that by the end of fiscal year 2010, DHS will have deployed an intelligence operations specialist to each of the 70 designated fusion centers.[52]

Although the fusion center initiative began in 2006, it has been plagued with criticism about its effectiveness.[53] While the federal government maintains that it uses fusion centers as focal points to disseminate terrorism-related information to state and local governments, officials at the state and local levels counter that, although they provide information up to DHS, they do not feel that they receive adequate reports from the federal government. A 2008 congressional hearing revealed that DHS was not consistently sharing counterterrorism details with state and local governments and was not establishing an environment that promoted information sharing.[54] Secretary Napolitano has stated that DHS needs to better use information collected by state fusion centers as part of its counterterrorism operations: "A key challenge for us is to share information with state and local governments better and how we get information back from them."[55]

In March 2009, DHS held the National Fusion Center Conference whose theme was "Achieving Baseline Capabilities." Although the fusion centers are three years old, the purpose of the conference was to ensure that all the fusion centers maintain the same level of baseline capabilities to operate an integrated national network.[56] Secretary Napolitano stated at the conference: "I believe that Fusion Centers will be the centerpiece of state, local, federal intelligence-sharing for the future and that the Department of Homeland Security will be working and aiming its programs to underlie Fusion Centers."[57] She emphasized that the priority was not in sharing isolated facts but in converting the information into products that could be used at the federal as well as state and local levels. While recognizing that technology is an important facilitator of sharing information (the Homeland Secure Data Network was installed in approximately 29 fusion centers by March 2009), she emphasized that it cannot replace the "brainpower assisted by education and training" needed to analyze the data to make sure intelligence products are being created and disseminated as opposed to pieces of information being passed on.[58]

Significantly, Secretary Napolitano has a broad view of fusion centers that is consistent with her message that homeland security is beyond terrorism. As she explained at the conference, some fusion centers may focus on a serial killer or gangs and not just terrorists. Furthermore, she expressed her view and that the fusion centers need to include "capacity for response and recovery" and act as "collaborative space" where information can be shared across different disciplines, such as law enforcement, fire, public health, emergency management, and critical infrastructure protection, as well as the private sector.[59] Yet, despite their potential, fusion centers are still a work in progress, and a 2009 report by the Markle Foundation concluded that "the role and future of these [fusion] centers is uncertain and the sharing of information with them has been uneven."[60] Nonetheless, while clear improvement is needed, it appears that fusion centers will play an integral role in this administration's commitment to information sharing.

The ITACG, discussed next, is another DHS initiative focused on information sharing. While it too has had its share of obstacles, it appears to be a priority to this new administration.

ITACG

The ITACG brings together state, local, and tribal law enforcement and intelligence analysts to work in NCTC. As recommended by the 9/11 Commission and as part of the 9/11 Act and the *National Strategy for Information Sharing*, the ITACG advocates for state, local, and tribal interests at the federal level to ensure that federally coordinated intelligence is available to domestic law enforcement.[61] In essence, the ITACG is supposed to shape intelligence products to make them more relevant and useful for state and local governments by providing local perspective and bringing nonfederal information to federal analysts. While achieving initial operability in October 2007, the ITACG became fully operational in January 2008.

The ITACG had a rocky beginning, mainly because it appeared that DHS's I&A was not committed to its success. According to House Homeland Security Committee officials, DHS delayed signing the ITACG agreement for more than two months, although the FBI, ISE, and NCTC had approved the memorandum.[62] According to a Congressional Research Service report, DHS officials may have felt that bringing in state and local officials to the NCTC would create unnecessary confusion.[63] Although DHS signed the agreement in September 2007, several congressmen wrote a letter to former secretary Chertoff asking for an explanation about the initial delay in creating the ITACG, fearing that it demonstrated a lack of commitment on behalf of DHS:

While Mr. Thompson and Ms. Harman are delighted that the department is now apparently doing what it's supposed to do, they are mindful of the fact that the devil will be in the details. . . . No turn of phrase or creative interpretation of either the 9/11 Act or the [memorandum of agreement] will be permitted to undermine Congress' intent: a full partnership of state, local and tribal law enforcement officers and homeland security advisers situated in the NCTC who inform the national intelligence cycle by bringing state, local and tribal perspectives to what intelligence is most helpful to police and sheriffs' officers on America's front lines; how to write that intelligence in a way that makes sense to that state and local audience; and to whom in that audience any particular intelligence product should be disseminated.[64]

In the letter, the lawmakers further stated that it seemed that DHS viewed the ITACG as a threat to I&A instead of as an opportunity to share more information.[65]

By February 2008, Intelligence Subcommittee Chair Jane Harman expressed dismay that I&A was not meeting the needs of state and local governments. According to Harman, she took issue with "I&A's endless refusal to take the ITACG seriously and to build a robust State, local, and tribal presence at the National Counterterrorism Center (NCTC) that makes the intelligence production process for State and locals better."[66] Harman admonished that DHS wanted to control what information should be disseminated to state and local governments instead of seeking input from them. Specifically, Harman noted that I&A was not allowing state and local officials detailed to the ITACG to become involved in creating the analytic products.[67] Homeland Security Committee Chairman Bernie Thompson similarly expressed concern with the lack of progress with the ITACG: "The message, Mr. Allen, is clear: get the ITACG done right and get it done right now. With your new authorities and influence, we expect nothing less than your total commitment to the success of the ITACG."[68]

Former chief intelligence officer Allen, however, disagreed with Harman's and Thompson's criticism of I&A's commitment to the ITACG. He testified in February 2008 that a "major emphasis of the Office of Intelligence and Analysis has been the establishment of the Interagency Threat Assessment Coordination Group (ITACG)" and that his office had provided two senior officers along with two from the FBI to "lead the stand-up" of the organization.[69] He further testified that current staffing requirements had been met in that "four federal and four state personnel, as well as contractor officers, are working in dedicated spaces with essential systems connectivity in NCTC."[70]

By March 2008, Allen stated that I&A was working to harmonize DHS and FBI sponsorship programs so that state and local governments did not have to pay a financial price for sending officials to serve in the ITACG.[71] He further expressed that he wanted to expand the ITACG's local representation to include a broader array of homeland security disciplines to include fire and safety, health, law enforcement intelligence analysis, and state-level homeland security management. He noted, however, that it was difficult to find people willing to obtain security clearances and uproot families to move to Washington, D.C., for a year.[72] While DHS's commitment to the ITACG may have appeared tenuous at first, it appears that the ITACG has become a significant part of DHS's information-sharing priorities.

Concluding Thoughts

Jennifer Sims and Burton Gerber observe in *Transforming U.S. Intelligence* that "transformation involves less the editing of blue prints for where intelligence officers should sit than the description of what they might best seek to accomplish"[73] As they observe, "[t]rue intelligence transformation fuses wit, creative business practices, and selected technologies for the purpose of achieving strategic advantage."[74] In some sense, DHS was a bureaucratic redesign, and it is an outstanding question to what extent it has "transformed U.S. intelligence." Yet, the expansion of the State and Local Fusion Centers and the development of the ITACG appear to have the potential to truly transform intelligence by combining technology with vertical and horizontal information sharing. It seems that with the right leadership and adequate protection of privacy and civil liberties, these initiatives, working together, could provide the United States with a strategic advantage.

THE FUTURE OF DHS AND INTELLIGENCE

On January 29, 2009, President Barack Obama issued Intelligence Community Directive 501, which stipulates that the IC shall treat intelligence as "national assets" and shall have a "responsibility to provide," "responsibility to discover," and "responsibility to request" intelligence. Central to and consistent with these tenets is DHS's commitment to information sharing. In 2005, former vice chair of the 9/11 Commission, Lee H. Hamilton, testified:

[W]e have made minimal progress toward the establishment of a seamless information sharing system. You can change the law, you can change the technology, but you still need to change the culture; you need to motivate institutions and individuals to share information."[75]

In 2009, the Markle Foundation published a report that concluded that the "President and Congress must reaffirm information sharing as a top priority, ensuring that policymakers have the best information to inform their decisions." It observed that there is "unfinished business in implementing an information sharing framework across all agencies that have information important to national security (including state and local organizations)."[76] Hence, to the extent the Markle report is accurate, it appears that four years later, we have made minimal progress, and Hamilton's concerns about needing to motivate institutions and individuals are still applicable today.

Yet, despite the Markle report's criticism, it is clear that Secretary Napolitano has made fusion centers and information sharing a priority for her administration. In February 2009, she stated: "This is the first time there has been a transition of administrations where a Department of Homeland Security [is in place] from day one. . . . I believe the department right now is fully a partner in intelligence sharing. And if it is not, I'll be fighting for that."[77] Along the same lines, Director Riegle testified to Congress in April 2009, "[a]s fusion centers continue to mature, we expect to continue to grow the pool of analysts capable of connecting the dots and conducting information sharing and analysis in the manner intended by Congress."[78] And there is some heartening news. While in 2007 only 42 percent of respondents of the National Governors Association Center for Best Practices expressed satisfaction with their communications with DHS, by 2008 that percentage had grown to more than 75 percent.[79]

It can hardly be disputed that the creation of DHS in 2002 was a direct response to the 9/11 terrorist attacks. While DHS initially focused on counterterrorism, by 2009 the role of intelligence had broadened to include more of an all-hazards focus.[80] From the outset, Secretary Napolitano has stressed the civilian management role of DHS (e.g., natural disaster recovery, defending infrastructure) more than her two predecessors who had focused on preventing terrorist attacks.[81] If DHS continues to become more of an all-hazard organization, one question will be how that broader purpose will affect information sharing and the priority of gathering intelligence to prevent terrorist attacks.

While DHS has had its successes and failures throughout its relatively short existence, it plays a critical role in collecting, analyzing, and disseminating homeland security intelligence. It has overcome significant obstacles, a lack of respect, bureaucratic turf wars, and substantial criticism of many of its key initiatives. Moreover, information sharing—the lack of which was seen as the main contributor to 9/11—is one of DHS's top priorities. As with most challenging endeavors, the devil will be in the details as DHS continues to grow, but DHS's priorities and the commitment of its employees should not be underestimated.

In September 2009, Secretary Napolitano announced a realignment of I&A to strengthen information sharing and the delivery of useful and actionable intelligence products. Specifically, she outlined before Congress a plan to create the Joint Fusion Center Program Management Office within I&A to enhance coordination across all DHS components toward strengthening fusion centers and DHS intelligence products. As of this writing, the reorganization is in its infancy, but it is clear that information sharing is a top priority of her administration.

NOTES

The views in this chapter are the author's and do not necessarily represent the views of the U.S. government, including the Department of Homeland Security or the Department of Justice.

Epigraph. Prepared testimony of Secretary Michael Chertoff, *U.S. Department Of Homeland Security Before the United States Senate Committee On Commerce, Science and Transportation,* July 19, 2005, http://www.dhs.gov/xnews/testimony/testimony_0039.shtm (last accessed April 24, 2009).

1. *The 9/11 Commission Report: Final Report of the National Commission on Terrorist Attacks Upon the United States* (New York: W.W. Norton, n.d.), 408, 416.

2. The 9/11 Commissioners noted it was a "failure of imagination." *9/11 Commission Report,* 339. Nevertheless, Judge Richard Posner questions whether 9/11 was a failure as opposed to an "inevitability" given that not all surprise attacks are preventable. And to the extent it was a failure, he suggests that the problem was managerial and not organizational/structural. Richard Posner, *Preventing Surprise Attacks, Intelligence Reform in the Wake of 9/11* (Stanford, Calif.: Hoover Institution, 2005), 32, 42, 127. Similarly, Mark Lowenthal questions whether 9/11 was an intelligence failure. In an editorial to the *Washington Post,* he notes "Even if every 'dot' had been connected, they would not have led to the tactical intelligence needed to stop those four planes on that Tuesday morning." Mark Lowenthal, "Behind U.S. Intelligence Failures," *Washingtonpost.com,* May 25, 2008, B1.

3. Richard Best, Jr., "Homeland Security: Intelligence Support," *Congressional Research Service Report for Congress* (CRS Order Code RS21283), February 23, 2004, 1.

4. Prepared statement of George Tenet, *Testimony of the Director of Central Intelligence Before the Government Affairs Subcommittee,* June 27, 2002, https://www.cia.gov/news-information/speeches-testimony/2002/dci_speech_06272002.html (last accessed April 24, 2009).

5. Ibid.

6. Ibid. (emphasis in original).

7. Tenet, *Testimony of the Director of Central Intelligence Before the Government Affairs Subcommittee.*

8. Pub. L. No. 107–296, 116 Stat. 2135 (November 25, 2002).

9. George W. Bush, President, Department of Homeland Security, June 2002, www.dhs.gov/xlibrary/assets/book.pdf (last accessed December 28, 2009).

10. *Homeland Security Act of 2002,* 6 U.S.C. §111. Part (D) includes carrying "out all functions of entities transferred to the Department, including by acting as a focal point regarding natural and manmade crises and emergency planning." As explained in note 11, *infra,* natural disasters became more of a focus in the 2007 *National Strategy for Homeland Security.*

11. While DHS's mission was initially focused on terrorism, it has emerged to have more of an all-hazard focus, especially after Hurricanes Katrina and Rita. In fact, the 2007 *National Strategy for Homeland Security* emphasized an all-hazards

approach, noting that "certain non-terrorist events that reach catastrophic levels can have significant implications for homeland security." Homeland Security Counsel, *National Strategy for Homeland Security*, October 2007, 3, http://www. dhs.gov/xlibrary/assets/nat_strat_homelandsecurity_2007.pdf (last accessed April 25, 2009). Secretary Napolitano has also focused on the civilian manage- ment role of DHS more than counterterrorism. See generally "New Homeland Security Boss Calls for Sweeping Review," *therawstory*, February 25, 2009, http:// rawstory.com/news/afp/New_Homeland_Security_boss_calls_sw_02252009. html (last accessed April 24, 2009).

12. Best, "Homeland Security: Intelligence Support," 3–5.

13. "Nation At Risk: Policy Makers Need Better Information to Protect the Country," *Markle Foundation Task Force*, March 2009, 5, http://www.markle.org/ downloadable_assets/20090304_mtf_report.pdf (last accessed April 24, 2009).

14. Ralph Norman Channell, "Intelligence and the Department of Homeland Security," *Strategic Insight*, Center for Contemporary Conflict, August 9, 2002, 1, http://www.ccc.nps.navy.mil/si/aug02/homeland2.asp (last accessed April 26, 2009).

15. Paul Lowe, "DHS Nominee Departs Arizona Stage to Mixed Reviews," *AINonline*, January 1, 2009, http://www.ainonline.com/news/single-news-page/ article/dhs-nominee-departs-arizona-stage-to-mixed-reviews/ (last accessed April 26, 2009).

16. See, for example, Mickey McCarter, "Fugate: Leave FEMA in DHS," *Homeland Security Today*, April 22, 2009, http://www.hstoday.us/index2.php?option=com_ content&do_pdf=1&id=8197 (last accessed April 26, 2009); "FEMA to Remain within DHS, Nominee Says," *CNN Politics.com*, April 22, 2009, http://politicalticker.blogs. cnn.com/2009/04/22/fema-to-remain-within-dhs-nominee-says/ (last accessed April 26, 2009).

17. John Mintz, "At Homeland Security, Doubts Arise Over Intelligence," *Washington Post*, July 21, 2003, http://www.commondreams.org/headlines03/0721–05. htm (last accessed April 26, 2009).

18. Ibid.

19. Ibid.

20. Best, "Homeland Security: Intelligence Support," 4.

21. Mintz, "At Homeland Security, Doubts Arise Over Intelligence."

22. Best, "Homeland Security: Intelligence Support," 1, 3.

23. Mintz, "At Homeland Security, Doubts Arise Over Intelligence."

24. White House Fact Sheet, "Strengthening Intelligence to Better Protect America," January 28, 2003, http://www.fas.org/irp/news/2003/01/wh012803. html (last accessed April 26, 2009).

25. Written Statement for the Record of John O. Brennan Director, *Terrorist Threat Integration Center on Law Enforcement and the Intelligence Community before the National Commission on Terrorist Attacks Upon the United States Washington, D.C.*, April 14, 2004, http://www.fas.org/irp/congress/2004_hr/041404brennan.html (last accessed April 26, 2009). The TTIC was composed of elements of the DHS, the FBI's Counterterrorism Division, the DCI's Counterterrorist Center, the Depart- ment of Defense, and other U.S. government agencies. It reported to the DCI.

26. Ibid.

27. Best, "Homeland Security: Intelligence Support," 1, 4–5. See also Chris Strohm, "House Chair Says DHS Should Lead Intelligence Analysis,"

GovernmentExecutive.com, June 7, 2004, http://www.govexec.com/dailyfed/0604/060704c1.htm (last accessed April 26, 2009).

28. April 13, 2004, letter to Senators Carl Levin and Susan Collins, http://hsgac.senate.gov/public/_files/040413ttic.pdf (last accessed April 26, 2009).

29. Ibid.

30. Ibid.

31. The TSC, overseen by the FBI, is responsible for running the watch list information gathered from various databases. For more information, see http://www.fbi.gov/terrorinfo/counterrorism/tsc.htm (last accessed April 26, 2009).

32. James Carafano, "Terrorist Intelligence Centers Need Reform Now," *Heritage Foundation Executive Memorandum* #930, May 10, 2004, http://www.heritage.org/research/homelandsecurity/em930.cfm (last accessed April 26, 2009).

33. Ibid.

34. See generally, Prepared testimony by Charles Allen, *DHS Under Secretary for Intelligence and Analysis Charles E. Allen Address to the Washington Institute for Near East Policy*, May 6, 2008, http://www.dhs.gov/xnews/speeches/sp_1210107524856.shtm (last accessed April 26, 2009), listing the staggering amount of data DHS component agencies obtain on a daily basis.

35. DHS Office of Inspector General, *Survey of DHS Intelligence Collection and Dissemination (Unclassified Summary)*, June 2007, 2, http://www.fas.org/irp/agency/dhs/ig-intel-0607.pdf (last accessed April 26, 2009).

36. Senate Committee on Homeland Security Governmental Affairs, *Senators Collins & Lieberman Invite Input from Secretary Chertoff on IAIP Role, Senators Concerned over Lack of Clarity of Current Role*, April 13, 2005, http://hsgac.senate.gov/public/index.cfm?FuseAction=PressReleases.Detail&Affiliation=C&PresRelease_id=dfa980e6–1e52–4d86–9365–3ce6f879e168&Month=4&Year=2005 (last accessed April 26, 2009).

37. Prepared testimony of Secretary Michael Chertoff, *U.S. Department Of Homeland Security Before the United States Senate Committee On Commerce, Science and Transportation*. I&A is formally part of the IC, and the IC at large is also a customer of the I&A. Furthermore, I&A serves as a member to the DNI's Executive Committee, contributes to the President's National Intelligence Priorities Framework, and prepares assessments for President's Daily Brief and National Terrorism Bulletin.

38. The Homeland Security Council coordinates homeland security-related efforts across executive departments and agencies of all levels throughout the country. It also implements DHS's policies through 11 policy coordination committees.

39. Allen held this position until January 20, 2009. As of July 2009, Bart Johnson is the acting assistant secretary for information analysis.

40. Greta Wodele, "DHS Intelligence Chief Seeks Improved Information Sharing," *GovernmentExecutive.com*, October 20, 2005, http://www.govexec.com/dailyfed/1005/102005cdam2.htm (last accessed April 26, 2009).

41. Prepared remarks by Charles Allen, *Testimony of Charles E. Allen before the U.S. House of Representatives Committee on Homeland Security, Subcommittee on Intelligence, Information Sharing and Terrorism Risk Assessment*, September 24, 2008, http://www.dhs.gov/xnews/testimony/testimony_1222268051417.shtm (last accessed April 26, 2009).

42. Ibid.

43. DHS Office of Inspector General, *Survey of DHS Intelligence Collection and Dissemination (Unclassified Summary)*, 3.

44. See DHS Intelligence Enterprise Strategic Plan, October 2006, 3, http://www.fas.org/irp/agency/dhs/stratplan.pdf (last accessed April 26, 2009).

45. Prepared remarks of Charles Allen, *Statement of Charles E. Allen, Under Secretary for Intelligence and Analysis Before the Subcommittee on Intelligence, Information Sharing, and Terrorism Risk Assessment Committee on Homeland Security U.S. House of Representatives*, February 24, 2008, http://homeland.house.gov/SiteDocuments/20080226165154–47048.pdf (last accessed April 26, 2009).

46. Prepared testimony by Charles Allen, *DHS Under Secretary for Intelligence and Analysis Charles E. Allen Address to the Washington Institute for Near East Policy.*

47. White House, *National Strategy for Information Sharing, Success and Challenges in Improving Terrorism-Related Information Sharing*, October 2007, 20, http://georgewbush-whitehouse.archives.gov/nsc/infosharing/NSIS_book.pdf (last accessed April 26, 2009).

48. Ibid., A1–1.

49. Office of the Press Secretary, "DHS Secretary Napolitano, Missouri Governor Nixon Address Annual National Fusion Center Conference," March 11, 2009, http://www.dhs.gov/ynews/releases/pr_1236792314990.shtm (last accessed April 26, 2009).

50. Office of the Press Secretary, "DHS Secretary Napolitano, Missouri Governor Nixon Address Annual National Fusion Center Conference."

51. Prepared remarks by Robert Riegle, *Testimony of Director Robert Riegle, State and Local Program Office, Office of Intelligence and Analysis, before the Committee on Homeland Security, Subcommittee on Intelligence, Information Sharing, and Terrorism Risk Assessment, "The Future of Fusion Centers: Potential Promise and Dangers,"* April 2, 2009, http://www.dhs.gov/ynews/testimony/testimony_1238597287040.shtm (last accessed April 26, 2009).

52. Ibid.

53. A comprehensive evaluation of fusion centers is beyond the scope of this chapter. For a summary of key issues with fusion centers, see Todd Masse and John Rollins, *A Summary of Fusion Centers: Core Issues and Options for Congress*, Congressional Research Service, September 19, 2007, http://www.fas.org/sgp/crs/intel/RL34177.pdf (last accessed May 10, 2009) and the DHS Inspector General's report entitled "DHS' Role in State and Local Fusion Centers is Evolving," December 2008, http://www.dhs.gov/xoig/assets/mgmtrpts/OIG_09–12_Dec08.pdf (last accessed May 10, 2009). For a report on problems with fusion centers, see the American Civil Liberties Union (ACLU)'s report entitled "What's Wrong with Fusion Centers," December 5, 2007, http://www.aclu.org/privacy/gen/32966pub20071205.html (last accessed May 10, 2009).

54. Jill Aitoro, "DHS Secretary Promises More Information Sharing," *nextgov*, February 25, 2009, http://www.nextgov.com/nextgov/ng_20090225_3153.php (last accessed April 24, 2009).

55. Jason Miller, "DHS Considering Giving TSA Employees Rights," *Federal News Radio*, February 26, 2009, http://www.federalnewsradio.com/index.php?nid=35&sid=1610981 (last accessed April 26, 2009).

56. *FACT SHEET: 2009 National Fusion Center Conference*, March 10, 2009, http://www.zibb.com/article/5032812/FACT+SHEET:+2009+National+Fusion+Center+Conference?expired=4545256 (last accessed April 27, 2009).

57. "Remarks by Homeland Security Secretary Janet Napolitano to the National Fusion Center Conference in Kansas City, MO," March 11, 2009,

www.dhs.gov/ynews/speeches/sp_1236975404263.shtm (last accessed December 28, 2009).

58. Ibid.

59. Ibid.

60. "Nation At Risk: Policy Makers Need Better Information to Protect the Country," 29.

61. Prepared testimony of Charles Allen, *Statement of Charles E. Allen, Under Secretary for Intelligence and Analysis Before the Subcommittee on Intelligence, Information Sharing, and Terrorism Risk Assessment Committee on Homeland Security U.S. House of Representatives*, March 13, 2008, http://homeland.house.gov/SiteDocuments/20080313104349–34499.pdf (last accessed April 27, 2009).

62. Jason Miller, "DHS Signs On to Create Threat Assessment Coordination Group," *Federal Computer Week*, October 1, 2007, http://fcw.com/Articles/2007/10/01/DHS-signs-on-to-create-threat-assessment-coordination-group.aspx?p=1 (last accessed April 27, 2009).

63. Ibid.

64. Ibid.

65. Ibid.

66. Statement of Chair Jane Harman Committee on Homeland Security Subcommittee on Intelligence, Information Sharing & Terrorism Risk Assessment, *Homeland Security Intelligence at a Crossroads: the Office of Intelligence & Analysis' Vision for 2008,* http://homeland.house.gov/SiteDocuments/20080227111045–34957.pdf (last accessed April 27, 2009).

67. Ibid.

68. Statement of Chairman Bennie G. Thompson, *Homeland Security Intelligence at a Crossroads: the Office of Intelligence & Analysis' Vision for 2008,* http://homeland.house.gov/SiteDocuments/20080226165143–20925.pdf (last accessed April 27, 2009).

69. Prepared statement of Charles Allen, *Statement of Charles E. Allen, Under Secretary for Intelligence and Analysis Before the Subcommittee on Intelligence, Information Sharing, and Terrorism Risk Assessment Committee on Homeland Security U.S. House of Representatives*, February 14, 2008, http://homeland.house.gov/SiteDocuments/20080226165154–47048.pdf (last accessed April 27, 2009).

70. Ibid.

71. Prepared statement of Charles Allen, *Statement of Charles E. Allen, Under Secretary for Intelligence and Analysis Before the Subcommittee on Intelligence, Information Sharing, and Terrorism Risk Assessment Committee on Homeland Security U.S. House of Representatives*, March 13, 2008, http://homeland.house.gov/SiteDocuments/20080313104349–34499.pdf (last accessed April 27, 2009).

72. Ibid.

73. Jennifer Sims and Burton Gerber, *Transforming U.S. Intelligence* (Washington, D.C.: Georgetown University Press, 2005).

74. Ibid.

75. Best, "Homeland Security: Intelligence Support," 14.

76. "Nation At Risk: Policy Makers Need Better Information to Protect the Country," Executive Summary.

77. Aitoro, "DHS Secretary Promises More Information Sharing."

78. Testimony of Director Robert Riegle, *State and Local Program Office, Office of Intelligence and Analysis, before the Committee on Homeland Security, Subcommittee on*

Intelligence, Information Sharing, and Terrorism Risk Assessment, "The Future of Fusion Centers: Potential Promise and Dangers."

79. Ibid.

80. See note 11, supra.

81. See Carter Yang, "Napolitano Not Talking Terror," *CBS News*, February 26, 2008, http://www.cbsnews.com/blogs/2009/02/26/politics/politicalhotsheet/entry4830824.shtml (last accessed April 27, 2009).

6

Military Intelligence

Louis H. Liotti

> I must have precise information to adjust my movement and formulate my plan.
>
> —Napoleon Bonaparte

When dealing with the subject of military intelligence, one is always tempted to consider the well-worn, but misbegotten, joke that passes for knowing humor in some circles. The joke that military intelligence is an oxymoron betrays not only a sneering, uninformed contempt for the military, but also a profound ignorance of the topic of intelligence.

The subject of military intelligence is so immense and arcane as to be beyond encompassing within a brief chapter such as this one. Whole libraries, both physical and in cyberspace, can be, and are, devoted to the subject. Moreover, much of the subject, despite recent attempts at declassification, remains obscured from the average or survey reader by the demands of secrecy. Usually, immediate interest in the subject of military intelligence is reserved to consumers of the information produced, to professionals, and to scholars in the field. There are also those whose interest is tangential in that the subject is of concern only in so far as it is a component of, or impacts upon, a larger historical or political inquiry.

Of course, as a side note and not to be treated here, are the legions of fans of fictional military intelligence exploits. The ancestor of these stories, as far as students of American literature are concerned, is George Washington's itinerant peddler, Harvey Birch of *The Spy*, published by James Fenimore Cooper in 1821. As with so much of fiction about intelligence matters, the character of Harvey Birch is based upon a real-life individual, Enoch Crosby, who provided intelligence to Washington and his army in what was then the wilds of the "No Man's Land," or the neutral ground, of New York's Westchester County, between Tories and Rebels. Later on there were the adventures of U.S. Army Intelligence Officer Captain (later Colonel) Hugh North. This hero of fiction was created by F. Van Wyck Mason, an adventurer and world traveler in his own right, in the early 1930s and continued into the 1950s. A number of the events depicted in the North series prefigured subsequent historical events.

For the reader who does not possess a security clearance there are a surprising number of open sources (i.e., generally available to the public on an unclassified basis) from which to pursue an in-depth review of the subject of military intelligence. These sources include the Web sites of the various intelligence agencies, including the military services' own intelligence components. They also include such nongovernment sources as the Federation of American Scientists' (FAS') Intelligence Resource Program. While the latter site reflects the skeptical prism of its progenitor, it contains a wealth of original documents and references pertaining to the subject of military intelligence.

In general terms, in order to define military intelligence, we need to look at some of its legal underpinnings and review the structure of the intelligence components of the armed services of the United States—the army, navy, air force, Marine Corps, and coast guard. Of necessity, a brief overview of the Defense Intelligence Agency (DIA) and the National Security Agency (NSA) are also included, as those agencies, separate from the armed services, come under the rubric of military intelligence.

A WORKING DEFINITION
OF MILITARY INTELLIGENCE

The first question is, what is military intelligence? William E. Odom, in his excellent volume, *Fixing Intelligence—For a More Secure America*, divides military intelligence into two subsets. Odom, a former director of the NSA speaks of "material and force development," which is broadly defined as the need for each military service to obtain information about foreign weapons and forces that a particular service might have to overcome in time of conflict.[1] If the navy of Iran were to develop and send to sea a new submarine, the U.S. Navy would most certainly want to know all that was possible about that vessel's capabilities. This type of intelligence is anticipatory, in that the information obtained goes to shaping one's own forces, but is not being put to use immediately.

Contrast this intelligence with information that is used to develop and/or implement a specific battle plan. An example of this type of military intelligence is that used by American forces in the Battle of Midway. Having cracked the Japanese naval codes, the commander in chief of the

U.S. Pacific Fleet, Admiral Nimitz, was able to direct and position his forces to counter, and ultimately, defeat a much larger Japanese fleet.[2] This kind of military intelligence is, with no pun intended, of a fleeting nature. It is information of the moment; the positioning, makeup, and movement of an enemy. It is intelligence of an ephemeral nature that, if not acted upon immediately, has no lasting value. It is *tactical* intelligence; that is, information used to maneuver forces to gain a specific end. In this instance, the objective is to defeat a particular enemy force and prevent it from advancing or achieving its goal. In a ground combat situation, it might be the composition and placement of an enemy formation which might make it more difficult, or perhaps easier, to seize a particular objective. This sort of intelligence, which is short lived, would be in the second category of military intelligence as, defined by Odom, support for ongoing military operations.[3]

Somewhat more than two generations ago, the then principal adversary of the United States, the Soviet Union, would have taken our example of a new type of Iranian submarine and categorized it as *strategic intelligence*. This definition speaks to the ability of a nation to develop information on a possible adversary's overall capabilities and plans.[4] The purpose of this information is to permit a party to make preparations for an attack before it occurs and to make the best decisions, under real-time conditions, concerning the conduct of operations from the beginning of a conflict.[5]

It is necessary to digress briefly in order to comment on the difference between information and intelligence. They are not the same. Information is a component of intelligence. It is the raw data which, when analyzed, compared with other data and interpreted becomes intelligence.[6] To use the historical example of the Battle of Midway, the existence of a Japanese fleet in a particular location could be considered information useful perhaps, but limited in and of itself. To know the types of armaments carried, the fleet's heading, its level of training, and its orders makes that information intelligence—a product upon which decisions can be made and actions taken.

The search for a definition of military intelligence could extend well beyond the length of this limited treatment. For our purposes, it is the end result of collecting information about the military capabilities of foreign adversaries, assessing and analyzing that information so that it becomes meaningful knowledge for a decision maker.[7]

Military intelligence can be *tactical*, in that it concerns itself with knowledge that usually has a short shelf life and forms the basis for making decisions to achieve a limited goal, for example, the locations of the opponent's vessels (or rocket launchers), what are they capable of, and how best to defeat them. Another subset is operational intelligence, which deals with a more expanded scope of knowledge that permits the decision maker to conduct a large-scale endeavor that can be a component of ultimate success against an opponent.[8] An example of operational intelligence might be the number and type of enemy forma- tions (i.e., divisions) defending a beach head that is to be the entry point of an invasion (e.g., D-day at Normandy).

As mentioned above, there is also *strategic intelligence,* which is knowl- edge derived about an opponent's overall capabilities, capacities, and intentions so that the decision-making authority can formulate national plans and policies, but not necessarily at the time of conflict. Strategic intelligence can also involve assessing the capabilities and intentions of possible allies.[9]

Military intelligence is not an end in itself. The decision maker, the consumer of the intelligence product, uses it and acts upon it. For that reason it behooves the military intelligence officer to remain objective in his or her analysis of the information at hand. More importantly, he or she must be as dispassionate and nonpartisan as possible when provid- ing the intelligence to the decision maker. To fail to be independent and objective can lead to catastrophe.

One famous example in American military history of an intelligence failure caused by a lack of objectivity and independence came during the Korean War. In midautumn 1950, U.N. forces, composed mainly of U.S. troops, under the command of General of the Army Douglas MacArthur, had fought their way north of the 38th parallel. They had done so after precarious fighting throughout that summer following the invasion of South Korea by North Korean forces in June 1950. Now U.S. forces, marines and soldiers, were poised to strike north to the Yalu River, the border between North Korea and Manchuria, part of Communist China. In October 1950, MacArthur and President Harry S. Truman met at Wake Island in the mid–Pacific Ocean. At that meet- ing, the general assured the president that the Communist Chinese army would not come into North Korea and enter the war on the side of the North Koreans.[10] As a result of those assurances, U.N. forces were cleared to continue their drive north, which had begun about a week before the conference.[11] The resolute certitude of MacArthur notwithstanding, the Chinese infiltrated in massive numbers over the Yalu, setting the stage for the human-wave attacks that drove the American-led U.N. forces back.

It might have been prevented had not MacArthur's G-2 (the gen- eral staff officer in charge of intelligence) decided that it was his job to make the intelligence fit his superior's view of the world, rather than acquaint him with the truth. Major General Charles Willoughby, the G-2 in question, appears to have acted as a filter, keeping information of the presence of sizable numbers of Chinese troops in North Korea that autumn away from MacArthur's headquarters in Tokyo. In doing so, it has been suggested that Willoughby was trying to bolster his boss's con- tentions.[12] It appears in this instance that the intelligence officer acted as a partisan on behalf of the decision maker rather than an honest broker of good intelligence. The results were a near disaster for the troops.

It is imperative that an intelligence officer refrain from skewing intelligence into that which the officer thinks his decision maker wants to hear. For any policy or decision to have a sound basis, its underpinning must be the most accurate information available, delivered in a timely fashion without fear or favor. Of course, even the best military intelligence operations may not be understood by the decision makers. In such cases, the nation can suffer equally as when the intelligence officers seek to tailor their product to what they believe their bosses want to hear. A famous historical example of the decision maker not understanding the intelligence process is what has been termed the American Black Chamber.

In the World War I, the U.S. Army, then under the Department of War, set up a cryptanalysis unit under H. O. Yardley, the War Department's intelligence officer.[13] Cryptanalysis involves intercepting and breaking codes, in this case both those of enemies and of friendly nations or allies.[14] The unit continued its work after the war with substantial funding also provided by the U.S. State Department.[15] It is said that the United States was then able to use the information in the naval disarmament negotiations of the 1920s.[16] In 1929 the then U.S. secretary of state, Henry L. Stimson, decided to no longer provide State Department contributions. The unit known as the Black Chamber was disbanded. Stimson apparently had trouble with the ethics of reading the messages and cables being sent to diplomats in this country from their governments with which the United States was then at peace. As Stimson colorfully put it to a biographer, after World War II where he had rendered distinguished service as U.S. secretary of war, "Gentlemen do not read each other's mail."[17] Odom, in his book *Fixing Intelligence* advances the argument that the break-up of this intelligence unit contributed to the United States being caught unawares at Pearl Harbor some 12 years later.[18] Whether this assertion is valid is a debate best left to a more penetrating analysis by historians. The brief discussion of the Black Chamber is given here as an example of the proposition that military intelligence is a tool to be used, or misused, by the decisions makers.

LEGAL UNDERPINNINGS

Prior to World War II, the legal basis for military intelligence was not codified in any meaningful way. The collection, analysis, and dissemination of information by the military services were subject only to the regulations promulgated by those military services. There was no statute that regulated the conduct of intelligence by the armed forces, with the possible exception of the Posse Comitatus Act of 1878.

This law generally prohibited the use of the army and its units for civilian law enforcement. It was supposed to have been understood that the military was not to be used against civilian U.S. citizens engaged in purely domestic activities. There have been statutory exceptions, such as the Insurrection Act, which came about in the time of the Civil War. The Insurrection Act allows the president of the United States to use the armed forces to suppress rebellion and enforce federal laws. The law requires a declaration by the president of an insurrection. The line about when and where military intelligence can be used in domestic situations, never very clear, has been transgressed over the years. A good treatment of this issue can be found in a recent issue of *The American Scholar* in an article "Spies Among Us" by Clay Risen.[19]

At the end of World War II, it was determined that our national security apparatus had grown too complex and unwieldy to be administered by the federal departments that had arisen under the Constitution some 158 years earlier. The result was the National Security Act of 1947 [Pub. L. No. 235, 80 Cong., 61 Stat. 496 (July 26, 1947) as amended on August 10, 1949]. This legislation is now found in Title 50 of the U.S. Code. The act (as amended), recognizing the modern realities of war, created a separate Department of the Air Force, Department of Army, and Department of the Navy (including the U.S. Marine Corps) into one Department of Defense (DOD) under the authority of the secretary of defense.

In addition, the act created the Central Intelligence Agency (CIA) and a Director of Central Intelligence (DCI). It was the DCI's responsibility to oversee the intelligence community (IC) and serve as the director of the CIA. The secretary of defense had direct command authority of the various military intelligence agencies. The DCI managed the input from the various intelligence agencies and the military services and provided the intelligence product for the president and officials who comprised the National Command Authority. Collectively, all of the various intelligence agencies, civilian (such as the FBI) and military, are known as the IC. Since the 1947 act, and until the legislative reforms mentioned below, the DCI served as the IC coordinator. It was not until the attacks of September 11, 2001, that so shocked the nation as to its vulnerability to perceived intelligence failures that Congress and the president were compelled to reorganize the IC.

The result was the Intelligence Reform and Terrorism Prevention Act of 2004 (Pub. L. 108–458, 108 Cong., 118 ST 3638). The most salient feature of this law was to separate the DCI from the CIA. The DCI was transformed into the director of national intelligence (DNI)[20] within the Office of the Director of National Intelligence (ODNI). This officer, as defined by the executive orders (E.O.) issued to implement the legislation, is the "head of the Intelligence Community" and is the principal adviser to the president and for intelligence matters related to national security, and is empowered to oversee and direct the "National Intelligence Program."[21] The legislation that established then reorganized the IC, including the military intelligence agencies, has been implemented principally by means of executive orders issued by the president.

The executive order that provided for the structure and duties of the IC prior to 9/11 was E.O. 12333 issued on December 4, 1981, under President Ronald Reagan. On July 30, 2008, President George W. Bush issued amendments to E.O. 12333 in order to implement the reorganization that occurred as a result of the Intelligence Reform and Terrorism Prevention Act of 2004. E.O. 12333, as amended, defines the IC so as to include the NSA; the DIA; the intelligence and counterintelligence elements of the army, the navy, the air force, and the Marine Corps as well as other offices within the DOD that collect specialized national foreign intelligence through reconnaissance programs (electronic warfare).[22] That same order includes the coast guard as a separate listing because that service is, normally, a component of the Department of Homeland Security. In times of declared conflict, the coast guard operates as a specialized service within the Department of the Navy much in the same way as the Marine Corps. An interesting sidelight to E.O. 12333 is that it specifically defines the conduct of covert action as being limited to the CIA *and* the armed forces in time of declared war, or during a period specified by the president to the Congress pursuant to the War Powers Resolution (Pub. L. 93–148).[23] As noted, there are some agencies that are under the command authority of the DOD as opposed to the rubric of the individual services.

DEFENSE INTELLIGENCE ENTITIES

The NSA

This agency is this country's premier cryptologic structure. It collects, through all means, analyzes and disseminates signals intelligence which is known by the acronym as SIGINT.[24] E.O. 12333 specifies that the NSA is to perform its tasks for foreign intelligence and counterintelligence purposes. Immediately following the 9/11 attacks Congress authorized the president to use "all necessary and appropriate force against those nations, organizations, or persons he determines . . . aided those attacks" for the purpose of preventing future acts of international terrorism against the United States.[25] The Bush administration interpreted that legislation to authorize the NSA to intercept communications into or out of the United States, without a warrant, of persons, including U.S. citizens, linked to al-Qaeda or affiliated terrorist organizations.[26] This interpretation of the NSA's powers has proved to be controversial to say the least.

The NSA's duties also include protecting all sensitive or classified information that passes through U.S. government equipment. This protection responsibility of the NSA is the information assurance (IA) mission.[27] The NSA is expert in the fields of cryptanalysis (code breaking), cryptography (code making), computer science, mathematics, and foreign language analysis.

The National Reconnaissance Office (NRO)

The NRO is charged with the duty to research, develop, deploy, and operate this country's overhead collection systems (signals and imagery reconnaissance satellites).[28] For over 30 years after its establishment in September 1961, the NRO was a highly classified agency within the DOD. It is a joint agency in that its personnel are drawn, for the most part, from the navy, the air force, and the CIA, with contributions from other services on an as-needed basis. NRO satellites collect information that is used to produce monitoring weapons of mass destruction, enforcing treaties such as arms control, assessing disasters both natural and man-made and to provide warnings of potential military attacks.[29]

The National Geospatial-Intelligence Agency (NGA)

The NGA collects, analyzes, and disseminates about the geography of the earth for purposes of U.S. military operations, national security interests, navigation, and humanitarian assistance missions.[30] Although it is a primary combat-support office within the DOD, it is also a sitting member of the U.S. IC providing intelligence to the IC's component members. It develops cartographic intelligence for use by the military services, in aids to navigation and for homeland security purposes on the national and local level. The DNI considers the NGA to be the primary resource for the production, analysis, interpretation, and dissemination of information and imagery concerning the earth's geophysical state.[31] The NGA supports combat operations by providing its product in real-time to the National Command Authority and to commanders in the field. It supports humanitarian operations by providing information to first responders and federal agencies designated as lead agencies in disaster relief and recovery. The NRO, the NGA, and the NSA all carry out their duties under the aegis of the secretary of defense.

The DIA

The DIA provides the primary intelligence advice to the secretary of defense and the chairman of the Joint Chiefs of Staff. It is considered by the DNI to be the major producer and manager of intelligence about foreign militaries. It will collect and analyze information from all sources, including the individual services, to provide assessments of military threats, on a global scale, that are not particular to the needs or focus of any specific service. It has established a task force to produce intelligence on terrorism-related threats. The intelligence product provided by the

DIA is used to develop U.S. weapons systems to counter foreign large-scale threats such as nuclear, chemical, and biological weapons. The DIA also maintains an office to detect and assess foreign countries' hardened and underground critical facilities.[32] The DIA established the Defense Intelligence Operations Coordination Center (DIOCC) in late 2007 to integrate and better manage collaboration among all DOD intelligence resources and components.[33]

The DIA also manages the Joint Functional Component Command for Intelligence, Surveillance and Reconnaissance (JFCC-ISR). Despite its James Bondian, Ian Fleming-like name (ala S.P.E.C.T.R.E.), this DIA command monitors the needs of the combatant commanders for ISR, essentially intelligence derived from aerial and space-based reconnaissance; obtains the greatest coverage by ISR means; and corrects any gaps in that coverage. It acts as the contact by other IC members to the DOD's ISR capabilities. The DIA, by means of the JFCC-ISR, establishes specific task forces to deal in real time with events unfolding during a crisis. The DIA's Missile and Space Intelligence Center develops intelligence concerning foreign missile and space-based defense systems.[34] Through its Directorate of Human Intelligence (DH), the DIA manages the worldwide Defense Attaché program. The DH also collects intelligence not otherwise available from technical means, essentially spies in place.[35] The DIA, by means of its National Center for Medical Intelligence, produces medical assessments and profiles on global health conditions and hazards in support of overseas U.S. military operations (e.g., is there an epidemic where U.S. troops are operating and how to counter that threat). Medical Intelligence will also provide information useful in humanitarian assistance operations such as the naval relief effort to the Indian Ocean tsunami catastrophe in 2004.[36] Through its National Defense Intelligence College, the DIA provides well-trained intelligence professionals who receive fully accredited degrees.[37]

Army Intelligence

Each army unit, down to the company level, has an intelligence staff officer "the 2" as in G-2 (generally division-level and above) or S-2 (generally battalion-level and below). These are the officers responsible for collecting and disseminating immediate battlefield intelligence. The major army command that conducts overall global intelligence operations is the U.S. Army Intelligence and Security Command, known as INSCOM, formed in 1977. It has subordinate brigades and groups dispersed throughout the globe. These subordinate units provide intelligence support to both U.S. Army forces in a particular geographic location, such as Iraq, and to the large joint command, such as the U.S. Central Command (CENTCOM), within which those forces operate. Some of these units are tasked with assisting other DOD agencies with specialized technical support such as the 116th Military Intelligence Group that provides support for the NSA.[38] In 2007 the army promulgated Army Regulation 381–10 (effective June 3, 2007). This regulation implemented E.O. 12333. The regulation established responsibility for intelligence gathering with regard to U.S. nationals both within and without the territory of the United States.

Navy Intelligence

The Office of Naval Intelligence (ONI) was established in 1882. It has as its primary mission to provide timely intelligence about the global maritime environment in which the United States operates so that decision makers from national leaders to tactical operators can act on it in a meaningful way. Because of the nature of the ocean environment, naval intelligence personnel and equipment are an integral part of each command ashore and afloat. Naval intelligence is derived, in part, from dedicated elements such as the former Naval Security Group (NAVSECGRU) units that had navy-wide responsibility for cryptology operations. Naval units that have other primary functions also have intelligence functions, for example, a naval vessel at sea transmitting a contact report about a foreign naval vessel.[39] Intelligence collection capabilities are integral parts of almost all naval assets from the cameras in naval aircraft to the advanced radar and sonar systems of the ships and submarines. The ONI collects and assesses information from all sources, whether its own dedicated units or outside naval assets, to provide a finished intelligence product.[40]

In February 2009, the navy created the National Maritime Intelligence Center as the core of its Nimitz Operational Intelligence Center in Suitland, Maryland.[41] The facility was set up in part to answer criticism heard in the fleet that the ODNI was less interested in providing intelligence useful to tactical commanders at sea. The center was established so the fleet could access real-time intelligence for its ongoing operations at sea. It acts as a round-the-clock watch center integrate all sources of intelligence for use by naval commanders in particular and the IC in general. It is staffed by navy and coast guard personnel.[42]

Air Force Intelligence

The primary intelligence function within the U.S. Air Force resides in the Air Force Intelligence, Surveillance and Reconnaissance Agency (AF/ISR). This command operates out of Lackland AFB in Texas. Its main focus is to conduct intelligence and surveillance operations in order to permit air force combatant commanders to conduct operations with full situational awareness.[43] The agency assesses and processes information collected from all air force elements, including aircraft, ground installations and satellites in carrying out its responsibility. It does not limit itself to its own dedicated assets.[44]

Marine Corps Intelligence

As with the other services, Marine Corps Intelligence is specifically enumerated in E.O. 12333 as an established member of the IC. The point of focus for Marine Corps intelligence activities is Headquarters, U.S. Marine Corps Intelligence Department. The officer who heads this department, the director, is the principal intelligence staff officer to the commandant of the Marine Corps. The department manages all cryptologic and intelligence activities carried out by the corps.[45] At the operational level, the marines have dedicated units carrying out specialized functions, such as imagery analysis, which carry out their missions alongside and, as necessary, embedded within the marine operational forces. The primary focus of Marine Corps intelligence forces is to provide actionable information for the battlefield commander. As with the army, each marine aviation and ground combat unit has an organic intelligence staff officer.

Coast Guard Intelligence (CGI)

The coast guard, even though it is a subordinate unit under the authority of the Department of Homeland Security, is now a part of the IC, on equal footing with the army and the navy.[46] While it is a recognized armed service, it is also the lead federal maritime law enforcement agency. It operates as the principal U.S. law enforcement authority on the high seas and the contiguous navigable waters of the United States. CGI is focused on facilitating the coast guard missions relating to environmental protection, port security, enforcement of narcotics and immigration laws, and maritime security and safety, known collectively as Maritime Domain Awareness (MDA).[47] CGI functions are contained within the CG-2 directorate in its Intelligence and Criminal Investigations Program. This program encompasses the coast guard's Criminal Investigations Service, its Counterintelligence Service, its Cryptologic Service, and its Intelligence Coordination Center.[48] Coast guard personnel serve in the National Maritime Intelligence Center operated by the ONI.

CGI provides a finished intelligence product to the service's operational and tactical commanders to support the guard's military and law enforcement responsibilities. In the past several years, the coast guard has focused more intently to the problem of countering the threat posed by those vessels, which because of their size and nondescript appearance, might otherwise have escaped scrutiny, known as the "small boats" threat.[49] The small boat threat has been encountered in the piracy occurring in the maritime choke points of the world, such as off the coast of Somalia or in the Straits of Malacca. It was in such small boats from which the terrorists initiated their attacks in Mumbai, India, in 2009.

CONCLUSION

The complexities of the subject of military intelligence are such as to defy capture within a single survey treatment of the type we have attempted here. It is not a static topic. It is so broad and deep that its components engender whole fields of study and volumes. What is true today of its forms and functions changes tomorrow with each new challenge or threat presented. Yet we cannot stop trying. We must always strive to know and understand what is out there. For as the wise man said, "Eternal vigilance is the price of Liberty."

NOTES

Epigraph. "Instructions for General Bertrand—25 August 1805," in *New Letters of Napoleon I*, trans. Lady Mary Lloyd (New York: D. Appleton and Company, 1897).

1. William E. Odom, *Fixing Intelligence* (New Haven, Conn.: Yale University Press, 2003), 91–92.

2. See John Keegan, *Intelligence in War* (New York: Vintage Book, Random House, 2002), 200–220.

3. Odom, supra note 1, at 8–12, 90–91.

4. *Soviet Military Strategy*, V. D. Sokolovskii, ed., Herbert Dinerstein, Leon Goure, and Thomas W. Wolfe, trans. (Santa Monica, Calif.: The Rand Corporation, 1963), 446–49 (http://www.rand.org/pubs/reports/R416/).

5. Id. at 446.

6. *Naval Intelligence*, Naval Doctrine Publication 2 (NDP2) (Norfolk, Va.: Naval Doctrine Command, Department of the Navy, 1996), 4–5.

7. *Intelligence*, Marine Corps Doctrinal Publication 2 (MCDP2) (Washington, D.C.: Headquarters United States Marine Corps, Department of the Navy, 1997), 5–12.

8. Id. at 52.

9. NDP2, supra note 6, at 6.

10. David Halberstam, *The Coldest Winter* (New York: Hyperion, 2007), 366–67.

11. Id. at 345, 366–69.

12. Id. at 373–83.

13. Odom, supra, at 40, 127–28.

14. Geoffrey Hodgson, *The Colonel—The Life and Times of Henry Stimson* (New York: Alfred A. Knopf, 1990), 203.

15. Id. at 203.

16. Hodgson, supra, at 203. See also Odom, supra, at 40–41.

17. Hodgson, supra, at 203.

18. Odom, supra, at xii and 128.

19. Clay Risen, "Spies Among Us," *The American Scholar* (Winter 2009): 49–60.

20. Pub. L. 108–487, Title VII, §803, December 23, 2004, 118 Stat 3962(a).

21. Executive Order (E.O.) No. 12333, as amended, July 30, 2008.

22. E.O. 12333, as amended, July 30, 2008, Section 3.5.

23. Id., at Section 1.7(a)(4).

24. Id., at Section 1.7(c)(1).

25. Authorization for Use of Military Force, Pub. L, 107–40, Sec. 2(a), 115 Stat 224 (September 18, 2001).

26. "Legal Authorities Supporting the Activities of the National Security Agency Described by the President," U.S. Department of Justice, January 19, 2006.

27. "Introduction to NSA/CSS," http://www.nsa.gov/about/index/cfm.

28. "United States Intelligence Community—Who We Are," http://www. intelligence.gov/1-members.shtml. See also, E.O. 12333, Id. at Sect. 1(d)(1)-(2).

29. National Reconnaissance Office, http://www.nro.gov. See also "An Overview of the United States Intelligence Community for the 111th Congress" (2009), Office of the Director of National Intelligence, 11.

30. Id. at E.O. 12333 (United States Intelligence Activities) at Sect. 1(e)(1)-(4), December 4, 1981.

31. National Geospatial-Intelligence Agewncy, http://www1.nga.mil/About. See also "An Overview of the United States Intelligence Community for the 111th Congress," 9, 10.

32. Defense Intelligence Agency, http://www.dia.mil/thisisdia. See also "An Overview of the United States Intelligence Community for the 111th Congress," 5, 6.

33. Id.

34. Id.

35. Id.

36. Id.

37. Id.

38. "United States Army Intelligence and Security Command," http://www. inscom.army.mil.

39. Office of Naval Intelligence, http://www.nmic.navy.mil/our_mission. html. See also, NDP2, supra, at 6–8, 29–31.

40. NDP2, supra, at 5.

41. Commander Mike Studeman, USN, "7 Myths of Intelligence," *Proceedings (U.S. Naval Institute)* 135 (February 2009): 64, 68.

42. Id. at 68.

43. *Intelligence, Surveillance, and Reconnaissance Operations,* Air Force Doctrine Document 2–5.2 (Washington, D.C.: Headquarters Air Force Doctrine Center, April 21, 1999), 1–7.

44. Id., at 29–37.

45. "Headquarters, U.S. Marine Corps Intelligence Department, Mission & Functions," (Washington, D.C.: U.S. Marine Corps), http://hqinet001.hqmc.usmc. mil/DIRINT/mission.html.

46. E.O. 12333, supra, Sect. 1(h)(1)-(4).

47. Coast Guard Organization, http://www.USCG. mil/top.

48. *Homeland Security Leadership Journal,* http://www. dhs.gov/journal/leadership/(December 9, 2008). See also "An Overview of the United States Intelligence Community for the 111th Congress," 24, 25.

49. Admiral Thad Allen, U.S. Coast Guard, "Friend or Foe? Tough to Tell," *Proceedings (U.S Naval Institute)* 134 (October 2008), http://www.usni.org/magazines/proceedings/story.asp?STORY_ID=1615.

Connecting Police Intelligence with Military and National Intelligence

Gary Cordner and Kathryn Scarborough

This chapter discusses the intersection of police, military, and national intelligence.[1] Police intelligence had relatively little common ground with military and national intelligence prior to 9/11, but the situation has shifted rather dramatically now that international terrorism is a priority threat for all three sectors. This chapter reviews features of U.S. policing that greatly complicate any effort to develop a coherent and coordinated system of information sharing and intelligence analysis. This includes the fragmented nature of the U.S. police structure, but also the characteristics of police work, police culture, and the checkered history of interagency relationships among local police, state police, and federal law enforcement agencies.

OVERVIEW

This chapter describes and discusses the terrain on which police, military, and national intelligence intersect. After 9/11, there were concerns about inadequate information sharing[2] and intelligence analysis (National Commission, 2004), together with subsequent initiatives aimed at better integration of homeland security intelligence activity (White House, 2007b; DNI, 2008b; ISE, 2008). The military's new Northern Command (NORTHCOM) recognizes the need for a better understanding of law enforcement intelligence practices and capacities in order to better prepare for its civil support and homeland defense responsibilities (Bowman, 2003; Bowman and Crowhurst, 2006; Cronin, 2007).

By *police intelligence* we mean those activities that law enforcement agencies[3] engage in to collect information and produce intelligence. Police intelligence today is dynamically evolving with the newer priorities of homeland security and terrorism. The current emphasis on intelligence is reflected in the latest police strategy, intelligence-led policing (NJSP, 2006; Ratcliffe, 2008). In the modern era, law enforcement agencies necessarily engage in a range of intelligence-related activities associated with their broad crime control and public safety missions.

Military intelligence has traditionally been focused on determining the military capabilities and intentions of our nation's enemies, while national intelligence has focused more broadly on the military, economic, and political intentions of all nations, friend and foe alike. More recently, the significant threats posed by nonstate actors have caused both military and national intelligence to focus more intently on international terrorism.

Prior to 9/11, local and state police tended to focus primarily on domestic crime and emergencies, while federal law enforcement focused on federal crimes and transnational crimes (Table 7.1). Neither the military nor the national intelligence community had much of a role in these criminal matters. With the exception of the FBI's counterintelligence responsibilities, police missions had relatively little in common with military or national intelligence missions.

Post-9/11, with heightened concern about terrorism and homeland security, the situation has shifted significantly, causing police intelligence to overlap more with military and national intelligence. Besides overlapping concerns, more frequent interactions and greater interdependencies also seem to have developed (CSG, 2005). It is suddenly more likely that the national intelligence community might need a bit of information picked up by an ordinary patrol officer somewhere in middle America. Similarly, it now seems more likely that terrorist plans found by a U.S. soldier in a cave in central Asia might have implications for a police chief back in the United States.

A BRIEF HISTORY

Military and national intelligence have much longer histories than police intelligence, since armies and nation states preceded organized, paid police forces by many centuries. It is also true that ancient rulers utilized spies and *agents provocateur* to help maintain internal control within their countries and empires. These secret police and the abuses they perpetrated (1) are an often unacknowledged part of police history; (2) help account for the reluctance to form organized police forces in England and its former colonies, until urbanization spawned increased crime and disorder in the early 1800s; and (3) continue to account for mixed emotions among the public and political leaders toward the practice of police intelligence.

Police intelligence in the United States began largely as a dossier system for collecting, retrieving, and sharing information about known criminals, especially bank robbers, train robbers, counterfeiters, and other mobile offenders (Carter, 2004). Prior to the 20th century, the nation's

Table 7.1 Summary of Operational Roles and Responsibilities in Relation to Particular Threats and Problems

	Domestic Crime	Transnational Crime	Terrorism
Local Police	Primary responsibility for prevention, response, and investigation.	Growing problem associated with globalization and Internet. Limited by resources and jurisdiction.	Eyes and ears throughout the country. Closest to the public (human intelligence). First responders and infrastructure protection.
State Police	Varies by state. Some primary and some secondary responsibilities. Important support roles—crime labs, criminal records systems, and so forth.	Growing problem associated with globalization and Internet. Limited by resources and jurisdiction.	Eyes and ears, information collection and analysis. First responders and infrastructure protection.
Federal Law Enforcement	Investigation of federal crimes, protection of federal property. Important support roles—crime labs, criminal records, special expertise.	Long-standing focus with regard to drugs, smuggling, customs, border control, and so forth. Becoming even more salient due to globalization and Internet.	Primary responsibility for investigation and operations within the United States. Information collection and analysis. Liaison to national intelligence agencies.
Federal and State Homeland Security	Little or no federal homeland security role. State fusion centers adopting all-crimes approach.	Important focus for state fusion centers. Some federal focus due to the nexus between crime and terrorism.	Intelligence analysis and information sharing.
National Intelligence	Little or no role. Restricted by law.	Little or no role except when connected with terrorism.	Investigation and operations outside the United States. Intelligence analysis and information sharing.
Military	Little or no role except on military bases or involving military personnel. Restricted by law.	Support role over the past 20 years with regard to drug smuggling. Otherwise limited to military bases and military personnel.	Military operations outside the United States. Homeland defense. Military operations within the United States through NORTHCOM.

most complete records and files were maintained by the Pinkerton private detective agency. It was not until 1924 that an effective national repository for fingerprint cards and criminal records was established in the DOJ and later the FBI (SEARCH, 2001). This repository became the National Division of Identification and Information and is now the National Repository of Criminal History Records and Criminal History Data (FBI, 2008).

The dossier system of police intelligence led local and federal law enforcement agencies into serious trouble in the years before World War I, then again between the world wars, and yet again in the 1950s, 1960s, and 1970s. Agencies were found to have collected information and maintained files on suspected communists, civil rights leaders, and antiwar activists, and individuals and groups critical of the government, but not necessarily engaged in crime. As a result, Congress and many state legislatures passed laws regulating the collection, storage, and sharing of intelligence information, particular in relation to domestic intelligence and U.S. citizens (Carter, 2004).

Despite these challenges, the importance of an effective intelligence function has consistently been recognized as an important component of modern police operations and administration. The President's Crime Commission in 1967 and the National Advisory Commission on Criminal Justice Standards and Goals in 1971 both recommended improved local and state law enforcement intelligence functions (Carter, 2004). Today's law enforcement agency accreditation program notes that "intelligence-gathering activities are important in all agencies, regardless of size" and that "activities should include information gathering, analysis, and dissemination to the appropriate functions/components" (CALEA, 2006: 42–43). Accreditation standards specify that "the agency maintains liaison with other organizations for the exchange of information relating to terrorism" and require agencies to have "procedures for reporting and relaying terrorism related intelligence/information to the proper task force or agency" (CALEA, 2006: 46–46).

Since the 1980s, police intelligence activities have focused mainly on drugs, gangs, and organized crime, with the more recent addition of terrorism (Cordner and Scarborough, 2007). Most federal, state, and local law enforcement agencies do not seem to have developed intelligence operations that can be described as effective or sophisticated.

THE STRUCTURE OF U.S. POLICING

The most distinctive feature of U.S. policing is fragmentation (Table 7.2). Under federalism, the primary responsibility for policing is delegated by the U.S. Constitution to the states. In turn, states have delegated policing authority to cities, towns, and counties. As a result, policing is primarily a function of local government. The United States has almost 18,000 separate law enforcement agencies, roughly 16,000 of which are local. Of the remaining 2,000 agencies, the vast majority represent special jurisdictions

Table 7.2 Summary of Key Participants in the Homeland Security Intelligence Arena

Local Police	• 17,876 separate agencies (71% local, 17% sheriff, 11% special jurisdiction) • 674,000 full-time sworn employees, 314,000 nonsworn • Some 50 percent of agencies have fewer than 10 full-time sworn officers. • Largest municipal agency is NYPD (36,118 sworn); largest sheriff agency is Los Angeles County (8,239 sworn).
State Police	• 49 primary state law enforcement agencies (mix of state police and highway patrol) • Primary state agencies employ 58,000 full-time sworn officers and 31,000 nonsworn. • In addition, there is a mix of state investigation bureaus and special jurisdiction law enforcement agencies. • Largest state agency is California highway patrol (7,085 sworn); largest investigation bureau is FDLE (531 sworn).
Federal Law Enforcement	• 65 nonmilitary federal agencies with law enforcement personnel • There are 106,000 nonmilitary full-time sworn personnel stationed within the United States. • 38 percent primarily investigation/enforcement, 21 percent response/patrol, 16 percent inspections, 25 percent other • Some 75 percent are DHS or DOJ; the largest are CBP (27,705 sworn), BOP, FBI, and ICE.
Federal and State Homeland Security	• DHS: 208,000 employees • Homeland Security Information Network (HSIN) • Protected Critical Infrastructure Information Program (PCII) • 58 state and local fusion centers (mostly state)
National Intelligence	• Director of National Intelligence (ODNI) • National Counterterrorism Center (NCTC) • CIA • FBI, DEA • DOE, State, Treasury, coast guard
Military	• DIA • air force, army, marines, navy • NSA, NRO, NGA

Sources: Reaves, 2006; Reaves, 2007; DHS, 2008a; DNI, 2008a.

(university police, transit police, park police, etc.), followed by state agencies, and lastly by federal nonmilitary agencies. Out of 837,000 full-time sworn police personnel (armed with arrest authority), 74 percent work for local agencies, while 26 percent work for special jurisdiction, state, and federal agencies.[4]

This overall distribution of U.S. police between different types of agencies masks a substantial amount of variation among the 50 states. The two largest components of U.S. policing are both local—municipal police departments (cities, towns, townships, boroughs, villages, etc.) and county sheriff's offices.[5] Two characteristics of these types of law enforcement agencies are absolutely essential for understanding their capabilities and contexts:

- *Most of these local agencies are small.* The median size local police department has nine full-time sworn officers, and 77 percent have fewer than 25 full-time sworn (Reaves, 2007). On average, sheriff's offices are slightly larger, but even so, 60 percent have fewer than 25 full-time sworn personnel.[6]
- *All of these local agencies are independent of each other.* Local police chiefs report to mayors, councils, or city/town managers. Sheriffs are almost all elected and therefore report to county voters. These agencies answer to local interests and are bound much more by local and state statutes than by federal law.

State police agencies are larger (averaging over 1,000 sworn) than the vast majority of local agencies, and they typically answer to state governors or cabinet secretaries. An important distinction is the difference between state police and highway patrol agencies. State police usually have relatively broad jurisdiction throughout their states, whereas highway patrol agencies have narrower jurisdiction. Pennsylvania, Maryland, and Kentucky are examples of state police agencies, whereas California, Ohio, and Florida are examples of highway patrol. The exact jurisdiction and practices of each state agency are a function of that state's laws and traditions.

The FBI was the largest nonmilitary federal law enforcement agency until recent growth in federal prisons and then the mergers associated with the establishment of the Department of Homeland Security. The largest federal law enforcement agency is now Customs and Border Protection (28,200 sworn), followed by the Federal Bureau of Prisons (15,361 sworn), the FBI (12,414 sworn), Immigration and Customs Enforcement (10,691 sworn), and the Secret Service (4,780 sworn).

From this brief description of the structure of U.S. policing, here are a few observations likely to be pertinent to information sharing among police, military, and national intelligence agencies:

- The U.S. police system is extremely fragmented—much more so than the military or national intelligence systems.
- Most police agencies and most police officers are found at the local level.
- Most local police agencies are small.
- All local police agencies are independent of each other (and of state and federal law enforcement agencies).
- The landscape of policing varies among the 50 states—in particular, the relative market share represented by sheriffs, state police, and/or federal agencies is negligible in some states and quite substantial in others.

Following from these observations, we can identify a few ramifications for information and intelligence sharing:

- The situation is highly complex—any one of 18,000 separate and independent agencies might possess information of value to others or might need information possessed by some other agency. None of these agencies necessarily knows who might need its information or who might have information it needs.

- Most of these agencies are too small to have full-time investigators, much less intelligence analysts.
- Substantial variation among agencies and among the states makes it unlikely that any one-size-fits-all solutions will be acceptable or effective.
- There is no chain of command between agencies in this system.[7] Local agencies answer to local authorities, state agencies answer to state authorities, and so forth. The levels of federalism (federal, state, local) should not be mistaken for levels of authority. No police chief, and certainly no sheriff, considers any state or federal law enforcement official to be his or her boss or superior.

POLICE WORK AND POLICE CULTURE

The following are a few characteristics of police work that might have implications for information sharing and police intelligence activity: *discretion, reaction,* and *territoriality.*[8] One central feature of police work is discretion. Despite reams and reams of constitutional law, case law, statutes, policies, procedures, and rules, individual police officers have considerable leeway when deciding whether to intervene in a situation, how to handle a dispute, whether to issue a citation or make an arrest, what techniques to use in a particular investigation, and so forth. Particularly at the local and state levels, officers in the field frequently act alone and without immediate supervision.

If an officer's decision does not result in a report or arrest, it probably will not be reviewed or produce any official information for later analysis. As Manning (1992: 370) notes, "information in police departments can best be characterized as systematically decentralized. Often, primary data known to one officer are not available to other officers" because they are stored in the officer's head or personal notes. Moreover, "all essential police knowledge is thought to be contextual, substantive, detailed, concrete, temporally bounded, and particularistic" while information in official reports and files is often viewed by officers and investigators as trivial, having been created and manipulated for bureaucratic purposes.

Another characteristic of modern police work is that it tends to be reactive. Most local police agencies devote at least 90 percent of their resources to motorized patrol, response to calls, and reactive investigations. Local police, in particular, are most often mobilized by a call from a citizen, and most police investigations are initiated after a citizen reports a crime. Two things provide a significant counterbalance to this reactive tendency. First, patrol officers everywhere, even in the busiest jurisdictions, have free time when they are not answering calls. During this free patrol time they are supposed to engage in preventive activities (such as patrolling), proactive enforcement (such as traffic stops), and public contact. Research conducted since the 1970s has demonstrated rather convincingly that traditional reactive policing methods are not very effective. As a result, more proactive strategies and tactics have been widely implemented, including repeat offender programs, differential responses, directed patrol, hot spots policing, broken windows policing, community policing, problem-oriented policing, and intelligence-led policing.

A third feature of police work is territoriality. Police agencies have traditionally assigned patrol officers to beats, and larger agencies usually divide their jurisdiction into precincts or districts, each with its own commander. Officers were expected to be knowledgeable about their beats and even take some degree of ownership for them. When motorized patrol and rapid response became dominant strategies, however, the importance of territoriality diminished.

Most police agencies have tried to reassert the influence of territoriality since the 1980s and 1990s. Foot patrol, community policing, permanent beat assignment, beat management, area detectives, crime mapping, and Compstat are all aimed at establishing a greater degree of patrol officer, detective, and commander familiarity, responsibility, and accountability for defined geographic areas. Officers who are knowledgeable about a local area are better able to differentiate between suspicious and ordinary behavior. Also, officers who are known and trusted by local residents are better able to gather information, engage the community, solve problems, and take other necessary actions.

From these characteristics of police work we might draw a few implications for information sharing and intelligence activity:

- Police, especially local police officers, are used to exercising discretion. They are comfortable making decisions and consequently tend to resist encroachments on their flexibility and professional judgment.
- The common tendency in policing is toward reaction, that is, waiting for something to happen. Modern strategies promote a more proactive approach.
- The reemphasis on territoriality in modern policing seeks to maximize place-based knowledge and accountability. This seems likely to increase the quantity and quality of bits of information collected by police officers. The corresponding challenge within and across police agencies is compiling and analyzing these bits of information in order to identify patterns, trends, and the bigger picture. In other words, geographically focused policing produces more observations about pieces and parts of the elephant, but does not automatically recognize the elephant for what it is.

Policing is also influenced by occupational and organizational cultures. There are several themes within police culture that seem to have important consequences for police intelligence activity and information sharing.

- Police agencies and police culture tend to celebrate and reward good arrests. Arrests are closely tied to the core law enforcement function of policing, plus they are tangible and easily quantifiable. Information and intelligence, by themselves, are not traditional units of police work, they are not measured, and producing them is not rewarded.

- The traditional units of police work are incidents, crimes, and cases. Each one of these tends to be regarded as a separate and discrete event deserving attention and, if possible, closure. Information that is not directly connected to an incident, crime, or case does not have a natural home in the traditional police records system—there is no file to put it in.
- Incidents, crimes, and cases are traditionally assigned to individual officers (or detectives), and individuals are evaluated on how well they handle and dispose of these events. Consequently, the tendency is for officers and detectives to hold information closely in order to enhance their own productivity. This pertains as well to information not yet connected to a case—officers tend to keep it to themselves in case it might lead to productive action later.
- Local and state policing have modernized significantly over the past several decades, but there is still a tendency toward parochialism. Local practices are often justified on the basis that "our situation is unique." Also, in spite of globalization, most crime is still local. Thus, many police do not demonstrate much interest in information that originates elsewhere, and do not always recognize that information they have gathered might be relevant to someone else.

In addition to these observations, we can note some characteristics of different types of agencies that may be applicable to intelligence activity and information sharing:

- Sheriff's offices tend to be particularly responsive to the public, since the sheriff is an elected official, a politician by definition, and someone who is always preparing for reelection.
- State police agencies, in comparison to local agencies, tend to have a more legalistic, no-nonsense orientation. This probably derives from the high priority they have historically given to traffic enforcement,[9] as well as their insulation from local political and community pressures.
- The various federal law enforcement agencies tend to have distinct cultures. For example, the FBI has traditionally emphasized making cases for prosecution, primarily through reactive investigation (National Commission, 2004; Posner, 2005). The DEA, by contrast, has historically put more emphasis on intelligence and proactive investigation—not surprising since drug crimes are rarely reported to authorities, but rather have to be discovered (Wilson, 1978).

INFORMATION AND INTELLIGENCE SHARING PRE-9/11

At the risk of overgeneralizing, information and intelligence sharing within the law enforcement community has traditionally been inadequate, while the flow of information between law enforcement agencies and military and national intelligence agencies has been nearly nonexistent. The latter was due mainly to disparate missions prior to 9/11. While police were focused mainly on domestic and transnational crime, the military and national intelligence agencies were focused mainly on threats to national security posed by other nations. Within the community of law enforcement agencies, the lack of information sharing was more a function of the structural, occupational, and cultural factors noted above. Table 7.3 identifies the complete set of interrelationships among the various types of agencies under consideration in this chapter. Disregarding homeland security agencies, which did not exist prior to 9/11, we can draw some of the key issues and themes pertinent to information and intelligence sharing from the table.

Sharing by Local Police

Local police agencies are generally predisposed to share information with each other, but several complications have historically interfered with good intentions. The biggest is simply the fragmentation of the U.S. police system, making even local information sharing very complicated. A few regional information systems have been created (ARJIS in San Diego and CLEAR in Chicago, for example), and it is common in some areas to hold monthly or quarterly regional meetings of chiefs, investigators, and/ or intelligence specialists. Still, in such a fragmented system, it is difficult to determine whom to share your information or intelligence with (who needs it) and to determine whom to contact in search of particular information or intelligence.

Local police have routinely shared basic information with state police, other state agencies, and some federal agencies, especially the FBI. This is because state agencies and the FBI maintain the official repositories and databases of fingerprint cards, criminal histories, wanted persons, stolen cars, and other stolen property. In addition, state police typically oversee registration systems for handgun permits and sex offenders, while state motor vehicle agencies maintain records related to driver licenses and vehicle registrations. The Uniform Crime Reporting (UCR) system is run by the FBI; the process involves local agencies submitting their reports to their state police, or some other state agency, which combines the information and forwards it on to the FBI.[10] While local police have traditionally shared these kinds of basic information with state police and federal agencies on a routine basis, sharing of other information and intelligence has not always been routine. Local police often complain about a one-way flow of information in their relations with both state and federal agencies; they provide information, but they never get anything back. Resentment builds up, leading to less information sharing by local agencies.

Conflict between local police and state police agencies is exacerbated by several factors. One is that the state police frequently has public corruption in its mission; as a result, state police occasionally investigate local police and sheriffs. Another factor is that state police often compete with sheriffs and local police for market share.[11] In the investigative arena state agencies may have the luxury of picking their cases, whereas local police are stuck with every crime reported to them. Local police sometimes accuse state police of poaching the easiest or most sensational cases, leaving

Table 7.3 Summary of Information and Intelligence-Sharing Considerations between and among Agencies in the Homeland Security Intelligence Arena

To the Agencies Below	From These Agencies					
	Local Police	State Police	Federal Law Enforcement	Federal and State Homeland Security	National Intelligence	Military
Local Police	No major obstacles, but limited by parochialism and complicated by fragmented system.	Usually provide state criminal records and link to NCIC. Sharing of intelligence historically limited.	Sharing of information and intelligence historically limited. Distrust, need to know, and lack of clearances. Some improvement via JTTFs.	Fusion centers intended to be the link. Time will tell if they can overcome one-way flow and need to know.	Little or no direct connection. Need to know. Lack of clearances. NCTC may help.	Historically, little or no direct connection except through MPs at local bases.
State Police	Natural channel for official records. Some resistance to sharing other information.	Good contacts between state police in various states.	Sharing of information and intelligence historically limited. Distrust, need to know, and lack of clearances. Some improvement via JTTFs.	Fusion centers are closely tied to state police. Time will tell if federal-to-state information flow improves.	Little or no direct connection. Need to know. Lack of clearances. NCTC may help.	Historically, little or no direct connection except through MPs at local bases.
Federal Law Enforcement	Historical resistance due to one-way flow. Often overcome through personal relationships.	Natural channel for official records. Some resistance to sharing other information.	Significant resistance due to jealousies, turf protection, and federal agency politics.	Competition between FBI and DHS. Mixing of staff in fusion centers should help.	Competition between FBI and CIA. ODNI and NCTC may help.	Unknown. ODNI should provide link.

Federal and State Homeland Security	Fusion centers intended to be the link. Time will tell if they succeed.	Closely tied to state fusion centers. Time will tell if sharing with federal agencies improves.	Major competition between FBI and DHS inhibits information sharing. Federal staff in state fusion centers may help.	National network of fusion centers should improve information sharing. Time will tell if federal-to-state information flow improves.	Fusion centers intended to be the link. CIA staff in some fusion centers. ODNI also a link.	Military advisor in DHS. National Guard in many fusion centers. Role for NORTHCOM.
National Intelligence	Historically, little or no direct connection.	Historically, little or no direct connection.	Competition between FBI and CIA. ODNI may help.	ODNI should provide link.	ODNI designed to overcome barriers.	ODNI designed to overcome barriers.
Military	Historically, little or no direct connection except through MPs at local bases.	Historically, little or no direct connection except through MPs at local bases.	Unknown. ODNI should provide link.	ODNI should provide link.	ODNI designed to overcome barriers.	Role for Joint Chiefs, DIA, DJIOC, and NMJIC.

the rest for the locals to handle. Another factor that greatly influences local-state relations and information sharing has to do with the size and prominence of the local agency. It is quite common for the state police and a few of the largest local police agencies in the state to compete for status and prestige. Typically, big city police departments ignore their state police. The smallest local police agencies often work closely with the state police, relying on them for radio communications, crime scene processing, accident reconstruction, and special operations response.

 The one-way information flow problem that discouraged local police information sharing with state police agencies also applied to federal law enforcement agencies, particularly the FBI. Historically, the FBI was also prone to poaching local cases, as well as taking credit for arrests and recoveries actually made by local police. In more recent years, well before 9/11, the FBI, DEA, and Secret Service all created local-area federal task forces on which local police routinely participated. These violent crime, major drugs, and electronic crimes task forces enhanced operational cooperation as well as information and intelligence sharing. Those local police agencies participating in task forces often used them as their principal channels for information sharing with federal law enforcement agencies. Over 7,000 law enforcement agencies joined six regional (multistate) intelligence networks established to facilitate sharing of criminal intelligence (RISS, 2007). In addition, local, state, and federal agencies jointly operated 31 regional and border HIDTAs (high intensity drug trafficking areas) that emphasized drug-related information sharing and intelligence production (ONDCP, 2008).

 Local police agencies have not traditionally engaged in much information sharing with the military, with the important exception of jurisdictions adjacent to a military installation. Information sharing between local police and military police about crimes, drugs, and hot spots on and around military bases has been fairly routine in the past (Cronin, 2007). Local police contacts with military police in matters involving military personnel (such as AWOL cases) were not uncommon. However, systematic sharing of other information or intelligence from local police to the military has not been common, because police did not imagine that their information would be relevant to the military's mission. Even less likely was information sharing with national intelligence agencies.

Sharing by State Police

The principal means of state police information sharing with local police has been through the databases and information systems that the state police operate. These systems are now mostly automated. When local police want to know if someone is wanted, if a car is stolen, or if an arrestee's fingerprints match the name he has given, they typically check first within state systems, and then use those same state systems to access national systems.

Most state police and/or state investigation bureaus traditionally housed some kind of intelligence unit. Unfortunately, some of these units adhered to the one-way flow phenomenon noted above. There are probably several reasons for this: (1) they may have seen themselves primarily as the *state police* intelligence unit, rather than a *statewide* intelligence unit, and therefore did not regard local police as important customers; (2) they may have embraced the need-to-know philosophy rather than the need-to-share philosophy; and (3) they may have held local police in low regard or even distrusted their ethics or professionalism.

It seems inevitable in our federal system that state officials often see themselves as superior in some ways to local officials. Their jurisdictions are broader, their numbers (personnel, budgets) are usually greater, and they work for a higher level of government. This is exactly the same kind of thinking that gets federal officials in trouble too, of course. This mentality may not always be conscious or intentional, but anyone who listens closely will hear clues in rhetoric and discourse that reveal the pecking order as many state and federal officials see it.

Information and intelligence sharing between different state police agencies (state to state) has traditionally been routine and effective. Each state has but one primary state police agency, plus perhaps one primary investigative agency. Thus the number of agencies is small—if the state police in Illinois obtain information about a crime or suspicious individual who lives in Pennsylvania, it is easy for them to figure out whom to share the information with. They also have small but effective national groups (the State and Provincial Police Division of IACP and the Association of State Criminal Investigative Agencies, ASCIA) that enhance networking and information sharing.

Traditional information sharing from state police to federal law enforcement, military, and national intelligence agencies would have been similar in many ways to that experienced by local police agencies, with one important exception. Since state police typically had their own dedicated intelligence units, these were always logical points of contact within each state for federal, military, and national agencies. Personnel in these state police units were more likely to obtain security clearances and to develop contacts and networks with other intelligence personnel. Having an effective link to these other agencies and systems probably made it more likely, in turn, that state police information and intelligence would be shared with them.

Sharing by Federal Law Enforcement

The FBI played a vital role in enhancing information sharing for U.S. law enforcement. The FBI oversaw the development of the national criminal identification (fingerprint) repository, the National Crime Information Center (NCIC) that received and stored information from police agencies on wanted persons and stolen property, and the UCR. The FBI also developed the National Academy (NA), one of the first training programs for selected police officials from all over the country. The NA became one of the most effective networks for information sharing in law enforcement.

Despite these contributions, the FBI's culture and tradition generally interfered with information and intelligence sharing with other agencies (Best, 2001; National Commission, 2004). FBI culture celebrated solving cases and presenting winning evidence to U.S. attorneys, not intelligence work. The differences between investigation and intelligence are quite profound (Posner, 2005: 14–15):

Criminal investigation is case-oriented, backward-looking, information-hugging, and fastidious (for fear of wrecking a prosecution). Intelligence, in contrast, is forward-looking, threat- rather than case-oriented, free-wheeling. Its focus is on identifying and maintaining surveillance of suspicious characters and on patiently assembling masses of seeming unrelated data into patterns that are suggestive of an emergent threat but may be based on speculative hypotheses far removed from probable cause, let alone from proof beyond a reasonable doubt.

In the realm of interagency relations, the FBI has never had a reputation for collaborating well with others. In its early years, the FBI routinely took credit for arrests and recovery of stolen property when other agencies had actually made the cases. Information was seen primarily as having value for individual and agency success, and therefore not something to be readily shared. At least two other factors came into play that hindered FBI information sharing: (1) an emphasis on need-to-know and security clearances; and (2) the FBI's role in investigating public corruption and civil rights allegations, which made the agency a potential threat to local and state police.

The most fundamental issue affecting information sharing by federal law enforcement agencies is, once again, federalism. This superior and paternalistic mentality leads federal officials to doubt whether state and local officials really need, or can be trusted with, sensitive information. In turn, it causes resentment among state and local officials. This is all the more ironic since the U.S. policing system is primarily local, not federal. Interrelationships and information sharing within the community of federal law enforcement agencies have also been notoriously problematic.

Information sharing between federal law enforcement agencies and national intelligence agencies suffers many of the same issues endemic to the federal bureaucracy, including some long-standing conflicts between the FBI and CIA related to the lines between domestic and foreign intelligence, and between counterintelligence and intelligence. These two agencies also fundamentally clash along the fault lines of investigative culture versus intelligence culture. An example from the 1990s pertains directly to obstacles limiting information sharing from the FBI to the National Security Council and State Department (Best, 2001: 20–21):

The distinction between law enforcement and intelligence can lead to potentially important difficulties. For instance, in March 1997, according to media reports, the FBI, out of concern for an ongoing criminal investigation, was unwilling to share information with the NSC staff about alleged contacts between Chinese officials and U.S. political fundraisers. Reports further indicate that such information was not shared with the Secretary of State, who was then preparing for an official visit to China. Samuel Berger, President Clinton's National Security Adviser was recalled as "sputtering in a profane rage," and his deputy, James Steinberg, subsequently recalled that the problem of insufficient information-sharing was "commonplace."

Sharing by National Intelligence Agencies and the Military

To the extent that information and intelligence sharing did occur from national intelligence agencies and the military to police, it was mainly to and through federal law enforcement agencies, primarily the FBI. Information sharing directly to state or local police was probably fairly uncommon, except in regard to criminal matters involving military personnel or domestic military bases.

In addition to the kinds of federal bureaucratic issues, such as agency cultures and politics, one of the biggest obstacles limiting intelligence sharing by national intelligence agencies and the military has been security clearances and information classification practices (National Commission, 2004). Different agencies, including the military, established their own security practices using categories such as confidential, classified, secret, and top secret. Classified information could then only be shared with officials who had the necessary security clearances as well as a need to know. Moreover, security clearances issued by one agency were not always recognized by another agency as valid. The net effect of these practices was to err on the side of protecting the information, rather than sharing it. This system made sense to those inside the classified circle, especially as a means to protect the sources of information. However, there tended to be few people inside the circle, while many officials outside the circle came to believe, correctly or incorrectly, that they were being denied a lot of important information and intelligence.[12]

This traditionally restricted flow of information and intelligence from national intelligence agencies and the military, due to security practices and clearances and the need-to-know philosophy, effectively turned off the spigot for state and local police. It was rare for state or local officials to have the necessary clearances to receive the information, plus unlikely that federal officials would determine they had the need to know.

POST-9/11 REFORMS

Following the events of September 11, 2001, a substantial number of reforms and other changes pertinent to intelligence and information sharing have been implemented. Some of the most important of these are noted below.

- Passage of the USA PATRIOT Act in 2001 expanding (and/or clarifying) some law enforcement and intelligence authorities related to counterterrorism
- Creation of U.S. Northern Command (NORTHCOM) in 2002
- Publication of a *National Strategy for Homeland Security* (White House, 2002)
- Creation of the Joint Regional Information Exchange System (JRIES) in 2002
- Creation of the Department of Homeland Security (DHS) in 2002 (operational in 2003)
- Publication of a National Criminal Intelligence Sharing Plan (GIWG, 2003)
- Creation of the Criminal Intelligence Coordinating Council (CICC) in 2004
- Creation of the Homeland Security Information Network (HSIN) to replace JRIES in 2004
- Creation of the Office of Director of National Intelligence (ODNI or DNI) in 2004
- Creation of the National Counterterrorism Center (NCTC) in 2004
- Establishment of 100 Joint Terrorism Task Forces (JTTFs) around the country, headed by the FBI with active participation from local and state police as well as other federal agencies (FBI, 2004)
- Passage of the *Intelligence Reform and Terrorism Prevention Act* establishing an Information Sharing Environment (ISE) in 2004
- Publication of an updated *National Strategy for Homeland Security* (White House, 2007a)
- Publication of a *National Strategy for Information Sharing* (White House, 2007b)
- Passage of the 9/11 Commission Act establishing the Interagency Threat Assessment and Coordination Group (ITACG) in 2007
- Publication of an Intelligence Community Information Sharing Strategy (DNI, 2008b)
- Creation of 58 state and local information fusion centers (DHS, 2008b)

Not surprisingly, these changes have not seemed to immediately solve all of the information- and intelligence-sharing problems associated with terrorism and homeland security. Local and state police have consistently complained that national plans were too often really federal plans—created without state and local input, not responsive to state and local needs, often asserting federal control, and often creating new and unfunded state and local mandates (PERF, 2003; IACP, 2005). Similarly, the most recent national intelligence community information-sharing strategy describes conditions largely unchanged from 2001 (DNI, 2008b: 11):

The "need-to-know" culture led to practices that inhibit information sharing today. Multiple organizations establish their own classification rules and procedures, resulting in inconsistent use and understanding of security markings. Differing requirements for access and certification and accreditation inhibit trust across the Intelligence Community agencies.

INFORMATION AND INTELLIGENCE SHARING POST-9/11

While obstacles and challenges remain, it is also the case that significant changes have occurred. Within one or two years after 9/11, local and state police were reporting increased responsibilities related to homeland security, increased contacts with a range of federal agencies, better relationships with federal authorities, and more open and effective information sharing (CSG, 2005; PERF, 2003; PERF, 2005). More JTTFs were created (increasing from 35 to 100) with more state and local participation, and federal participation within state and local fusion centers became common. The overall trend has undoubtedly been in the direction of more information sharing.

One of the early sources of frustration, from the state and local perspective, was a lack of coordination, and the existence of competition, between DHS and the FBI (Eack, 2008). State and local police found that they received threat information from both sources, but it was not always consistent (nor timely, as they sometimes got it from CNN first). Also, both DHS and the FBI advocated their own information networks (JRIES/HSIN for DHS, LEO for the FBI) as the proper channels for terrorism-related information and intelligence sharing (DHS, 2006). In this scenario, DHS had the advantage of billions of dollars in grants to give, whereas the FBI had the advantage of an operational counterterrorism role with which state and local police could more readily identify, including JTTFs on which they could participate.

Another early frustration related to security clearances (GAO, 2004). As DHS and the FBI tried to ramp up information and intelligence sharing from the federal level, they bumped into the problem that many state and local police executives lacked clearances and could not receive classified information. A crash program was initiated to conduct background checks in order to process these security clearances, but it was a slow process. It was also perceived as demeaning by many state and local police executives; from their perspective, they were ultimately responsible for protecting their jurisdictions from terrorism, not to mention crime and disorder, yet they had to undergo lengthy scrutiny by federal investigators who shouldered far less responsibility and were often far less senior. To make matters worse, there was often a quota on how many security clearances would be processed.

A third general issue that arose concerned intelligence analysts. The vast majority of large local police agencies, state police, and the new state and local information fusion centers realized that they needed to add and/or upgrade intelligence analysis capabilities. However, few criteria existed for selecting these analysts, little training was available, and competition for trained and experienced analysts was stiff. This competition was exacerbated by the fact that federal law enforcement agencies, including the FBI, also began recruiting and hiring more analysts. An added problem, especially for fusion centers, was that DHS grant monies could not usually be used to pay staff salaries and benefits, so analyst positions had to be funded with state and local dollars.

Sharing by and with Local Police

The post-9/11 focus on local police has mainly been on their role as eyes and ears in local communities throughout the nation. In this respect they are seen as very important collectors of information, of raw data, that can be fed into the intelligence process in order to help analysts and others connect the dots. Officers have been given training and also checklists to help them identify and report suspicious behavior that might have some connection to terrorism (BJA, 2008; Meyer, 2008). Community policing is seen as an ideal local police strategy because it helps officers get to know their communities and builds trust, making it more likely that residents will share important information with the police (PERF, 2001; Scheider and Chapman, 2003).

It can be noted that this eyes-and-ears role may be perceived as somewhat insulting if not presented correctly. If all local police are asked to do is collect information and send it up to the state fusion center or federal authorities, the suggestion is that local police are not capable of more significant activity, or a more substantial role is not necessary. A more sophisticated message has been to refer to local police as *first preventers* who are most likely to be in a position to prevent a terrorist act, both by gathering information and by taking action, when appropriate. This first preventer role is paired with the more familiar *first responder* role to make a logical and meaningful package that demonstrates the synergy between effective crime reduction tactics and counterterrorism, and it encourages local police to take their counterterrorism role more seriously (Kelling and Bratton, 2006).

The *National Strategy for Information Sharing* (White House, 2007a: 10) reiterated this expanded role for local police and provided a few specific examples:

These partners are now a critical component of our Nation's security capability as both "first preventers" and "first responders," and their efforts have achieved concrete results within their communities, as the following examples illustrate:

- A narcotics investigation—conducted by Federal, State, and local law enforcement officials and resulting in multiple arrests—revealed that a Canadian-based organization supplying precursor chemicals to Mexican methamphetamine producers was in fact a Hezbollah support cell.
- A local police detective investigating a gas station robbery uncovered a homegrown jihadist cell planning a series of attacks.
- An investigation into cigarette smuggling initiated by a county sheriff's department uncovered a Hezbollah support cell operating in several States.

Sharing by and with State Police

Each state has set up some type of homeland security apparatus to advise the governor and the legislature, oversee statewide threat assessment and infrastructure protection, receive and distribute DHS funds, provide training and assistance to local jurisdictions, and so forth. In many if not most states, the state police have naturally assumed a large role in these activities, since they are usually the largest state public safety agency. The development of state fusion centers has also typically been with substantial state police involvement. The state police usually had a preexisting intelligence unit (Eack, 2008) and they were often already serving as a principal point of contact for federal law enforcement and national intelligence agencies.

Despite this potentially heightened role for state agencies, several factors may account for a lower level of state police involvement in the new information-sharing environment than might be expected. State fusion centers may be superseding state police agencies as the principal state-level cogs in the information-sharing system. Additionally, many local agencies have their own direct connections to the JTTF, FBI, or other federal agencies, so that state-level involvement is not needed in many situations. From an efficiency standpoint this direct local-federal connection may be desirable, however, it might limit information sharing and intelligence development if pertinent information does not also find its way to broader networks such as the state fusion centers or the NCTC.

It seems absolutely essential in the new information-sharing environment that state fusion centers function as statewide entities rather than merely as state police entities. In the former mode, they stand a chance of being perceived as serving all agencies in the state; and if they in fact disseminate useful information and products to all agencies, they should become critical assets for both intrastate and national information sharing (Rollins and Connors, 2007; Larence, 2008).

Sharing by and with Federal Law Enforcement

The new information-sharing environment (ISE, 2008) is supposed to put greater emphasis on need to share. One method for doing that is to funnel information to the NCTC, from which it would presumably be shared with other agencies as deemed appropriate. Another avenue would be to enter pertinent information in the NCIC VGOTF file. The former method would theoretically be more proactive, since it might result in intelligence being widely shared with agencies that could then use it in a variety of ways. The latter method would be more reactive—if an officer stopped a vehicle or person somewhere and made a NCIC query, they could be notified of the possible terrorism connection.

There remains a good bit of skepticism about the free flow of information from federal law enforcement agencies. Improved systems for information sharing have been established but they are not always used. The National Strategy for Information Sharing (White House, 2007b) and Information Sharing Environment (ISE, 2008) provide additional enhancements that should continue the improvements already made. Traditional obstacles and barriers certainly remain, even though progress has been made (Kelling and Bratton, 2006):

Since 9/11, information sharing between the federal government and state and locals has improved. Most of the improvement has come through the FBI's Joint Terrorism Task Force (JTTF), which has tripled in number from 34 before September 11 to 100 today. In Los Angeles and other large departments across the country, there are active levels of communication and cooperation with the Department of Homeland Security and the FBI.

Despite this progress, the level of cooperation seems to vary greatly, depending on the personalities of individual bureau and police chiefs. Too often, the FBI cuts itself off from local police manpower, expertise, and intelligence. More than 6,000 state and local police now have federal security clearances, but the historical lack of trust is still an issue. For example, many police chiefs complain of calls they get from their JTTF alerting them to a potential threat, but when they ask for the detailed information needed to launch an investigation, they are told by the bureau: "We can't tell you" or "You don't need to know."

Sharing by and with National Intelligence Agencies and the Military

The National Counterterrorism Center (NCTC, 2008) was established in 2004 and includes federal law enforcement agencies, national intelligence agencies, and the military among its partner organizations. As described on the NCTC Web site (http://www.nctc.gov/about_us/what_we_do.html):

NCTC serves as the primary organization in the United States Government for integrating and analyzing all intelligence pertaining to terrorism possessed or acquired by the United States Government (except purely domestic terrorism); serves as the central and shared knowledge bank on terrorism information; [and] provides all-source intelligence support to government-wide counterterrorism activities.

The NCTC is assisted by the ITACG, which specifically represents the interests of state and local law enforcement and related officials. Its purpose is to enable and facilitate the production of federally coordinated terrorism-related information and products that are shared through existing channels with state and local agencies.

Together, these new entities along with the National Strategy for Information Sharing (White House, 2007b) and the Intelligence Community Information Sharing Strategy (DNI, 2008b) are supposed to assure that terrorism-related information and intelligence are shared more effectively among all the counterterrorism players, including state and local police, federal law enforcement, federal and state homeland security operations, the IC, and the military.

CHALLENGES AND PROSPECTS

Ten years ago, few would have seen very much common ground between police intelligence, on the one hand, and either military intelligence or national intelligence. The threat and reality of international terrorism have shifted the terrain substantially. Everyone now recognizes the common ground between police, military, and national intelligence. Figuring out how best to operate on this common ground is proving to be a challenge, but significant progress is apparent. At the federal level, new information-sharing strategies and the new architecture of the ODNI, NCTC, and ISE hold great promise, if traditional interagency competition can be overcome. At the state level, fusion centers have been created and are beginning to operate as the linking pin with federal agencies and networks.

But it is the local level that presents the greatest challenges. U.S. policing is mainly local and extremely fragmented, police work has not traditionally emphasized intelligence gathering and sharing, and local police relations with state and federal agencies have always been tenuous. Local police are ready to be first responders to terrorism and can probably be convinced that they should also be first preventers. Convincing them to become the eyes and ears for an intelligence apparatus that is mainly situated at the state and federal levels is a harder sell, however. The current situation needs a concerted effort at remarketing to convince local police that the new institutions and networks truly serve statewide and national interests, not state police and federal interests. This will take more than public relations and spin. Local police will be watching for demonstrations of real respect and genuine collaboration.

NOTES

1. Preparation of this work was sponsored in part by the Homeland Security Defense Education Consortium (HSDEC). Any errors or misrepresentations in the chapter are solely the responsibility of the authors. Points of view expressed in the chapter are the authors' and do not represent the views of HSDEC or the Department of Defense.

2. This chapter addresses both information sharing and intelligence sharing. Generally, information refers to raw data (a person's address, a criminal record, or an informant's report that a person carries a gun in the glove box of his car),

whereas intelligence refers to data that has been evaluated, analyzed, interpreted, and preferably collated with other data.

3. We use the terms *police* and *law enforcement* interchangeably in this chapter. One can make a compelling argument in favor of the term *police* since it is a better descriptor than *law enforcement* of the traditionally broad mission of policing agencies. However, some sheriff personnel resent the term *police* because it does not seem to include them. Similarly, most federal police have such a narrower role that *law enforcement* does fit them better. Despite these intricacies, though, many practitioners as well as the public tend to use the two terms, *police* and *law enforcement*, interchangeably.

4. These proportions were calculated using data presented in Reaves (2006) and Reaves (2007).

5. It is common to refer to sheriff's departments and sheriff's agencies, but purists prefer the term *sheriff's offices,* since sheriff is an office to which one is elected (usually) or appointed (occasionally). In the United States, the office of sheriff is typically established within state constitutions, leading sheriffs to identify themselves as constitutional officers, a sign of prestige and sometimes authority.

6. These figures include only law enforcement personnel in sheriff's offices, not corrections (jail) personnel also in the sheriff's employ.

7. Of course, there are chains of command *within* each agency. But between agencies, in interagency relationships, authority is typically absent. This is one of the reasons why the development of mutual aid agreements, interstate compacts, the incident command system, and NIMS has been so important.

8. The interested reader is referred to Cordner and Scarborough (2007), especially chapters 2, 8, and 13, for additional explanation and extensive references on police work, police strategies, and police culture.

9. In fact, many state police and highway patrol agencies were founded in the early to middle 1900s specifically to handle problems created by that newfangled invention, the automobile.

10. Federal law does not require local agencies to participate in the UCR. For the past 20 years, an enhancement to the UCR, the National Incident Based Reporting System (NIBRS), has been gradually implemented on a voluntary basis. In this system, agencies report incident-level data instead of aggregate data. Only about 25 percent of reported crime is currently submitted via NIBRS, while the other 75 percent is still submitted in traditional aggregate UCR format (JRSA, 2007).

11. This consideration applies in those states with full-service state police agencies, but probably not in states with highway patrol agencies.

12. Most of the post-9/11 discussion about information and intelligence sharing presumes that the CIA or the FBI or some other agency has a lot of really useful information that it never shares. It is also possible that the information just is not there (PERF, 2003).

REFERENCES

Best, Richard A., Jr. 2001. "Intelligence and Law Enforcement: Countering Transnational Threats to the U.S." *Report for Congress* RL30252. Washington, D.C.: Congressional Research Service.

BJA. 2008. State and Local Anti-Terrorism Training Program. Bureau of Justice Assistance. Information online at https://www.slatt.org/Default.aspx.

Bowman, Steve. 2003. "Homeland Security: The Department of Defense's Role." *Report for Congress* RL31615. Washington, D.C.: Congressional Research Service.

Bowman, Steve, and James Crowhurst. 2006. "Homeland Security: Evolving Roles and Missions for United States Northern Command." *Report for Congress* RS21322. Washington, D.C.: Congressional Research Service.

CALEA. 2006. *Standards for Law Enforcement Agencies,* 5th ed. Fairfax, Va.: Commission on Accreditation for Law Enforcement Agencies.

Carter, David L. 2004. *Law Enforcement Intelligence: A Guide for State, Local, and Tribal Law Enforcement Agencies.* Washington, D.C.: Office of Community Oriented Policing Services.

CICC. 2008. Criminal Intelligence Coordinating Council. Information online at http://www.iir.com/global/council.htm.

Cordner, Gary, and Kathryn Scarborough. 2007. *Police Administration,* 6th ed. Newark, N.J.: Matthew Bender/LexisNexis.

Cronin, R. Barry. 2007. "U.S. Northern Command & Defense Support of Civil Authorities." *The Police Chief* (April): 152–59.

CSG. 2005. *The Impact of Terrorism on State Law Enforcement: Adjusting to New Roles and Changing Conditions.* Lexington, Ky.: Council of State Governments.

DHS. 2006. "Homeland Security Information Network Could Support Information Sharing More Effectively." Washington, D.C.: Office of Inspector General, Department of Homeland Security. Available online at http://www.dhs.gov/xoig/assets/mgmtrpts/OIG_06–38_Jun06.pdf.

DHS. 2008a. Office of Intelligence & Analysis. Department of Homeland Security. Information online at http://www.dhs.gov/xinfoshare/.

DHS. 2008b. State and Local Fusion Centers. Department of Homeland Security. Information online at http://www.dhs.gov/xinfoshare/programs/gc_1156877184684.shtm.

DNI. 2008a. "An Overview of the United States Intelligence Community." Washington, D.C.: Office of the Director of National Intelligence. Available online at http://www.dni.gov/overview.pdf.

DNI. 2008b. "Intelligence Community Information Sharing Strategy." Washington, D.C.: Office of the Director of National Intelligence. Available online at http://www.dni.gov/reports/IC_Information_Sharing_Strategy.pdf.

Eack, Kevin D. 2008. "State and Local Fusion Centers: Emerging Trends and Issues." *Homeland Security Affairs,* Suppl. no. 2. Available online at http://www.hsaj.org/pages/supplement/issue2/pdfs/supplement.2.3.pdf.

FBI. 2004. Protecting America Against Terrorist Attack: A Closer Look At the FBI's Joint Terrorism Task Forces. Federal Bureau of Investigation. Information online at http://www.fbi.gov/page2/dec04/jttf120114.htm.

FBI. 2008. Fingerprint Identification. Federal Bureau of Investigation. Information online at http://www.fbi.gov/hq/cjisd/ident.pdf.

GAO. 2004. "Security Clearances: FBI Has Enhanced Its Process for State and Local Law Enforcement Officials," GAO-04–596. Washington, D.C.: General Accounting Office. Available online at http://www.gao.gov/new.items/d04596.pdf.

GAO. 2008. "U.S. Northern Command Has Made Progress but Needs to Address Force Allocation, Readiness Tracking Gaps, and Other Issues," GAO-08–251. Washington, D.C.: Government Accountability Office. Available online at http://www.gao.gov/new.items/d08251.pdf.

GIWG. 2003. *The National Criminal Intelligence Sharing Plan.* Global Intelligence Working Group. Washington, D.C.: Bureau of Justice Assistance. Available online at http://it.ojp.gov/documents/NCISP_Plan.pdf.

IACP. 1985. *Law Enforcement Policy on the Management of Criminal Intelligence.* Gaithersburg, Md.: International Association of Chiefs of Police.

IACP. 2005. "From Hometown Security to Homeland Security." Alexandria, Va.: International Association of Chiefs of Police. Available online at http://www.theiacp.org/leg_policy/HomelandSecurityWP.PDF.

ISE. 2008. Information Sharing Environment. Information online at http://www.ise.gov/.

ITACG. 2008. Interagency Threat Assessment Coordination Group. Information online at http://www.ise.gov/pages/partner-itacg.html.

JRSA. 2007. Status of NIBRS in the States. Justice Research & Statistics Association. Information online at http://www.jrsa.org/ibrrc/background-status/nibrs_states.shtml.

Kelling, George L., and William J. Bratton. 2006. "Policing Terrorism." *Civic Bulletin* no. 43. New York: Manhattan Institute for Policy Research. Available online at http://www.manhattan-institute.org/html/cb_43.htm.

Larence, Eileen R. 2008. "Federal Efforts Are Helping to Address Some Challenges Faced by State and Local Fusion Centers," GAO-08–636T. Testimony before the Ad Hoc Subcommittee on State, Local, and Private Sector Preparedness and Integration, Committee on Homeland security and Governmental Affairs, U.S. Senate. Washington, D.C.: Government Accountability Office.

Manning, Peter K. 1992. "Information Technologies and the Police." In *Modern Policing,* ed. Michael Tonry and Norval Morris. Chicago: University of Chicago Press.

Markon, Jerry. 2008. "FBI, ATF Battle for Control of Cases." *The Washington Post* (May 10). Available online at http://www.washingtonpost.com/wp-dyn/content/article/2008/05/09/AR2008050903096.html.

Meyer, Josh. 2008. "LAPD Leads the Way in Local Counter-Terrorism." *Los Angeles Times* (April 14). Available online at http://www.latimes.com/news/local/la-me-counterterror14apr14,1,5682393.story.

National Commission. 2004. *The 9/11 Commission Report: Final Report of the National Commission on Terrorist Attacks Upon the United States.* New York: W.W. Norton.

NCTC. 2008. National Counterterrorism Center. Information online at http://www.nctc.gov/.

NJSP. 2006. *Practical Guide to Intelligence-Led Policing.* New Jersey State Police. New York: Center for Policing Terrorism, Manhattan Institute. Available online at http://www.cpt-mi.org/pdf/NJPoliceGuide.pdf.

ONDCP. 2008. High Intensity Drug Trafficking Areas. Office of National Drug Control Policy. Information online at http://www.whitehousedrugpolicy.gov/HIDTA/.

PERF. 2001. "Local Law Enforcement's Role in Preventing and responding to Terrorism." Washington, D.C.: Police Executive Research Forum. Available online at http://www.policeforum.org/upload/terrorismfinal%5B1%5D_715866088_12302005135139.pdf.

PERF. 2003. *Protecting Your Community from Terrorism: Improving Local-Federal Partnerships.* Washington, D.C.: Police Executive Research Forum. Available online at http://www.policeforum.org/upload/wp1_925579737_32200614297.pdf.

PERF. 2005. *Protecting Your Community from Terrorism: The Production and Sharing of Intelligence.* Washington, D.C.: Police Executive Research Forum. Available online at http://www.policeforum.org/upload/wp4_925579737_322006144658.pdf.

Posner, Richard. 2005. *Remaking Domestic Intelligence.* Stanford, Calif.: Hoover Institution Press.

Ratcliffe, Jerry H. 2008. *Intelligence-Led Policing.* Devon, UK: Willan Publishing.

Reaves, Brian A. 2006. "Federal Law Enforcement Officers, 2004." Washington, D.C.: Bureau of Justice Statistics. Available online at http://www.ojp.usdoj.gov/bjs/pub/pdf/fleo04.pdf.

Reaves, Brian A. 2007. "Census of State and Local Law Enforcement Agencies, 2004." Washington, D.C.: Bureau of Justice Statistics. Available online at http://www.ojp.usdoj.gov/bjs/pub/pdf/csllea04.pdf.

Reuss-Ianni, Elizabeth. 1983. *Two Cultures of Policing: Street Cops and Management Cops.* New Brunswick, N.J.: Transaction Books.

RISS. 2007. Regional Information Sharing Systems. Information online at http://www.riss.net/.

Rollins, John, and Timothy Connors. 2007. "State Fusion Center Processes and Procedures: Best Practices and Recommendations." *Policing Terrorism Report No. 2.* New York: Manhattan Institute for Policy Research. Available online at http://www.manhattan-institute.org/html/ptr_02.htm.

Scheider, Matthew, and Robert Chapman. 2003. "Community Policing and Terrorism." *Journal of Homeland Security* (April). Available online at http://www.homelandsecurity.org/newjournal/articles/scheider-chapman.html.

Schmitt, Richard B. 2008. "FBI Is Called Slow to Join the Terrorism Fight." *Los Angeles Times* (May 9). Available online at http://www.latimes.com/news/nationworld/nation/la-na-intel9-2008may09,0,7865641.story.

SEARCH. 2001. *Use and Management of Criminal History Record Information: A Comprehensive Report, 2001 Update.* Washington, D.C.: Bureau of Justice Statistics.

Tucker, Nancy Bernkopf. 2008. "The Cultural Revolution in Intelligence: Interim Report." *The Washington Quarterly* (Spring): 47–61.

White House. 2002. *National Strategy for Homeland Security.* Washington, D.C.: Office of Homeland Security. Available online at http://www.dhs.gov/xlibrary/assets/nat_strat_hls.pdf.

White House. 2007a. *National Strategy for Homeland Security.* Washington, D.C.: Homeland Security Council. Available online at http://www.dhs.gov/xlibrary/assets/nat_strat_homelandsecurity_2007.pdf.

White House. 2007b. *National Strategy for Information Sharing: Successes and Challenges in Improving Terrorism-Related Information Sharing.* Washington, D.C.: White House. Available online at http://www.whitehouse.gov/nsc/infosharing/NSIS_book.pdf.

Wilson, James Q. 1978. *The Investigators: Managing FBI and Narcotics Agents.* New York: Basic Books.

8

Private Security Intelligence and Homeland Security

Pamela A. Collins and Ryan K. Baggett

We will build a national environment that enables the sharing of essential homeland security information. We must build a "system of systems" that can provide the right information to the right people at all times. Information will be shared "horizontally" across each level of government and "vertically" among federal, state, and local governments, *private industry*, and citizens. (Office of Homeland Security, 2002)

The U.S. Department of Homeland Security's (DHS) Office of Intelligence and Analysis (OIA), a member of the national intelligence community (IC), ensures that information related to homeland security threats is collected, analyzed, and disseminated to the full spectrum of homeland security customers in the department, at the state, local, and tribal levels, to the private sector, and within the IC. The office has five analytic thrusts, aligned with the principal threats to the homeland addressed by the DHS.

The first is *threats related to border security* (to include all borders: air, land, sea, and virtual), analyzing a range of interlocking threats to include narcotics trafficking, alien and human smuggling, money laundering, and other illicit transnational threats. This includes the monitoring of foreign government initiatives that affect border security.

The second is the *threat of radicalization and extremism*. This focus is on domestic groups, including radicalized Islam and other types of radicalized domestic groups. The OIA does not monitor known extremists and their activities. Instead, OIA is interested in the radicalization process: why and how people who are attracted to radical beliefs cross the line into violence.

The third is *threats from particular groups entering the United States.* These are the groups that could be exploited by terrorists or criminals to enter the homeland legally or to bring in harmful materials. The office further focuses on travel-related issues of interest to the department, such as visa categories and the Visa Waiver Program.

, The fourth is *threats to the homeland's critical infrastructure and key resources,* in which all source intelligence from the IC is merged with information from critical infrastructure owners and operators and shared with the State and Local Fusion Centers. This approach provides a comprehensive tactical and strategic understanding of physical and cyberthreats to the critical infrastructure, including threats from nation-states, international and domestic terrorism, and criminal enterprises. Threat assessments are integrated with other assessments of infrastructure vulnerabilities and the consequences of an incident to define all hazard infrastructure risk for risk-based prioritization and decision making.

• The last and fifth thrust area is *weapons of mass destruction (WMDs) and health threats.* This includes evaluating and establishing a baseline of the actors, their claims, and their plans to conduct attacks involving chemical, biological, radiological, and nuclear materials against the homeland (U.S. Department of Homeland Security, 2009).

This chapter focuses on the fourth thrust area of the OIA, the *threats to the homeland's critical infrastructure and key resources.* It is this area in which the collection and analysis of intelligence involves and greatly depends upon the ability and cooperation of the private sector.

BACKGROUND

The fact that the private sector controls the vast majority of U.S. critical infrastructure and key resources (CI/KR) makes collaboration between the federal government, specifically DHS and the private sector, a necessity. Since the events of September 11, 2001, there has been considerable progress made in bridging the gap between the private sector and the federal government; however, much remains to be done. One of the primary stumbling blocks to creating a collaborative relationship with the private sector is the government's inability to establish formal and effective methods of cooperation. A variety of legal and procedural obstacles have blocked the ability of both entities to successfully engage one another in a meaningful way for any sustained period of time. To address these obstacles, Executive Order (E.O.) 13231 was written in October of 2001. This E.O. on "Critical Infrastructure Protection in the Information Age" established the National Infrastructure Advisory Council (NIAC) (Bush, 2001).

The NIAC provides the secretary of homeland security with advice on the security of information systems for critical infrastructure (CI) supporting several sectors of the economy: banking and finance, transportation, energy, manufacturing, and emergency government services. The members of the NIAC represent the private sector, academia, and state and local government. Individuals selected from the private sector would normally hold the position of chief executive officers (CEOs), or equivalent, with responsibilities for security of information and infrastructure supporting the critical sectors of the economy. The purpose of this council is to enhance the partnership between public and private sectors in the protection of information systems for CI and to monitor the development of private sector Information Sharing and Analysis Centers (ISACs). Each CI industry has established an ISAC to communicate with its members, its government partners, and other ISACs about threat indications, vulnerabilities, and protective strategies. ISACs work together to better understand cross-industry dependencies and to account for them in emergency response planning.

OBSTACLES TO INTELLIGENCE INFORMATION SHARING

The NIAC conducted a study in 2006 to determine whether the federal government and its private sector partners could improve coordination between the IC and CI owners and operators. A similar study, entitled *Homeland Security Information Sharing between Government and the Private Sector* was conducted a year earlier by the Homeland Security Advisory Council's (HSAC) Private Sector Information Sharing Task Force, in August of 2005. The HSAC provides advice and recommendations to the DHS secretary on matters related to homeland security. The HSAC is composed of leaders from state and local government, first responder communities, the private sector, and academia. The HSAC Task Force was charged with developing a better understanding of the legal and procedural obstacles that appeared to be hampering the free flow of information between the federal government and private sector. Many of the key findings, described below, were useful information for the NIAC study that followed.

The key findings from the HSAC study suggest that while there have been significant information-sharing initiatives and projects within DHS, and in both public and private sector agencies, there did not appear to be any particular alignment or architecture to these efforts, nor was there a clear understanding as to whose responsibility it was to create one. It was also concluded that it would take significant work to align relationships between DHS and the private sector as well as different considerations made for sharing threat and vulnerability information. For example, considerations regarding statutory, regulatory, and policy would have to be addressed. Clearly, it would require the creation and maintenance of a trusted partnership between the government and the private sector for successful intelligence and information sharing to occur. Interestingly, the study found that relationships and interaction between the private sector and state and local agencies are less problematic than those with DHS. (Homeland Security Advisory Council, Private Sector Information Sharing Task Force, 2005)

Using this study, and other works that contributed to a better understanding of the dynamics involved in creating a climate and culture for sharing of intelligence between the federal government and the private sector, the NIAC created the Intelligence Coordination Working Group (Working Group). The Working Group identified more than 30 representative subject matter experts from the private sector and the IC to assist the NIAC in identifying information-sharing mechanisms within and between the government and the private sector. The NIAC study was significant since there had been a number of organizational and governance changes since the NIAC was originally formed in October 2001. The two most significant changes were the establishment of the Office of the Director of National Intelligence (ODNI) and the creation of the Critical Infrastructure Partnership Advisory Council (CIPAC). The two organizations were formed to provide the framework for establishing single points of contact for both the government and the private sector. The guidance given to the ODNI and heads of executive departments and agencies was to:

- Leverage ongoing information-sharing efforts in the development of the Information Sharing Environment (ISE)
- Define common standards for how information is acquired, accessed, shared, and used within the ISE
- Develop a common framework for the sharing of information between and among executive departments and agencies and state, local, and tribal governments, law enforcement agencies, and the private sector
- Standardize procedures for sensitive but unclassified information
- Facilitate information sharing between executive departments and agencies and foreign partners
- Protect the information privacy rights and other legal rights of Americans
- Promote a culture of information sharing (Bush, 2005)

The NIAC Working Group study provided additional guidance and recommendations to not only the ODNI, but also to CIPAC and the DHS. The findings from the Working Group study were segmented into eight specific areas of consideration:

1. *Personal relationships:* Due to the high turnover rate for public and private sector personnel there should be less of a dependence on personal relationships for

the flow of intelligence and information. These types of relationships should be institutionalized to the position rather than the person.

2. *Critical infrastructure subject matter expertise:* There was a significant lack of CI subject matter expertise that was detrimental to private sector intelligence analysis.

3. *Government's intelligence dissemination processes:* The necessary information is not consistently shared with the right people in the private sector in the time needed to respond.

4. *Private sector information-sharing mechanisms:* There is a lack of uniformity, capability, and maturity of intelligence information sharing between private sector agencies.

5. *Protected Critical Infrastructure Information (PCII) program:* The PCII is an information-protection program that was intended to enhance information sharing between the private sector and the government. The DHS and other federal, state, and local analysts use PCII to analyze and secure critical infrastructure and protected systems, identify vulnerabilities and develop risk assessments, and enhance recovery preparedness measures. However, according to the NIAC Working Group study, there is still considerable reluctance on the part of the private sector to share what they consider sensitive or proprietary intelligence information. This is important due to the fact that in order for full National Infrastructure Protection Plan (NIPP) implementation, the private sector must provide sensitive business or security information that could cause serious damage to private firms, the economy, public safety, or security through unauthorized disclosure or access. (Collins & Baggett, 2009) Until there is a legal challenge to PCII, there is the concern by the private sector that courts will not uphold the protections provided for in this program. Although the Critical Infrastructure Information (CII) Act of 2002 shields private sector from the Freedom of Information Act (FOIA) disclosure of CII, it does not provide sufficient assurances from legal challenges and "lacks tracking and accountability mechanisms for guaranteeing protection from disclosure." (Chambers & Gallegos, July 2006)

6. *Threat-information clearinghouse:* The Working Group has recommended the creation of a clearinghouse for the collection of threat and risk-based information. The idea is that the private sector could access the database to assist them in conducting intelligence analysis on information and data that comes into their possession. It would also improve their analysis by providing an opportunity to confirm or reject specific elements of information used to complete their analysis.

7. *Lack of an established process for intelligence information push and pull:* This finding refers to the inability of the IC and CI sectors to push, or provide information, as well as pull, or receive information, between the two entities within a common operating protocol.

8. *Sensitive but unclassified (SBU):* Due to the increased security following 9/11, there has been a tendency to overclassify information that otherwise would never have even been considered sensitive or for that matter having a sensitivity calling for government classification. The overclassification of unrestricted and unclassified government documents has severely inhibited information sharing between the federal government and the private sector. (Chambers & Gallegos, July 2006) The federal government has a statutory responsibility

to safeguard CI/KR protection-related information. DHS and other federal agencies use a number of programs and procedures, such as the PCII program, to ensure that security-related information is properly safeguarded.

RECOMMENDATIONS FOR IMPROVING INTELLIGENCE INFORMATION SHARING

Based upon the findings from the NIAC working group study, there were eight recommendations made to both the federal government and the private sector outlining how to improve the seamless transfer of intelligence information between them. The first recommendation called for a pilot project to test the viability of creating a voluntary executive-level information-sharing system between CI CEOs and senior intelligence officers. The focus is on the CEOs because even though there are a number of ongoing examples of intelligence exchange between the federal government and the private sector, the inclusion of the CEOs is considered one area in need of improvement. Part of the identified problem was that many CEOs were getting inconsistent information. The CEOs also suggested a system that would allow for the interaction and exchange directly between CEOs and IC leaders.

The second recommendation addressed the issue of laws regarding privacy and insider threats. This recommendation calls for the publication of a legal issues guide on privacy laws and counterterrorism laws involving employees. The CEOs indicated they wanted clear guidance on the protection of employee privacy while also protecting their organizations from insider threats.

The third recommendation calls for the leveraging of existing information sharing such as clearinghouses for information to and from critical infrastructure owners and operators. The organization considered best situated to process and in turn disseminate an initial notification of a possible threat is the Partnership for Critical Infrastructure Security (PCIS). Part of the difficulty now with information dissemination to the private sector is that because there are a number of different groups collecting various types of intelligence related information, such as ISACs, HSIN, HITRAC, NICC, PCII, and CIPAC, the private sector is often inundated with information, much of it they do not need to know or find no value in. By using the PCIS as the single point of entry to push advisory information and incident response to the private sector, the intelligence analysis can be more precise and effective. Because the CI owners have self-organized into sector-specific agencies (SSAs) that have self-organized into the PCIS for cross-sector coordination, they are best situated to interpret the intelligence and understand what the possible threats, risks, and interdependencies across the 18 DHS recognized CI sectors. (Collins & Baggett, 2009) In addition, the PCIS has the capability to protect sensitive information.

The fourth recommendation addresses the national-level fusion center capability that has been built up over the last five years. According to the *Fusion Center Guidelines: Developing and Sharing Information and Intelligence in a New Era,* a fusion center is "a collaborative effort of two or more agencies that provide resources, expertise, and information to the center with the goal of maximizing their ability to detect, prevent, investigate, and respond to criminal and terrorist activity." (U.S. Department of Justice, 2006) Some apply this definition broadly to include any multijurisdictional, anticrime, or response effort that may utilize intelligence and/or information, to include federally owned and operated collaborative efforts like FBI-led joint terrorism task forces (JTTFs) or high intensity drug trafficking areas (HIDTAs). As of February 2009, there were 58 fusion centers throughout the United States. Within these centers, DHS plans to have 70 professionals deployed by the end of 2009. Twenty-seven of these centers utilize the Homeland Security Data Network (HSDN). Through this network, the federal government has the capability to move classified information and intelligence to the states. In sum, DHS has provided more than $254 million from FY 2004–2007 to state and local governments to support the centers (State and Local Fusion Centers, 2009).

Despite the relationship that is building between the federal and state governments within fusion centers, the relationship and role of the private sector is a function that most state fusion centers have yet to fully define and/or embrace. A number of fusion centers have undertaken informational and security-related discussions with some of the major critical infrastructure owners and operators and data providers within their respective jurisdictions. While acknowledging that a comprehensive understanding of the risks to the state/region is impossible to attain without a viable relationship and consistent information flow, the vast majority of centers have yet to put the processes in place. Very few of the state and regional fusion centers have an infrastructure sector representative detailed to their organization and rely, in part, on open-source information, data provided by the federal government, or contract data vendors for information about threats to a critical infrastructure facility. Common reasons for the lack of a relationship between the fusion center and private sector entities are the following:

- Prioritizing the infrastructure sectors to be represented in the center based on risk
- A lack of appreciation as to the role and information a sector representative might provide
- The lack of a federal government strategy or recommendations regarding how the fusion center should incorporate private sector data into the analytic fusion process (Masse, O'Neil, & Rollins, 2007)

This recommendation is proposing that efforts should be undertaken by states to either establish or modify their existing government entities to operate both a national and statewide intelligence and information fusion capability that is focused more on critical infrastructure protection (CIP). The focus on CIP would require greater coordination between the fusion centers and the private sector. The good news is that there seems to be a significant increase in the interactions between the private sector and state law enforcement agencies since 9/11. Specifically, private companies are communicating with agencies about the security of their facilities and workers and their interactions with representatives of corporate security. (Council of State Governments; Eastern Kentucky University, 2005)

The fifth recommendation by the NIAC Working Group called for key intelligence agencies through the IC to create sector analysts, or specialist positions, at both the executive and operational levels. More specifically at an operational level, sector analysts would be tasked with establishing relationships with CI operational decision makers. The goal would be to create subject matter experts, allowing them to analyze the data coming into the fusion center and disseminate it quickly and appropriately. (Chambers & Gallegos, July 2006)

An additional, or sixth, recommendation would be the need for ongoing training and career development for these specialists. This would need to be required by DHS and made available to analysts from each of the 50 states. According to the Lessons Learned Information Sharing (LLIS) initiative, DHS found the following:

Domestic intelligence sharing is currently a predominantly law enforcement function; whereas state, local tribal, and private sector entities would prefer a broader, more inclusive homeland security intelligence-sharing framework. Public safety disciplines such as public health, fire, emergency medical services, and private sector security provide different types of information and different perspectives that are essential for a successful information and intelligence sharing process. (Lessons Learned Information Sharing, December 2005)

The seventh recommendation calls for the formalization of any request for information (RFI) be designed to account for the diversity among sectors. The IC should tailor information gathering and dissemination to the needs of each sector and state, local, and tribal security partners. It was also suggested that the CIPAC would be the logical vehicle for coordinating the development of the "bi-directional RFI process" (Chambers & Gallegos, July 2006).

The final recommendation by the NIAC Working Group was influenced by a Government Accountability Office (GAO) report, which recommended that the "Director of National Intelligence (DNI) assess progress, address barriers, and propose changes, and that the Office of Management and Budget (OMB) work with agencies on policies, procedures, and controls to help achieve more accountability" (Government Accountability Office, March 2006).

CONCLUSION

The tragedies of 9/11 signified a mandate for change due to the inability of the U.S. IC to "connect the dots" from a lack of efficient information-sharing mechanisms (National Commission on Terrorist Attacks upon the United States, 2003). These gaps led to a significant debate and subsequent changes in an attempt at improving the nation's intelligence system. The most significant changes were the creation of several national organizations: the DHS, the DNI, and the National Counter Terrorism Center (NCTC). These changes also include the FBI's efforts to restructure and upgrade its intelligence support to include the adoption of new operational practices, and the improvement of its information technology (Cumming & Masse, August 2004; Burch, 2008). As a result, the 9/11 attacks prompted the largest reorganization of the intelligence community since the National Security Act of 1947 and the Dulles Report of 1949 (Warner & McDonald, April 2005). These significant changes, along with an emphasis on information sharing and the development of state and local fusion centers, provide immense resources towards domestic intelligence.

Despite these changes, several facts have remained unchanged. First, the protection of critical infrastructure, as well as the response to an initial attack, is largely the responsibility of state, local, and private entities. Traditional intelligence-gathering and dissemination techniques, originating at the federal level, will not be sufficient for modern day threats against the United States. As indicated in the HSAC's *Report on the Future of the Terrorism Task Force*, "the evolving complexity of our adversaries challenges existing paradigms—walls separating state, local, and federal responders are counterproductive, and the bifurcation of homeland security from national security is no longer relevant" (Homeland Security Advisory Council, January 2007). Finally, increased globalization, advanced technology development, and information sharing indicates that the number and magnitude of terrorist acts on the United States will likely increase. It is essential to ensure that the federal government works with state, local, and tribal governments and the private sector as true partners in all aspects of prevention, mitigation, and response.

REFERENCES

Burch, J. (2008). The domestic intelligence gap: progress since 9/11? *Journal of Homeland Security Affairs* (Suppl. 2), http://www.hsaj.org/?special:article=supplement.2.2.

Bush, G. (2001, October 16). *Critical Infrastructure Protection in the Information Age.* Executive Order 13231. Retrieved February 16, 2009, from http://www.ncs.gov/library/policy_docs/eo_13231.pdf.

Bush, G. W. (2005). *Guidelines and Requirements in Support of the Information Sharing Environment: Memorandum for the Heads of Executive Departments and Agencies.*

http://georgewbush-whitehouse.archives.gov/news/releases/2008/05/20080509-6.html.

Chambers, J. T., & Gallegos, G. G. (July 2006). *Public-Private Sector Intelligence Coordination: Final Report and Recommendations by the Council.* National Infrastructure Advisory Council.

Collins, P. A., & Baggett, R. K. (2009). *Homeland Security and Critical Infrastructure Protection.* Westport, Conn.: Praeger Security International.

Council of State Governments; Eastern Kentucky University. (2005). *The Impact of Terrorism on State Law Enforcement.* Lexington, Ky.: CSG.

Cumming, A., & Masse, T. (August 2004). *FBI Intelligence Reform Since September 11, 2001: Options for Congress.* Washington, D.C.: Congressional Research Service.

Government Accountability Office. (March 2006). *The Federal Government Needs to Establish Policies and Processes for Sharing Terrorism Related and SBU Information.* Washington, D.C.: GAO.

Homeland Security Advisory Council. (January 2007). *Report of the Future of Terrorism Task Force.* Washington, D.C.: U.S. Department of Homeland Security.

Homeland Security Advisory Council, Private Sector Information Sharing Task Force. (2005). *Homeland Security Information Sharing Between Government and the Private Sector.* Washington, D.C.: U.S. Department of Homeland Security.

Lessons Learned Information Sharing. (December 2005). *Intelligence and Information Sharing Initiative: Homeland Security Intelligence Requirements Process.* Department of Homeland Security, https://www.llis.dhs.gov/index.do.

Masse, T., O'Neil, S., & Rollins, J. (2007). *Fusion Centers: Issues and Options for Congress.* Washington, D.C.: Congressional Research Service.

National Commission on Terrorist Attacks upon the United States. (2003). *The 9/11 Commission Report.* New York: W.W. Norton.

Office of Homeland Security. (2002). *The National Strategy for Homeland Security.* Washington, D.C.: GAO.

State and Local Fusion Centers. (2009, February 4). Retrieved February 28, 2009, from http://www.dhs.gov/xinfoshare/programs/gc_1156877184684.shtm.

U.S. Department of Homeland Security. (2009, January 20). *Office of Intelligence and Analysis.* Retrieved February 27, 2009, from http://www.dhs.gov/xabout/structure/gc_1220886590914.shtm.

U.S. Department of Justice. (2006, August). *Fusion Center Guidelines: Developing and Sharing Information and Intelligence in a New Era.* Retrieved January 22, 2009, from http://it.ojp.gov/documents/fusion_center_guidelines_law_enforcement.pdf.

Warner, M., & McDonald, J. K. (April 2005). *U.S. Intelligence Community Reform Studies Since 1947.* Washington, D.C.: Central Intelligence Agency.

Foreign Intelligence and Counterterrorism: An Israeli Perspective

Nadav Morag

Intelligence has always played a central role in the provision of security, both internal and external, for the State of Israel. Israel has had to rely on intelligence in order to cope with quantitatively superior enemies that possessed considerably more troops, tanks, aircraft, and the like. The collection and analysis of intelligence information, when the process worked properly, provided Israel not only with a wealth of enemy targets to hit, but also with the time to mobilize its largely reservist-based military. Intelligence has also played a critical role in Israel's counterterrorism efforts though for different reasons. Terrorist organizations, of course, do not present a quantitatively superior foe, and coping with them very rarely requires the large-scale mobilization of military forces. As far as equipment is concerned, the terrorist groups that threatened Israel over the years certainly did not possess the huge numbers of tanks, aircraft, ships, and artillery pieces that were at the disposal of the combined military forces of Israel's Arab state adversaries. In fact, these terrorist groups, at best, possess only arsenals of (usually inaccurate) rockets, antitank missiles, and small arms. Nevertheless, efforts to mitigate the terrorist threat require the allocation of significant intelligence resources and this for two reasons. First, though small, terrorist organizations have the advantage of a virtually limitless supply of possible targets (only a few of which can actually be defended in an efficient manner). Consequently, foreknowledge of terrorist actions and movements is critical in protecting a highly vulnerable citizenry. Second, since terrorists do not fight on the field of battle, their recruitment, training, planning, and provisioning all occur within highly populated areas; this means that neutralizing them requires pinpoint knowledge that will enable the security forces to either arrest or eliminate them without harming innocent people. Intelligence is thus a critical component and, arguably, the most significant element in a counterterrorism *order of battle* that includes components as diverse as army patrols, special forces arrest teams, attack helicopters, police officers, private security guards, and an alert citizenry.

THE THREAT

During the course of the present decade, Israel has faced two categories of terrorist threats: conventional and mass casualty. During most of this time period, Israel also had to cope with an increasing rocket threat directed at its border towns and villages near the Gaza Strip. While Israel has never experienced a terrorist attack that came close to approaching the magnitude of the September 11, 2001, attacks in the United States, there have been attempts at carrying out mass-casualty attacks, referred to in Israel as *megaterror* attacks. In 2002, there were two such attempts. The first involved Palestinian terrorists driving a van filled with explosives into the underground parking lot of the Azrieli Towers in central Tel Aviv, which were, at the time, the tallest skyscrapers in Israel and stand atop a large and very popular shopping mall. The terrorists were caught during the security check conducted when they tried to access the underground lot.

The second attempt involved a failed attack against a critical infrastructure target on the northernmost environs of Tel Aviv (known as Pi Glilot). This facility contained gasoline, propane, and other highly flammable liquids and gases. It was well guarded as the Israeli authorities were well aware that should there be a massive explosion at the site, a sizeable portion of the city of Tel Aviv (a city of close to 400,000 inhabitants) would have been decimated. In May of 2002, terrorists conducted a sophisticated operation in which they planted explosives on the undercarriage of a fuel truck that was able to pass inspection and access the site—whereupon the explosives were set off using a cell phone as a triggering mechanism. Luckily, the ensuing fire was put out before it could threaten the site and result in a huge catastrophe.

In addition, terrorist organizations have attempted to conduct very primitive attacks using chemical and biological weapons. The Israeli authorities suspect that on a few occasions, suicide bombers infected with hepatitis were chosen as primitive biological weapons with the hope being that their blood and tissue, blown far afield by the explosion, would infect their victims. Similarly, in a number of primitive chemical weapon attacks, suicide belts were laced with rat poison and other chemical agents in the hope that the otherwise minor injuries might be fatally toxic to their victims. None of these primitive WMD attacks had any impact beyond the damage wrought by the conventional explosion of the vest itself.

From 2001 on, Palestinian terrorist cells in the Gaza Strip employed homemade Kassam rockets to attack Israeli towns near the Strip. Only a few people have been killed by these primitive rockets (though they have become more sophisticated and accurate over time), but they have succeeded in terrorizing border communities and causing serious social and economic problems in those localities.

Of course, the most common, and therefore in practice the deadliest type of threat, is that of frequent small-scale attacks, many involving suicide terrorist attacks. The Palestinians refer to their suicide bombers as *smart bombs* designed to create a level playing field with Israel, which is in possession of precision guided munitions (a.k.a. smart bombs)—only the Palestinian smart bombs are seen to be smarter because they can change the target of the mission, if need be, at the last minute.

With the onset of what the Palestinians referred to as the Al-Aksa Intifadah in September 2000, the number of suicide and other terrorist attacks and the corresponding death and injury rate in Israel exploded. The Palestinians emptied their jails of suspected and convicted terrorists and allowed members of their security forces to actively engage in terrorist operations, this, in addition to carrying-out a low-level insurgency against the Israeli military in the West Bank and Gaza Strip. Israel's initial reluctance to operate inside Palestinian autonomous areas (both for fear of international condemnation at the violation of Palestinian territory and also because Israel did not relish the thought of having to reoccupy Palestinian cities and resume responsibility for the Palestinian population's needs), meant that terrorists could freely use those areas to organize attacks.

Eventually, Israel's strategic approach to the conflict changed, and it decided to reoccupy most of the Palestinian cities on the West Bank; this was, at the time, the largest military operation conducted since the 1982 Lebanon War. This military operation, known as Operation Defensive Shield and carried out from late March to mid-April of 2002, signified the beginnings of a more effective Israeli counterterrorism strategy that produced rapid results in terms of lowering the Israeli death rate. This was not surprising in view of the fact that military operations were conducted almost exclusively in urban areas; the death rate among innocent Palestinian noncombatants rose precipitously. One of the benefits, from a counterterrorism perspective, of reoccupying most of the Palestinian cities on the West Bank was that this facilitated access to existing human intelligence (HUMINT) assets living in those cities as well as the recruitment of new local HUMINT assets, thus providing Israel with a more accurate intelligence picture and serving as an important component in its overall counterterrorism intelligence effort. In sum, it is the nature of this threat environment that determined, in large part, the nature of Israel's counterterrorism and counterterrorism intelligence response.

ISRAELI COUNTERTERRORISM AND COUNTERTERRORISM INTELLIGENCE POLICIES

Israel's counterterrorism and counterterrorism intelligence policies are composed of three overarching components: legal, institutional, and strategic. These form the context within which Israel was able to develop, albeit after much trial and error, an effective counterterrorism and counterterrorism intelligence effort.

The Legal Component

Israel is a liberal democracy functioning under the rule of law that affords legal rights and protections to its inhabitants. The dominance of the cabinet over the parliament (where it almost always enjoys a majority) also means that there are, at least theoretically, fewer restrictions on policy planning and implementation in countries with similar systems.

Israel differs from Britain and most other parliamentary democracies, however, in the fact that no single party ever achieves a majority in the Israeli parliament (called the *Knesset*), and consequently, cabinets are formed by coalitions of parties. This sometimes makes Israeli cabinets somewhat chaotic, and Israeli prime ministers often have to act more as consensus builders than leaders in order to keep together coalitions of parties with different agendas and ideologies. One of the repercussions of this need to maintain coalitions is that long-range planning is highly difficult, as Israeli cabinets do not always last for their entire four-year term. The prime minister must be careful not to be seen as supporting positions that might irrevocably alienate his or her coalition partners in the cabinet causing them to leave the government and vote against it in the Knesset.[1]

Israel also possesses a highly centralized political structure with no state or county governments and very limited autonomy for municipalities or local or regional councils. Law enforcement, for example, is centralized, with one national police force acting as the sole law enforcement body in the country, and mayors or heads of regional councils having no formal control over the police. Intelligence is also centralized and is passed down within centrally structured organizations to those at the law enforcement level, thus obviating the need for fusion centers, joint terrorism task forces, and the like.

The Israeli military (Israel Defense Force, or the IDF), as in other democracies, is subordinate to the civilian political leadership. Nevertheless, the military's opinion carries great weight among the decision makers (some of whom are themselves ex-generals). The IDF's Planning Branch prepares strategic policy recommendations for the prime minister and the cabinet (not limited exclusively to military matters), and the IDF's Intelligence Branch (IB) provides the cabinet with the national intelligence estimate (therefore officially acting as the country's lead intelligence agency).

In terms of legislation, Israel has three categories of powerful legislative tools with which to conduct its counterterrorism and counterterrorism intelligence efforts. The first piece of legislation, the Prevention of Terrorism Ordinance, dates from 1948 (the year of Israel's inception) and allows for the prosecution of anyone suspected of membership in a terrorist organization, publishing propaganda for the organization, managing the organization, and fund-raising or transferring funds for the organization. The ordinance can only be in effect so long as Israel remains in a legal state of emergency.

The second piece of legislation, the Penal Law (updated 1996), allows for prosecution of terrorism suspects under ordinary criminal procedures. Some auxiliary pieces of criminal legislation, such as the Prohibition of Money Laundering Law (from 2000), the Combating Criminal Organizations Law (from 2003), or the 2001 amendment to the Extradition Law, may also be useful for the conduct of standard criminal prosecutions against terrorism suspects, or for facilitating extradition of suspected terrorists to other countries. The Penal Law, in addition to allowing prosecution for ordinary crimes, allows for prosecution of suspects trying to subvert the political order in Israel, through attempts to overthrow the lawful government by force or employment of sabotage against state property. The Penal Law remains in force regardless of whether Israel is in a state of emergency or not.

Finally, emergency legislation gives the security forces broad powers to disrupt the activities of terrorist organizations. Israel, in fact, has been in a legal state of emergency since its inception in May 1948—a status that is renewed annually.

Under the Defense Regulations and other emergency legislation, Israeli security bodies are given significant powers to deal with terrorism. Emergency legislation allows the IDF to detain Palestinian suspects for 12 days before being brought before a military magistrate and 4 days before allowing the suspect access to legal representation. Military law applies in the West Bank and with respect to Israeli operations in Gaza, but not in Israel itself. The IDF had initially issued an order in April 2002 authorizing its forces to detain suspects for 18 days prior to judicial review and access to legal representation, but public pressure and concern that the supreme court might intervene and force the military's hand led the IDF to modify its order. Within Israel, suspects can be detained under emergency legislation for no longer than 48 hours before being brought before a magistrate.[2] From an intelligence-gathering perspective, such detentions are useful in that they allow interrogators to isolate suspects. Frequently, the very act of isolation and initial interrogation leads suspects to understand that "the game is up" and to divulge information.[3]

Emergency legislation also allows suspects to be held for fixed periods of time without going through a normal conviction process. This is known as administrative detention and is primarily used to prevent potential attacks. Within Israel, only the minister of defense has the authority to issue administrative detention orders for up to six months, with the ability to renew these orders. In the West Bank, or in IDF operations within the Gaza Strip, the local military commander has the power to issue an administrative detention order for up to six months, which also can be renewed. All administrative detention orders are subject to review by the supreme court, should the detainees' lawyers choose to appeal these orders. The defense lawyers, incidentally, do not have the right to access to evidence gathered by the authorities against their clients, if disclosure of that evidence may compromise sensitive intelligence sources and methods. Administrative detention serves as a quick and efficient alternative to criminal proceedings because it does not require the investment in time necessary to gather sufficient evidence to charge an individual and because it allows the authorities to protect intelligence sources and methods while at the same time removing threats. In most cases, people held under administrative detention are eventually either released or tried (either by a civilian court in the case of Israeli citizens and some Palestinians, or by a military tribunal, in the case of most of the Palestinians).

Emergency legislation also allows for closures (ringing an area with checkpoints and limiting access to or from that location), curfews, confiscation of mail, closing of newspapers or publishing houses, the banning of public gatherings, and so forth. It should be noted that these powers are rarely used within Israel proper but are much more commonplace in the West Bank (and in Gaza when it was under Israeli occupation between 1967 and 2005).

Historically, the interrogation of terrorism suspects has often involved some degree of physical force. The Israeli approach traditionally made protecting the Israeli population from terrorist attack through the acquisition of intelligence from detainees a significantly higher value than safeguarding the rights of those detainees. In 1987, following widespread complaints of torture, a judicial commission created a set of recommendations (not made public) governing the interrogation process. It was found, however, that in a number of subsequent governmental studies (these too were not made public), that Israel's domestic intelligence service, the Israel Security Agency (ISA, also known as the Shin Bet or Shabak), was continuing to violate some of those guidelines. In 1999, the supreme court ruled that the ISA could not use physical torture, and the agency claims that it now employs exclusively psychological methods. This assertion, however, is disputed by human rights groups who claim that detainees are still subject to being put into uncomfortable positions for long periods of time, being held in filthy cells, being violently shaken, being exposed to blasts of cold air, being slapped, and being verbally abused and threatened.[4] In general then, Israeli law is very robust (some might argue *too* robust) in terms of the powers granted to the authorities to detain suspected terrorists, to use evidence obtained through general intelligence-gathering methods, and to protect sources and methods. In terms of the entities tasked with executing laws, gathering intelligence, and mitigating terrorist acts, those institutions too have proved quite robust.

The Institutional Component

Unlike the United States, Israel has only a small number of agencies that are actively engaged in various aspects of counterterrorism intelligence gathering, combat, and law enforcement. This does not necessarily mean, however, that Israel is entirely devoid of the type of institutional jealousies and hesitance to share information across agencies that frequently plagues U.S. counterterrorism efforts. Nevertheless, there is a fairly clear hierarchy and delineation of responsibilities between the primary agencies. Since there are only a few agencies engaged in counterterrorism and counter-terrorism intelligence collection and analysis, they are usually more than happy to leave activities outside their core mission to other agencies, thus facilitating interagency cooperation. For example, the only agency in Israel that has the authority to enforce laws within Israel proper (that is, not including the West Bank or Gaza Strip) is the Israel Police. While some intelligence officers in the ISA are granted police powers, the ISA, as a whole, is not a law enforcement agency.[5] The police are recognized as the lead agency in all matters relating to coping with run-of-the-mill crime. As none of the other agencies are interested in engaging in traditional law enforcement, they are more than happy to share any information that they come across in the criminal sphere with the police intelligence division, which in turn, focuses exclusively on criminal intelligence and turns over any information that it uncovers in the terrorism sphere to the ISA. Among the intelligence agencies, there is more room for overlap and for bureaucratic infighting; nevertheless, here too each agency has a clearly separate core mission, and the problems usually arrive at the fuzzy edges of each agency's mission, but not at the heart of their respective enterprises.

The IDF is a unitary military force (as opposed to the system of separate military branches practiced in the United States) and is subject to the orders of the IDF chief of staff, who in turn is subject to the authority of the cabinet. In Israel, the cabinet is the commander in chief rather than the prime minister (or the Israeli president, who serves in what is an almost exclusively ceremonial post). The IDF possesses the country's largest intelligence organization, the IB (also known by its Hebrew acronym—AMAN), as well as its most important strategic policy planning organization, the Planning Branch. The IDF also serves as the primary operational organization tasked with combating terrorism in the West Bank (where the police role is generally limited to policing Israeli citizens living in the Settlements and engaging in a few additional limited activities) and in the Gaza Strip. The IDF is the single largest and most powerful governmental agency in Israel with resources and personnel numbers that dwarf all of the other agencies mentioned here.

As noted earlier, the IB is also the country's lead intelligence agency and responsible for providing the national intelligence assessment, which acts as the basis for national security policy decisions, to the cabinet. It is the Israeli equivalent of the U.S. National Security Agency, which serves as Israel's primary signal intelligence (SIGINT) agency, and it is also housed within the IDF (known as Unit 8200). The IB includes departments that focus on the various Arab states, Iran, and terrorist organizations and monitors goings-on worldwide. It also includes a unit that conducts internal reviews for purposes of quality control. This entity reviews intelligence reports and assessments in order to vet them for the effectiveness of their use of raw intelligence, the logic of their analysis and conclusions, and whether they took into account differing interpretations of intelligence data.[6]

However, in terms of operating HUMINT resources within the West Bank and Gaza Strip, particularly in the area of recruiting Palestinian informants, the ISA, serves as the principle agency. The primary HUMINT-gathering agency had originally been the IB's Unit 504. But after its poor showing in the occupation of southern Lebanon in the wake of Israel's 1982 war in that country, the ISA quickly became central in counterterrorism HUMINT-gathering activities.[7] The ISA works closely with the IDF in the West Bank and Gaza, and the Israel Police in Israel proper, but its focus is intelligence gathering and analysis as opposed to law enforcement (though, as noted earlier, some of its personnel possess arrest powers). In the West Bank, for example, ISA personnel, who run assets in a given area and consequently know that area and its population intimately, will typically travel with IDF units (who themselves cycle in and out of particular geographic commands and hence do not necessarily have expert knowledge of specific locales) that are tasked with making arrests in order to help pinpoint the suspects to be arrested or the bomb-making facility to be destroyed. Moreover, within the ISA, the desk officer (who plays the role of analyst and researcher) also provides operational guidance and support to the ISA case officers and their military colleagues in the field.[8] The ISA has also been active in recruiting Palestinian inmates in Israeli prisons and detention facilities.[9]

In addition to being an intelligence organization, the ISA also plays an important security role. In addition to its other security duties, the ISA is also tasked with providing security guidance (regulations, training, practice drills) to police, ports and airports security officers, ministry security officers (education, industry, transportation, foreign ministry, energy, etc.), and private security firms working in the public sphere, such as Israeli airline security personnel. In other words, the ISA drafts regulations in matters of security and counterterrorism that a broad range of security agencies, including the police, must adhere to. A common agency to enforce procedures at the federal, state, and local levels as well as across much of the private sector is not something that exists in the United States, but it has proved its utility in the Israeli case as everyone follows the same or similar standard operating procedures and all are on the same page with respect to security procedures.

The Institute for Intelligence and Special Duties (more commonly known by the Hebrew word for "Institute"—*Mossad*), is Israel's premier foreign intelligence-gathering and analysis organization. Though the IB also engages in foreign intelligence gathering and analysis, it is usually with a focus on military issues. Among other issues, it also has an active interest in gathering intelligence on terrorist threats emanating from outside Israel's immediate geographic environment.

The Israel Police, as noted earlier, is the country's sole law enforcement agency. It is a national organization that, aside from times of acute military conflict when it is put under the overall command of the IDF, operates under the auspices of the cabinet, through the minister for public security, who in turn overseas the senior uniformed police commander, the police commissioner. The Israel Police is also the main terrorism prevention and terrorist interdiction agency within Israel proper and provides law enforcement services to Israeli settlements in the West Bank. The minister of defense, however, may declare a limited state of emergency, in which case authority for dealing with a particular incident within Israel proper is shifted to the military. This allows the military to enforce orders for people to stay in bomb shelters and shut down schools and places of employment as necessary. Moreover, the police have very limited capabilities in dealing with WMD events, and in such cases, the military's Home Front Command (HFC) would be authorized to manage the event under the framework of the overall military command.

Field personnel in the Israel Police are assigned to stations, which in turn form part of the subdistricts that make up the country's six police districts. While an individual patrol officer is assigned to a specific station, they are under a unified command structure and hence can be moved from location to location as needed. This allows the police commissioner to concentrate forces in certain locations when intelligence indicates probable threats to public safety (as in the case of terrorist threats, riots, large public events, and the like). The senior police command is privy to all of the terrorism-related intelligence information and analysis being generated by the intelligence agencies (primarily the ISA and the IB). That information is then made available to intelligence liaison officers, who are specially designated police officials based in each police district, subdistrict, and station, whose role is to then determine the ways and means of sanitizing and disseminating that information throughout their area of responsibility and down to the level of the patrolman/patrolwoman. In principle at least, every effort is made to provide as much terrorism-related intelligence to the average patrolman/patrolwoman as possible because the senior police commanders recognize that they are not going to prevent terrorists attacks themselves while sitting in their air-conditioned offices and that disruption and mitigation will occur at the level of the officer on the street.

The Israel Police has a mobile response component for special tasks and as a reserve when additional personnel are needed. The police force also includes a highly trained antiterrorism SWAT team, known by its acronym Yamam, which also carries out operations for the military in the West Bank. The Israel Police also includes a paramilitary component that acts as a national gendarmerie force, known as the border police or border guard. The personnel in this force have full police powers but specialize in patrols along Israel's borders (along with the military) and counterterrorism operations within Israel; they also act as a reserve force for additional police activities. In addition, the border police operate in the West Bank, where they are under army command and act as a supplement to military forces conducting counterterrorism operations in Palestinian areas.

Given the fairly streamlined institutional structure described above, it is not surprising that issues relating to information and intelligence sharing in Israel are far less complex than those being dealt with in the United States, given the bewildering array of American intelligence, military, law enforcement, and other governmental agencies. This does not mean, however, that Israel is immune to bureaucratic infighting and mutual reticence with regard to information sharing, only that there are fewer opportunities for this, and consequently, on the whole, information and intelligence sharing is both significant and effective. At the senior policy-making level, as Israeli cabinets are typically large (usually with over 20 ministers), most of the work conducted by the cabinet is carried out by smaller cabinet committees (called ministerial committees), which are authorized to make policy decisions for the full cabinet.

In matters of national security, Israel does not distinguish, as is done in the post-9/11 United States, between *national security* and *homeland security*. The Ministerial Committee for National Security Affairs (popularly known as the Security Cabinet) is authorized to make day-to-day decisions and consequently receives daily intelligence briefings and reports. As this ministerial committee is also fairly large, a smaller ad hoc body that has access to the most sensitive information carries out the day-to-day decisions. It has been variously known, throughout Israeli history, as the Kitchen Cabinet (thus named because the grandmotherly Israeli Prime Minister Golda Meir, who was prime minister between 1969 and 1974, used to hold meetings for this group in her kitchen, where she served the ministers coffee and cookies), the Inner Cabinet, and other such sobriquets.

The prime minister is primus inter pares (first among equals) and while formally wields one vote in the cabinet, in practice controls the cabinet and has the power to dismiss ministers. The prime minister is advised, if he so chooses, by the National Security Council and has direct authority over the ISA and the Mossad. Both of these civilian intelligence agencies report directly to the prime minister, who, via their respective heads, sets planning and collection priorities for those agencies, receives intelligence from them, and approves (along with colleagues in the Security Cabinet or a small ad hoc committee) special operations.

The minister of defense is in charge of overseeing the IDF, via the chief or staff of the IDF (though major military operations must be approved by the Security Cabinet and then by the full cabinet). The IB therefore operates under the authority of the chief of staff and his superior, the minister of defense. However, the IB, unlike any other component of the IDF, also reports directly to the cabinet (in the context of its aforementioned role in providing the national intelligence assessment). Consequently, the major general in charge of military intelligence, unlike any of his/her colleagues in the IDF general staff, operates both within the military command structure as well as outside it. This is true even of the brigadier general that heads the IB's research division as that individual is frequently called upon to act as an advisor to the cabinet. Since the IB is the largest intelligence agency in the country as well as the senior agency, it is also responsible for coordinating with the other two major intelligence agencies (within the framework of what is referred to as the Heads of Services Committee). Information sharing between the agencies is thus mandated, and a nominal pecking order exists in which the IB is given precedence. This does not mean, of course, that the agencies always agree, particularly with respect to their analysis and assessments of events, or that their sister agencies are kept abreast of ongoing operations in other agencies, only that the final intelligence product is vetted and submitted jointly, with the IB being responsible for bringing that assessment to the decision makers.

The police intelligence branch does not normally play a role in the national security-related intelligence coordination effort except when invited to do so in cases where criminal activities have a terrorism nexus. The Israel Police Intelligence Branch focuses almost exclusively on criminal intelligence in traditional realms such as drugs, organized crime, and the like. The streamlined and largely cooperative relationship between intelligence agencies and between those agencies and those tasked with the prevention and mitigation of terrorism has thus enabled Israel to develop, albeit in fits and starts with plenty of mistakes along the way, what is presently a highly effective counterterrorism strategy.

The Strategic Component

Israel's counterterrorism strategy focuses on five areas: deterrence, intelligence, prevention, arrests/executive action, and public cooperation efforts. Generally speaking, terrorists cannot be deterred from carrying out acts of terrorism by the knowledge that they may die or be incarcerated for long periods of time—particularly in the case of suicide terrorism. Israeli deterrence policy has traditionally focused in two different areas: the terrorist's family members and morale within the terrorist organization.

Israel had a long-standing policy, which has been challenged through judicial means both in Israel and internationally, of destroying the homes of arrested terrorists or those who died in the course of their attacks. This practice has recently formally been abrogated as a result of a policy reassessment. The logic behind this practice rested on the idea that while a terrorist might have been willing (or was planning to) sacrifice himself or herself, they would not want their family members to suffer undue harm, and the destruction of the family's home represents a significant financial loss that would cause the family to suffer. Over the years, however, Palestinian organizations and Arab governments routinely donated money to such families to cover the costs of rebuilding, and consequently, the adverse financial impact was minimized. Moreover, there was never any clear proof that this policy actually deterred terrorists from carrying out attacks (though there was some anecdotal evidence to this effect).[10] Indeed, during the height of the second intifadah, donations by Arab governments to families of terrorists created a small class of nouveau riche Palestinians, whose sons or daughters had blown themselves up in Israeli cities.

A marginally more effective Israeli policy has been the public exposure, from time to time, of the modus operandi of terrorist organizations. This policy is designed to show the terrorists that their organization has been infiltrated and that the Israeli authorities thus have access to the most sensitive information within the organization. This often leads to the development of a sense of mistrust within the organization and lowers morale. Israel's policy of large-scale arrests as well as of targeted assassinations (more of which will be discussed later in the module) is also designed, in part, to lower morale by proving to the members of the terrorist organization that the organization is incapable of protecting them and is thus weak in comparison with Israel's counterterrorism capabilities.

On the intelligence side, Israeli intelligence efforts focus on identifying potential threats at the organizational and individual levels, uncovering sources and methods for financing and provision of other infrastructure-related activities, and uncovering sources of arms and cooperation with like-minded intelligence services. As noted earlier, cooperation between intelligence agencies is generally good. Following the outbreak of the second intifadah, the ISA and IDF developed an effective system for real-time horizontal information sharing, which enabled tactical units in the field to exchange intelligence information instead of waiting for intelligence to be pushed up the chain of command and then crossover to the sister agency. This tactical-level information sharing has resulted in significant gains in terms of arrests of suspected terrorists and disruption of terrorist activities. Generally speaking, the IDF-ISA relationship revolves around the IDF providing personnel to go in and make arrests or destroy bomb-making facilities, tunnels, and the like, as well as providing much of the SIGINT intelligence gathering. The ISA focuses more on recruiting and running Palestinian agents and thus focuses on the HUMINT piece of the puzzle.

Interestingly though, despite the fact that the IDF developed an effective system of information sharing between the IB and the ISA, the IB did not always effectively provide information to IDF forces on the ground. This was less of a problem in the Palestinian arena, but the Second Lebanon War in the summer of 2006 represented, among other failures, the inability of the IDF to provide intelligence that was readily available at headquarters on Hizballah and its facilities to the units in the field.[11] During that ill-fated war, the IB did not possess a unit capable of pulling together all the available intelligence on Hizballah and translating that information into operational and tactical intelligence capable of guiding the troops in the field. Much of that intelligence was available to the Research and Analysis department of the IB as well as the IDF's Northern Command, but it had not been provided to divisions, brigades, and regiments fighting in Lebanon that were not part of the Northern Command.[12]

Despite the seriousness of some of these intelligence coordination problems, if Israeli intelligence has an Achilles' heel, it is with respect to strategic, rather than tactical, intelligence. Israel has, of course, faced tactical intelligence failures. In addition to the above example, during the 2006 war in Lebanon, the precise nature and location of bunkers and tunnels built by Hizballah on the Israeli-Lebanese border, the extent of the organization's antitank missile arsenal, and Hizballah's possession of C-802 shore-to-ship missiles were unknown to the IDF Intelligence Branch or other intelligence agencies.[13] At the same time, Israel has also enjoyed significant tactical intelligence successes, such as the pinpointing of virtually all of Hizballah's medium-range fixed missile launchers, which were destroyed early in the 2006 war. On the other hand, Israel has rarely been able to predict macro-events, such as the outbreak of both Palestinian intifadahs, or to understand the course such events are likely to take; consequently, it has not been able to plan policies, allocate resources, and build force structures proactively.[14] Improvements in Israeli counterterrorism efforts have appeared in the wake of learning curves rather than in anticipation of expected events. Over the years, Israeli intelligence agencies have also increasingly attempted to influence policy through assessments of strategic-level intelligence and the suggesting of initiatives.[15] This has sometimes led to poor policy decisions. For example, intelligence conveyed by the IB has frequently led to policy initiatives that emphasized threats over opportunities, thus resulting in conservative policies that may have led to missed opportunities. The emphasis on threats rather than opportunities is inherent in the IB by virtue of the fact that it is part of the military, and identifying and preparing for threats are core military missions.[16]

After intelligence-gathering efforts have borne fruit, the Israeli security establishment typically commences with preventive efforts. Israel's counterterrorism strategy is based on the assumption that if terrorists cannot be apprehended, killed, or otherwise have their work disrupted before they set off on their mission to attack Israel's population centers, then the terrorist will be successful and Israel's counterterrorism policy will be deemed a failure. Hence, preventative activities play a central role.

Preventive actions and policies are, of course, affected by the reality of the short geographic distances between the terrorists' base of operations in the villages and cities of the West Bank or Gaza Strip and Israeli urban centers (which, in the case of the West Bank, are often 10 to 30 minutes' drive away). If a terrorist and his/her handlers have already left their town or village on an operation, it will be difficult to apprehend them before they reach an Israeli urban center. And once they've entered an Israeli city, the Israeli security establishment considers them to have successfully completed their mission, particularly if it was a suicide mission. In other words, if a Palestinian terrorist with a suicide vest enters an Israeli city, the terrorist has won and Israel has lost because even if that terrorist does not get to his/her primary target, they will blow themselves up in a manner designed to kill innocent people. While there have been cases where private security guards (sometimes at the cost of their own lives) have prevented terrorists from entering shopping malls, cafés, and the like, these events have almost always resulted in casualties, and any innocent victim being harmed is viewed in Israel as a failure of the system. Even if such an occurrence ended without any innocent people being harmed (due to the rapid and effective reactions of security guards or police or a technical glitch in the suicide vest), this is considered a case of luck and is still viewed as a failure of the system.

Consequently, Israeli efforts focus heavily on neutralizing threats within and around Palestinian population centers in the West Bank. This has necessitated an Israeli military presence, usually ad hoc (i.e., per operation) inside Palestinian villages and cities as well as the more or less permanent deployment of troops outside Palestinian population areas and the creation of a system of checkpoints that ring Palestinian towns and lie along major Palestinian highways. The IDF presence in and around Palestinian villages and towns and the system of checkpoints has proved extremely burdensome for Palestinians and represents one of the more onerous and obvious signs of Israel's military domination over the Palestinians—thus contributing to Palestinian anger. Nevertheless, this military presence has proved effective in countering terrorist activities. As noted earlier, much of Israel's success in bringing down the frequency and destructiveness of attacks during the second Palestinian intifadah of 2000 to 2005 occurred after Israel had cut off and invaded most of the Palestinian cities in the West Bank during Operation Defensive Shield (March–April 2002). The ability of IDF forces based near Palestinian towns and villages to react rapidly and effectively when real-time intelligence information points to the whereabouts of suspected terrorists or other terrorist activity is infinitely greater than the IDF's capacity to send in units to accomplish the same mission from over the Green Line in Israel itself.[17] Moreover, one of the essential conditions for effective ISA HUMINT recruitment is access to the particular locality for which the case officer is responsible.

More recently, Israel has begun constructing a controversial barrier of fencing, with sections in or abutting urban areas made up of concrete slabs, within the West Bank designed to make it difficult, if not impossible, for terrorists to infiltrate into Israel. Despite the political, legal, and diplomatic argument over its actual location, the barrier has proved extremely effective in limiting access to Israel from the West Bank and thus in significantly reducing terrorist attacks.

The system of checkpoints, while unquestionably the most aggravating and unbearable aspect of Israel's military presence in terms of the day-to-day lives of Palestinians, has proved to be an effective tool in countering terrorism. A number of Palestinian detainees have reported aborting attacks due to what was perceived as increased security at checkpoints (when in reality, activity levels were normal), and checkpoints have been shown to force terrorists to change their behavior, thus potentially exposing them. In addition, checkpoints also allow the use of intelligence on suspected terrorists to be employed without compromising sources. Terrorist suspects detained at checkpoints may think that the soldiers were simply being thorough when, in reality, the security service or military intelligence was tipped off by a source. When terrorists are apprehended in the field, on the other hand, this suggests that someone in contact with the suspect tipped off the authorities and can thus lead to that source being burned.[18] In general, active military operations in Palestinian villages and cities as well as the widespread use of checkpoints disrupt the movement of terrorist materiel, funds, and personnel from area to area and drive terrorist organizations deeper underground, thus inhibiting their ability to function.

Within Israel, the police are the primary agency tasked with interdiction of terrorists. Once intelligence information points to terrorist infiltration of Israel proper, the police are given descriptions of the suspected terrorists provided by the ISA and filtered through the police intelligence-liaison officers. Police commanders instruct their personnel to set up ad hoc roadblocks along major arteries leading into a city or area where the terrorist is thought to be heading as well as to increase patrols within that area. Unlike the United States, Israel does not have a color-coded system of alerts, and the entire country never goes on alert due to terrorist threats. Instead, a specific city or police district will be put on alert since intelligence is usually accurate enough to provide a general sense of the terrorist's likely target. This policy of limiting the focus of response efforts is designed both to limit the sense of fear within the country as well as to avoid the kind of lackadaisical and laissez-faire attitude that invariably develops when entire regions are put on alert, even when the likelihood of a threat in other parts of that region is extremely low. In other words, Israeli citizens know that when the authorities have reasonably accurate information as to the immediate geographic area likely to be affected, they will provide the populous with this information, and, at the same time, they will not trouble others with warnings that will almost certainly prove to be empty and unnecessary.

The single most significant Israeli counterterrorism policy involves large-scale preventative detentions (often leading to subsequent prosecution) and executive actions (known in Israel as *targeted killings*). The targeted-killings policy has a number of advantages and disadvantages. At the outset, it should be made clear that Israel assassinates terrorists only fairly rarely, in comparison to the numbers of people that it arrests. Between 2000 and 2005, Israel targeted fewer than 200 terrorist suspects for assassination, while arresting or detaining, at one point or another, some 9,000 suspects thought to be involved in some manner in terrorist activities. Only those individuals that cannot be easily arrested will be put on the list or, in very unique cases (such as that of Hamas leader Ahmad Yassin), those that Israel cannot afford to arrest because their arrest would likely lead to heightened terrorism in order to try and obtain their release. They also need to fulfill the criteria of being *arch-terrorists,* in other words, senior leaders, planners, bomb makers, and the like whose removal would significantly undermine the terrorist organization's ability to function—at least temporarily.

All decisions to assassinate require the approval of the prime minister, acting for the cabinet as a whole, and a case must be made—including provision of a dossier with information implicating the individual to be assassinated with terrorist acts and with the potential for contributing to future acts of terrorism. In almost all cases, Israel will prefer to arrest terrorists rather than assassinating them, and this is for two primary reasons. First, as the saying goes "dead me don't talk." Capturing suspected terrorists usually yields a gold mine of information, whereas assassinated terrorists are clearly useless as intelligence sources. Second, targeted killings often result in international criticism, pressure on Israel, and greater anger and motivation for carrying out terrorist attacks on the Palestinian side.

Nevertheless, the policy of assassination, when coupled with an aggressive policy of detaining suspected terrorists, has proved highly useful in disrupting terrorist communications, freedom of movement, planning activities, and the like, as well as sowing distrust and fear within terrorist organizations. From time to time, key individuals, such as the notorious Hamas bomb maker Yihyeh Ayash, have been assassinated, thus resulting in at least a temporary incapacitation of a critical part of the terrorist organization's apparatus. Moreover, the policy of assassinating terrorists acts to reassure the Israeli public that terrorist leaders and other key individuals are not immune to Israeli retribution. Even though assassinations are not authorized for purposes of retribution, the policy is often viewed as based on retribution by the Israeli public, as well as Palestinians and international public opinion. The average Israeli citizen knows that the authorities cannot protect him/her from each and every terrorist threat, and the authorities, in fact, frequently remind the public that they cannot provide 100 percent security. At the same time, carrying out an active and aggressive policy of arresting and killing terrorists helps to create a public sense that something is being done, and this thus helps to reassure the public. As terrorism is more of a psychological phenomenon (in terms of creating fear across society) than a physical one (due to the comparatively small number of victims), reassuring the public and making it possible for them to go about their daily lives thus represents an important victory over terrorism. Perhaps the worst feeling an Israeli citizen can face is one in which he or she senses that Israelis can be killed with impunity while the authorities are powerless to strike back.

In general, whether Israel is arresting or killing suspected terrorists, the essence of the Israeli approach revolves around three key assumptions:

1. The number of dangerous terrorists is limited, and therefore it is possible to arrest most of them and assassinate those that are not as accessible. This also means that no matter how much rage is produced in Palestinian society as a result of aggressive Israeli counterterrorism policies (including targeted killings), the bottom line is that this will not translate into more terrorism because very few people possess the resourcefulness and capacity to develop expertise in some area of terrorist operations to become effective terrorists. In other words, more angry people does not equal more truly dangerous terrorists. Being a truly effective terrorist operative is a full-time professional enterprise that requires years of training and development and cannot be the preserve of enraged amateurs desperate to strike out at Israel. Those amateurs can and do fill the ranks of the suicide bombers; but the suicide bomber without an organization behind him or her to supply the wherewithal can only be a *potential* suicide bomber.

2. Not every terrorist has to be neutralized in order for the counterterrorism strategy to be deemed a success. Since terrorists almost always operate as part of a complex organization that involve logistic, internal security, recruitment, leadership, smuggling, bomb making, and other functions, neutralizing key individuals in one or more of these component areas of the organization can severely hobble the organization, at least temporarily.

3. Over time, an unrelenting policy of arrests can severely decrease the effectiveness of the organization; with most of the leadership in jail, lower-level operatives are left demoralized and directionless.[19]

Most terrorist organizations can be viewed as made up of several levels, with the strategic level providing the overall policy guidelines and priorities (as well as inciting the public to violence and glorification of terrorist values), the operational level providing most of the expertise for funding, organizing, and implementing terrorist activities, and the actual perpetrator who carries out the attack. Israeli counterterrorism policy has heavily emphasized the use of intelligence in order to ascertain who is involved at the operational level as well as to target those individuals for arrest or, in some cases, assassination. The goal in focusing at this level of the organization has been to destroy the capacity of the organization to actually produce terrorist attacks (though, of course, actual perpetrators planning or in the process of carrying out attacks, will also be targeted).

It should be borne in mind that Israel's policy in this sphere is not predicated on the assumption that effectively combating terrorism requires a one-time operation. Even if the operational level of a terrorist organization is emasculated as a result of a series of successful Israeli arrests or targeted killings, other members of the terrorist organization will step in to take their places and fill these functions. The point is that these new planners, bomb makers, couriers, recruiters, and so forth, will require a learning curve, and consequently, their initial operations will be less effective, which translates into fewer Israelis being killed or maimed in terrorist attacks. This has proved to be true, for example, as Israeli investigators found faulty wiring and poorly made explosives in suicide vests and car bombs used in terrorist operations in the wake of successful arrests or assassinations of key bomb makers. Of course, those individuals will eventually develop the necessary expertise to be effective terrorist operatives, but by that time, presumably, Israel will have been able to arrest or assassinate them as well, thus forcing the organization to produce yet another crop of new personnel to step in and fill the breech. Through a methodical and painstaking shaving off of these layers each time they surfaced, Israeli counterterrorism officials became convinced that terrorist organizations would become increasingly less effective and that these organizations did not have the capacity to forever produce new crops of personnel for the operational level.

On the negative side of the ledger, targeted killing often results in collateral damage, despite the use of unmanned aerial vehicles (UAVs) and other technical means to try to confirm a terrorist's identity and to assess whether civilians have entered the target's immediate area. For example, on July 23, 2002, Israel targeted Hamas leader Salah Shehada, an individual who was a key figure within the organization, and Israel believed that by taking him out, Hamas's ability to function would be disrupted for some time. His assassination had been approved by then prime minister Ariel Sharon, and the IDF was simply waiting for the opportunity to strike him when the likelihood of producing collateral damage would be smallest. Eventually, intelligence information came in suggesting that Shehada was in a Gaza City apartment building that was not occupied, at the time, by any innocent civilians. An Israeli air force F-16 was deployed, and it dropped a one-ton bomb on the building in order to ensure that Shehada would be killed. Unfortunately, Israeli intelligence proved faulty and 14 civilians were killed in the attack, including 9 children.[20]

Following this event, Israel shifted to the use of ordinance with lower yields. On September 6, 2003, Israel received intelligence indicating that the whole of the senior leadership echelon of Hamas, including the organization's leader, Ahmad Yassin, was meeting in a specific location. This represented a real intelligence coup and could have resulted, in one fell swoop, in a total decapitation of the organization. The air force carried out an attack dropping a 250 kg bomb (the aircraft could have used a 1,000 kg bomb) in order to minimize the risk of collateral damage and not repeat the debacle in Gaza City. The explosion, however, turned out to be too small, and the whole of the Hamas leadership succeeded in escaping with a few suffering only very minor injuries.[21]

The collateral damage issue thus represents a significant moral conundrum for Israel, something that will be familiar to all students of asymmetric conflict. On the one hand, Israel is a democratic country with professional armed forces and an intelligence apparatus that aspire to do a proficient job combating terrorists without hurting innocents in the process. At the same time, the Israeli military knows that its primary mission is to protect Israeli citizens, and failing to take out key terrorists (who invariably hide among innocent civilians) means that more Israelis will die or be injured in terrorist attacks. It comes down to the cruel determination as to whose lives are more valuable, those of one's own civilians or those of the other side.

In terms of the Israeli public, the authorities view it as an intelligence asset in counterterrorism efforts. The more eyes and ears available to spot suspicious behavior or suspicious objects, the greater likelihood that terrorist attacks can be stopped or their impact minimized. Accordingly, all Israelis are taught from a very young age (in school as well as through educational television programs, public service messages, and press accounts) to be aware of their surroundings including the presence of suspicious objects and the behavioral markers of terrorists.[22] As suicide terrorism became an increasing problem after 1994, people were also taught to look for markers suggesting potential suicide bombers (winter dress, including overcoats, during summertime and individuals standing out in some other way such as profusely sweating, eyes darting about nervously, erratic behavior, etc.).

As the public cannot be expected to have full situational awareness 24/7 over extended periods of time, Israel has developed a system whereby when intelligence suggests that a terrorist is headed for a particular Israeli city or specific geographic region, the public will be mobilized. They will be told that a terrorist is heading toward, or is thought to be in, a particular city and that the public should be on the lookout for suspicious individuals and report any and all suspicions to the police

immediately. There have been quite a number of cases in which public awareness has succeeded in preventing or reducing the impact of
terrorist attacks. This has taken the most frequent form of bystanders
immediately contacting the police and a rapid police response. In other
cases, however, bystanders have intervened directly either by physically
grabbing terrorists and preventing them from setting off their explosives or by shooting terrorists while they were in the midst of carrying
out firearm attacks (many Israelis possess firearm permits and go about
their daily business armed). Interestingly, while one might expect official
announcements that terrorists are headed to one's town to cause panic,
they produce guarded awareness instead.

CONCLUSION

Despite Israel's wealth of experience in intelligence gathering and
analysis and counterterrorism strategy, when the second Palestinian intifadah broke out in September 2000, Israel was largely unprepared and at
a loss with respect to what needed to be done to stem the massive tide of
terrorist attacks emanating from cities and villages under the control of
the Palestinian National Authority. Accordingly, the numbers of Israelis
killed in terrorist attacks increased radically during the first year and a
half of the conflict.

Eventually, Israel decided to adopt new approaches and reinvigorate
some of the older ones and adopted an aggressive policy of intelligence
gathering, the deployment of permanent and ad hoc checkpoints, arrests,
and targeted killings. This decision, and the subsequent one to begin
building a barrier to pedestrian and vehicular traffic from the West Bank
to Israel, resulted in a dramatic drop in the number of deaths. Overall,
the numbers of Israelis killed in terrorist attacks following the shift in
Israeli strategy in 2002, dropped from a high of 220 deaths in 2002, to
142 deaths in 2003, 55 deaths in 2004, 22 deaths in 2005, 15 deaths in 2006,
and 3 deaths in 2007.[23] Throughout this time period, the motivation on the
part of terrorist groups to carry out attacks remained very high, in part
due to harsh Israeli counterterrorism measures that all too frequently resulted in civilian casualties, but the capacity of terrorist organizations to
plan and execute attacks was severely reduced. While these policies did
not result in 100 percent success, it was estimated by the ISA that Israel
had succeeded in thwarting, on average, some 75 percent to 80 percent of
attacks over the five-year period of 2000–2005.[24]

The question of what constitutes a successful counterterrorism and
counterterrorism intelligence policy is still an issue to be hotly debated.
The Israeli experience, overall, suggests that terrorism is something that
can be brought down by a significant degree through a strong emphasis
on intelligence gathering, collection, and analysis coupled with aggressive
tactical measures. While this approach cannot defeat terrorism or solve

underlying political disputes, it can bring terrorism down to manageable levels while bolstering the resilience of society and the economy.

NOTES

1. Charles D. Freilich, "National Security Decision-Making in Israel: Processes, Pathologies, and Strengths," *Middle East Journal*. 60, no. 4 (Autumn 2006): 639–40, 645–46.

2. For information on Israeli counterterrorism legal practices see: Stephen J. Schulhofer, "Checks and Balances in Wartime: American, British and Israeli Experiences," *Michigan Law Review* 102, no. 8 (August 2004): 1919–31; Yigal Mersel, "Judicial Review of Counter-terrorism Measures: the Israeli Model for the Role of the Judiciary during the Terror Era," *NYU Journal of International Law and Politics* 38 (November 2006): 67–120; Stephanie Blum, "The Necessary Evil of Preventive Detention: A Plan for a More Moderate and Sustainable Solution" (master's thesis, Naval Postgraduate School, December 2008), 107–119; Amos N. Guiora, *Where Are Terrorists to Be Tried—A Comparative Analysis of Rights Granted to Suspected Terrorists*, Case Research Paper Series in Legal Studies, Working Paper 07–13 (Cleveland, Ohio: Case Western Reserve University, Case School of Law, 2007), 16–23; Emanuel Gross, "Democracy in the War Against Terrorism—The Israeli Experience," *Loyola of Los Angeles Law Review* 35 (March 2003): 1161–1216.

3. Lisa Hajjar, *Courting Conflict: The Israeli Military Court System in the West Bank and Gaza* (Berkeley: University of California Press, 2005), 204–205.

4. See Israeli Supreme Court, *Judgement on the Interrogation Methods Applied by the GSS*, September 6, 1999, http://www.derechos.org/human-rights/mena/doc/torture.html; United Nations, Office of the High Commissioner for Human Rights, *Concluding Observations of the Committee Against Torture: Israel* (Geneva: Office of the UN High Commissioner for Human Rights, 1997), http://www.unhchr.ch/tbs/doc.nsf/0/69b6685c93d9f25180256498005063da?Opendocument.

5. ISA Law, 2002, L.S.I. 8(B).

6. Amos Gilboa, "Intelligence Also Has a Devil's Advocate: The Role of Intelligence Review in the Intelligence Branch," *Israeli Intelligence and Heritage Commemoration Center Perspectives* 44 (March 2006): 18 (in Hebrew).

7. Ronen Bergman, *The Secret War with Iran: The 30-Year Clandestine Struggle Against the World's Most Dangerous Terrorist Power* (New York: Free Press, 2007), 77.

8. Colonel Zohar, "Counterterrorism Intelligence: Hizballah and the Palestinians," *Israeli Intelligence and Heritage Commemoration Center Perspectives* 47 (December 2006): 37 (in Hebrew).

9. Clive Jones, "'One Size Fits All': Israel, Intelligence, and the al-Aqsa Intifada," *Studies in Conflict and Terrorism* 26 (2003): 276.

10. For a discussion of this policy and its legal underpinnings, see Amos N. Guiora, *Transnational Comparative Analysis of Balancing Competing Interests in Counter-Terrorism*, Case Research Paper Series in Legal Studies, Working Paper 06–08 (Cleveland, Ohio: Case Western Reserve University, Case School of Law, 2006), 10–14.

11. Amos Harel and Avi Issacharoff, *34 Days: Israel, Hezbollah, and the War in Lebanon* (New York: Palgrave Macmillan, 2008), 133.

12. Amos Gilboa, "Coping with a Number of Intelligence Challenges: Lebanon as a Case Study," *Intelligence Readings* 1, no. 1 (October 2007): 18 (in Hebrew).

13. David Tzur, "How Things Appeared from the Perspective of the Branch's Command: An Interview with Chief Intelligence Commander Brigadier-General Yuval Chalamish," *Israeli Intelligence and Heritage Commemoration Center Perspectives* 47 (December 2006): 12 (in Hebrew).

14. For a discussion of strategic intelligence failures in the context of the Second Lebanon War of 2006, see: The Commission for the Investigation of the Battle in Lebanon in 2006 (Winograd Commission), *The Second Lebanon War: Interim Report* (Jerusalem: State of Israel, 2007) (in Hebrew); and, Uri Bar-Joseph, "Israel's Military Intelligence Performance in the Second Lebanon War," *International Journal of Intelligence and Counterintelligence* 20, no. 4 (Fall 2007): 583–601.

15. Efraim Halevy, *Man in the Shadows: Inside the Middle East Crisis with a Man Who Led the Mossad* (New York: St. Martin's Press, 2006), 231–32.

16. Gilboa, "Coping with a Number of Intelligence Challenges: Lebanon as a Case Study," 17 (in Hebrew).

17. Yaakov Amidror, *Winning Counterinsurgency War: The Israeli Experience*, Strategic Perspectives #2 (Jerusalem: Jerusalem Center for Public Affairs, 2008), 18.

18. Avi Dicter and Daniel L. Byman, *Israel's Lessons for Fighting Terrorists and Their Implications for the United States*, Analysis Paper, No. 8 (Washington, D.C.: The Saban Center at the Brookings Institution, 2006), 7.

19. Ibid., 11–12.

20. The Economist, "Anger and Assassination," *The Economist.com*, July 23, 2002, http://www.economist.com/agenda/displaystory.cfm?story_id=E1_TNQGPPG (accessed October 28, 2008).

21. CBS News, "Hamas Leaders 'Marked for Death,'" *CBSNews.com*, September 7, 2003, http://www.cbsnews.com/stories/2003/09/07/world/main571958.shtml (accessed October 15, 2008).

22. Ariel Merari, "Israel's Preparedness for High Consequence Terrorism," BCSIA Discussion Paper 2000–30, ESDP Discussion Paper ESDP-2000–02 (Cambridge, Mass.: John F. Kennedy School of Government, Harvard University, 2000), 7.

23. Israel Ministry of Foreign Affairs, *Suicide and Other Bombing Attacks in Israel Since The Declaration of Principles (Sept. 2003)* (Jerusalem: Ministry of Foreign Affairs, 2008), http://www.mfa.gov.il/MFA/Terrorism-+Obstacle+to+Peace/Palestinian+terror+since+2000/Suicide+and+Other+Bombing+Attacks+in+Israel+Since.htm (accessed October 28, 2008).

24. Intelligence and Terrorism Information Center at the Israel Intelligence Heritage and Commemoration Center, *Anti-Israeli Terrorism, 2006: Data, Analysis and Trends* (Tel Aviv: Israel Intelligence Heritage and Commemoration Center, 2007), 55.

PART III

Homeland Security and Intelligence—Does the New Structure Work?

After this brief but engaging look at the new structure of homeland security and the intelligence community (IC), the next point to consider is whether it is working as intended. There have been numerous questions raised about whether the checks and balances between the executive branch IC and the oversight committees in Congress and the courts is working. This has come to the forefront of the news, regarding the thoroughness of classified briefings, the disclosure of information, and the warrantless interception of communications. Several authors have discussed the issued of a domestic intelligence agency and the role of fusion centers; and others will question the effectiveness of those centers and present several considerations for our future security.

CHAPTER 10: CONGRESSIONAL OVERSIGHT OF U.S. INTELLIGENCE

In this chapter, the authors examine the efforts of the Congress to carry out effective oversight of the IC. The United States has struggled with the central paradox of intelligence oversight: good democratic governance requires transparency and public accountability, while intelligence gathering is only possible if secrecy is maintained. The question that remains is, how then can Congress hold the intelligence community publicly accountable without compromising the effectiveness of their operations? This chapter attempts to answer that question by reviewing both the institutional challenges and legislative history of intelligence oversight. Special attention is paid to modern legislation, such as the Foreign Intelligence Surveillance Act (FISA) and the USA PATRIOT Act, and the 9/11 Commission's proposals to amend the congressional oversight committee system. Thus far, the combination of acute security concerns following the 9/11 terrorist attacks and an institutional structure that encourages legislators to adopt a laissez-faire approach to oversight has produced an equipoise favoring the security needs of the IC.

CHAPTER 11: ASSESSING THE DOMESTIC INTELLIGENCE MODEL AND PROCESS

The author challenges the post-9/11 intelligence reforms and the need for a domestic intelligence agency. Given the highly decentralized organizational approach to conducting domestic intelligence activities; the effectiveness of preventing terrorism does not lie with the performance of one organization, but rather how effectively the various organizations operate together. The intelligence cycle is the common methodology for how the intelligence system is supposed to work together. It is also a methodology to assess the performance of the decentralized approach to conducting domestic intelligence. The creation of common architectures and approaches to unify the various organizations involved in domestic, or any other form of intelligence, unify the community as a whole. It also focuses on the real issues, such as improving information sharing and creating transparency. However, the creation of a single agency is not necessarily better at preventing terrorist attacks, but would result in having to resolve new organizational seams, ensure information sharing, and create additional oversight issues for Congress—the same issues that require resolution today.

CHAPTER 12: FUSION CENTERS AND BEYOND—THE FUTURE OF INTELLIGENCE ASSESSMENT IN AN INFORMATION-DELUGED ERA

Fusion centers are a recent bureaucratic response to the realization that henceforth the world will be run by synthesizers. The author is concerned that intelligence services, which began in their modern bureaucratic forms as World War II and cold war era entities confronting states, clear enemies, and shortages of information, are now faced with fluid, unclear, diverse threats within a complex adaptive environment, wherein information is abundant and is mostly open-sourced. The expertise necessary to understand such dynamic adaptive complexity cannot reside within the intelligence services. The author believes that these facts have fostered existential threats to intelligence bureaucracies, especially about changed product need and its continued relevance which fusion centers alone cannot adequately address. The chapter discusses the human talent aspect and organizational requirements of fusion centers within larger IC trends.

CHAPTER 13: DISRUPTING HUMAN NETWORKS— ANCIENT TOOLS FOR MODERN CHALLENGES

The future of war, conflict, and societal unrest will be increasingly defined by nonstate actors, who reject traditional notions of sovereignty, national identity, and international norms of behavior. The author explores ways to influence decision makers, who lead criminal and terror organizations, so as to effectively inhibit their ability to operate. Organizational and group behavior provides a perspective on where to find or develop these fissures. Operational human intelligence techniques provide the leverage to exploit these fissures in order the break the structure. The future is full of uncertainty and the implications are grave for the stability of nations who cherish freedom and the rule of law. Globalization and interconnectedness will fuel discontent in some regions, while dissuading disputes in others. Armed groups are merely one vestige of mankind's struggle in an increasingly smaller world. This chapter suggests human intelligence can inform us about armed group leaders and become an enabler to disrupt groups, thereafter neutralizing the danger from criminal and terrorist networks. The author's purpose in writing this chapter is to prepare ourselves for when we discover, unexpectedly, that the future is here.

10

Congressional Oversight of U.S. Intelligence

John Riley and Mary Kate Schneider

Caught between a democratic culture that values transparency and a task that demands opacity, the U.S. intelligence community (IC) and its congressional overseers have often stood at odds with one another. State intelligence agencies present a challenge to democracies that otherwise publicly scrutinize their executive agencies through legislative oversight, as public exposure of intelligence operations may ultimately undermine the effectiveness of those operations. How to monitor effectively the activities of the IC remains a concern for the U.S. Congress, in terms of both mechanisms and scope. This concern has become especially pressing in the aftermath of the 9/11 terrorist attacks and the intelligence community's assessment of Iraq's weapons of mass destruction (WMDs) capabilities before the U.S.-led invasion in 2003.

This chapter presents an introduction to the legislature's oversight of the intelligence community, noting its origins, implements, and institutional design. Following a brief discussion of how Congress influences the intelligence community, we discuss the history of congressional oversight since the inception of the modern intelligence community in 1947, highlighting major pieces of legislation. After placing intelligence oversight in historical context, we proceed to elaborate on the institutional challenges of oversight, including the current incentive structure and a review of proposed reforms. Noting historical legacies, incentive structures, and institutional flaws, we argue for a new model of congressional oversight that incorporates active surveillance and electoral incentives.

HISTORY AND MECHANISMS: AN OVERVIEW OF LEGISLATIVE OVERSIGHT

Legislative Leverage: How Congress Influences the Intelligence Community

There are three key mechanisms through which Congress can exert leverage over the IC. Foremost, Congress controls the flow of resources from the U.S. government to the intelligence agencies, is responsible for reviewing the agencies' budgets, and appropriates and authorizes funds through the annual Intelligence Authorization Act. Thus, Congress can threaten to withhold funds from the IC, and the intelligence community is obligated to justify its expenses to Congress. Although this sometimes "smacks of micromanagement,"[1] such leverage is a powerful tool in ensuring accountability, serving as both carrot and stick.

A second mechanism through which Congress influences the intelligence community is legal—that is, Congress has both the power and the obligation to pass legislation that authorizes, constrains, or otherwise affects the operations of intelligence agencies. Additionally, Congress is charged with the responsibility to monitor the IC's adherence to these laws and to the U.S. Constitution.

Third, Congress can shape the actions of the IC through "the power to go public."[2] Although leaking classified information would appear to be a threat to national security, S. Res. 400 (the resolution that created the Senate's intelligence oversight committee) includes provisions through which Congress can declassify information despite opposition from the executive branch.[3] Congress has never exercised these formal procedures, but at least one former director of central intelligence (DCI) has been accused of leaking information after a congressional hearing and then blaming the leak on Congress.[4]

Congressional Oversight throughout the Eras: 1947–1978

In its own review of congressional oversight, the Central Intelligence Agency (CIA) notes the irony in that the original American intelligence agency was the legislature itself, as the Continental Congress was responsible for all intelligence activities related to the Revolutionary War effort.[5] After the U.S. Constitution was drafted in 1787, intelligence activities were largely under the purview of the executive branch with little more than tacit approval from Congress. This laissez-faire arrangement underwent dramatic revision in the aftermath of World War II.

With the onset of the cold war, the need for a permanent national intelligence agency was readily apparent. As a result, the CIA was created pursuant to the National Security Act of 1947, which also established the National Security Council (NSC). This marks the beginning of what Loch Johnson calls the "Era of Trust,"[6] characterized by "benign neglect" on the part of Congress.[7] During this period, congressional oversight was conducted by the Armed Services Committee (as most intelligence work was done by agencies in the Defense Department) and the Appropriations Committee (as they control the funding) within the Senate and the House of Representatives. On this arrangement, Pat Holt remarks: "None of these subcommittees had much stomach for the task,"[8] and DCI reports to Congress were typically "sketchy, perfunctory, and often unwanted by lawmakers."[9] As the cold war progressed, a series of events evidenced a growing need for closer congressional oversight, among them the U-2 incident of 1960, the 1961 Bay of Pigs invasion, and the Vietnam War. George Pickett notes that "Congress made several attempts to oversee intelligence before 1970, only to have them collapse in divisions of opinion among members."[10]

The need to reform the system of congressional oversight, however, reached a crisis point in December 1974 when the *New York Times* published a series of articles revealing the CIA's Family Jewels, a collection of CIA documents that recorded a wide variety of violations of the agency's charter, such as warrantless wiretapping and foreign assassination plots.[11] One of the most serious abuses of power was Operation CHAOS, a consolidation of all domestic surveillance operations targeting antiwar activists and other U.S. citizens. The public unveiling of Family Jewels triggered a domestic shock that ushered in an era characterized by "uneasy partnership"[12] during which Congress took upon itself more responsibility for intelligence oversight than ever before. The circumstances that led to Congress's changed attitude cast a long shadow over the U.S. IC, as former DCI Richard Helms describes this period as the CIA's "lowest point."[13]

Congress's first response to the CIA's assortment of transgressions was to pass the Hughes-Ryan Act (an amendment to the Foreign Assistance Act of 1961) on December 31, 1974, just nine days after the first *New York Times* articles were published. The Hughes-Ryan Act placed new constraints on the executive branch, requiring that the president report all covert operations of the CIA to the appropriate congressional committee(s) "in a timely fashion."[14] The Hughes-Ryan Act is credited for "[supplying] the statutory recognition that had previously been lacking."[15]

In January 1975, President Gerald Ford appointed an executive-branch commission led by Vice President Nelson Rockefeller to investigate the allegations against the CIA.[16] Later known as the Rockefeller Commission, it conducted its investigation concurrently with the Pike Committee in the House, led by House Representative Otis Pike, and the Church Committee in the Senate, led by Senator Frank Church. Although the Pike Committee's final report was never published, its investigation led to the creation of a House Intelligence Oversight Committee, and in 1977 H.R. 658 was passed to create the House Permanent Select Committee on Intelligence (HPSCI).

The Church Committee holds the distinction of being the most extensive investigation of U.S. intelligence to date.[17] Its work led to the passage of S. Res. 400 in 1976, which created the Senate Select Committee on Intelligence: Oversight Subcommittee (SSCI). The SSCI and the HPSCI assumed the responsibility of oversight from the Senate and House Armed Services and Appropriations Committees, respectively, and they remain the two primary committees through which oversight of U.S. intelligence activities is undertaken. Beyond establishing the first permanent congressional committees to oversee intelligence operations, the most significant outcome of these investigations was the adoption of P.L. 95–511 on October 25, 1978, the Foreign Intelligence Surveillance Act (FISA).

The Foreign Intelligence Surveillance Act of 1978

Realizing that circumstances might arise under which the CIA would have legitimate cause to engage in domestic surveillance, the 95th Congress created FISA to establish a set of rules by which surveillance—including electronic surveillance, physical searches, pen registers, and trap and trace devices, and later amended in 1994 to include physical surveillance—could be conducted by the executive branch.[18] FISA gave broad latitude to the executive branch, stipulating that: "Notwithstanding any other law, the President, through the Attorney General, may authorize electronic surveillance without a court order under this title to acquire foreign intelligence information for periods of up to one year" provided that intercepted communications be "exclusively between or among foreign powers," and that "there is no substantial likelihood that the surveillance will acquire the contents of any communication to which a United States person is a party."[19] A "United States person" was defined as any U.S. citizen, resident alien, or non-foreign-affiliated U.S. corporation.[20] If a U.S. person were party to an intercepted communication, judicial authorization was required for any surveillance to continue beyond 72 hours.

FISA also created the FISA Court, or FISC, through which surveillance warrants would be obtained. Warrants requested through the FISA Court were subject to a secret hearing in front of one of seven federal district judges appointed by the chief justice of the United States. These hearings were closed to the public and proceedings were classified. Thus, through FISA, Congress established a procedure through which the executive branch could legally order domestic intelligence operations while bypassing the regular judicial process.

Congressional Oversight throughout the Eras: 1980–2004

Congress built upon the reforms of the 1970s by passing the Intelligence Oversight Act in 1980. This Act was an amendment to the Hughes-Ryan Act and obligated the IC to report covert actions to both the SSCI and the HPSCI prior to their implementation, unlike the ambiguous previous requirement of a timely manner. The Intelligence Oversight Act was noteworthy in that it constrained the intelligence community more than any previous legislation.

In 1987, a second major shock delivered a blow to public trust in the government when the Iran-Contra scandal was revealed, ushering in an "Era of Distrust" that was followed by divisive partisanship in the 1990s.[21] Both public distrust and legislative partisanship were deepened by the series of domestic shocks that reverberated through the 1990s and early 2000s: the 1993 intelligence failure in Somalia; the 9/11 terrorist attacks in 2001; and the absence of WMDs in Iraq, 2003–2004.[22] These shocks highlighted an urgent need for intelligence oversight reform not felt since 1975.

Contemporary Congressional Oversight

Characterized by "congressional ambivalence," Johnson describes the post-9/11 intelligence oversight milieu: "On the one hand, the mistakes of 9/11 and the errors over predicting the presence of [WMD] in Iraq could hardly be ignored. On the other hand, lawmakers rushed to increase the espionage funding and authority and otherwise aid the secret agencies in the struggle against global terrorism."[23] In short, Congress simultaneously condemned the intelligence community for its failures while rewarding it with unprecedented resources.

Among the legislation adopted in the post-9/11 era are the USA PATRIOT Act (October 24, 2001), S. Res. 445 (October 9, 2004), the Protect America Act (August 5, 2007), and the FISA Amendments Act of 2008 (July 10, 2008). The USA PATRIOT Act (formally known as the Uniting and Strengthening America by Providing Appropriate Tools Required to Intercept and Obstruct Terrorism Act of 2001) was the first major piece of post-9/11 intelligence legislation passed and was designed to prevent and punish terrorism. Among other provisions, the PATRIOT Act expanded the power of the FISC, increasing the number of judges from 7 to 11.

S. Res. 445 was adopted based on "perceived widespread public support for the recommendations of the 9/11 Commission."[24] Its operative clauses aimed to streamline the SSCI's oversight capacity, abolishing the eight-year term limit for Senators serving on the SSCI, reducing the size of the SSCI from 17 to 15 members, and expanding periodic reporting requirements between the SSCI and the Senate.[25]

The Protect America Act of 2007 and its successor, the FISA Amendments Act of 2008 (scheduled to sunset in 2012), introduced several highly controversial updates to FISA, including provisions for warrantless surveillance. Both the Protect America Act and the FISA Amendments Act limited the power of the FISC, the latter having been criticized by the American Civil Liberties Union (ACLU) for "trivializ[ing] court review by explicitly permitting the government to continue surveillance programs even if the application is denied by the court. The government has the authority to wiretap through the entire appeals process, and then keep and use whatever it gathered in the meantime."[26] Given that a preponderance of recent legislation has granted broader, rather than narrower, latitude to the intelligence community and the executive, it stands to reason that Congress's current attitude toward intelligence oversight is motivated by a palpable disinterest in effective oversight extending beyond the perfunctory.

REFORMING OVERSIGHT

Effective congressional oversight of the intelligence community requires members of Congress to have a high degree of access to ongoing intelligence operations, the authority to effect changes in operations or halt operations that have run aground of either constitutional or statutory prohibitions, the power to enforce their collective judgment, and the willingness to conduct oversight. In practice, however, these requirements are rarely met as numerous and powerful institutional impediments intertwine with an electoral incentive structure to limit Congress's role in day-to-day oversight.

Institutional Challenges

Effective oversight depends, at least in part, on the formal and informal channels linking the executive and legislative branches. As the branch directly managing all operations, the executive enjoys a default hegemonic position vis-à-vis Congress in two critical ways. First, and most obviously, Congress is dependent upon the executive to provide all information about ongoing operations. Johnson summed up the situation well: "Lawmakers only know about intelligence activities to the extent that the president, attorney general, and the DCI allow them to know."[27] For example, some DCIs have famously employed their own filibuster techniques by either consuming a large portion of a public hearing's time with opening statements or by delivering so much information that it becomes unusable.[28] Put differently, the issue often is not whether the congressional leadership has been granted access to the classified information as whether the material has been presented in a timely and forthcoming manner.

Executive-congressional relations have been further strained by the recent trend of turning to nontraditional actors to conduct intelligence operations. The Intelligence Authorization Act of FY 1991 defined a covert action as "an activity or activities conducted by an element of the United States Government to influence political, economic, or military conditions abroad so that the role of the United States Government is not intended to be apparent or acknowledged publicly."[29] As Charles Cogan observed, the language "an element of the United States Government" is an explicit acknowledgement that covert activities would no longer be the sole purview of the CIA and that the reporting provisions contained in the statute would apply to anyone employed by the United States who was conducting covert operations.[30] The application of the provision, however, has been far from seamless. For example, U.S. Special Operations Forces have played an increasingly important role in gathering intelligence in the post-9/11 counterterrorist efforts and in the Afghanistan and Iraq theaters. The Defense Department, however, draws a careful distinction between clandestine and covert efforts and maintains that it only conducts the former.[31] The consequence is that the intelligence committees have been effectively excluded from the oversight of this increasingly large and important aspect of intelligence gathering.

On the legislative side, the congressional committee system established in the 1970s creates a series of unique challenges for effective oversight. Following the traditional practice of dividing authorization and appropriation powers, both the SSCI and HPSCI have been granted the statutory authority to oversee and authorize intelligence activities, while appropriation of intelligence activities continues to reside with the defense appropriation subcommittees. The division of authorization and appropriation powers is the norm in American legislative history and at times has provided an important internal check, preventing power from becoming too centralized within any single congressional committee. The unique secrecy requirements of conducting intelligence activities, however, have made the application of this model to intelligence oversight difficult as some members of the intelligence community "take advantage of the fact that defense appropriators are mightily distracted from intelligence oversight because of their other responsibilities" and effectively circumvent the authorizing committee.[32] In such a scenario, effective oversight is only possible when there is an excellent flow of information between the intelligence and appropriations committees and leadership carefully coordinates their efforts—a requirement that is rarely met in an environment that is often highly politically charged, and is dependent upon legislators with numerous competing issues on their agendas.

Incentives

Access and authority to authorize or sanction will ultimately mean little if those who are charged with oversight are unwilling to take up the task. David Mayhew's classic work on congressional motivation suggests that legislators are motivated primarily by reelection concerns, a desire to gain influence and prestige in the chamber, and the goal to advance good public policy.[33] Certainly, maintenance of the United States' national security and advancement of its foreign policy is an objective that motivates most, if not all, members of Congress. To this end, the desire to help protect the public good is a strong motivating factor that moves many legislators to take an active role in intelligence oversight.

However, patriotism is tempered by the realities of the electoral process. Put simply, there are very few votes to be won by taking part in intelligence oversight. A process that takes place largely behind closed doors and rarely generates tangible benefits for a particular district or constituency will be of little help come reelection time. Moreover, to provide oversight is to be participating in a process and that could lead to culpability if something goes wrong. For example, much has been made of the extent to which the Speaker of the House of Representatives, Nancy Pelosi, was fully aware of water boarding and other enhanced techniques during the interrogation of some al-Qaeda suspects.[34] Moreover, like many other issues competing for legislators' attention, intelligence gathering and analysis involves a fairly complex set of issues, and as the authors of the *9/11 Commission's Report* noted, "few members of Congress have the broad knowledge of intelligence activities or the know-how about the technologies employed."[35]

Finally, overlaying these electoral disincentives to engage in active oversight is the general predisposition held by many congresspersons that suggests that intelligence gathering is a presidential prerogative. As Richard Posner puts it, "in a rational allocation of the responsibilities of an enterprise, the details, including organizational details, of policy implementation are properly assigned to the executive."[36] It is, after all, difficult for Congress to speak with a coherent voice, let alone initiate on foreign policy, and since the president is likely to be the first to be held accountable for any failure, it is best to let him lead.

In sum, oversight requires a high level of work and time on the congressperson's behalf, carries a high level of responsibility and therefore a measure of risk if an intelligence failure becomes a public scandal, and offers few electoral incentives. Consequently, "Congress is informed to the degree that Congress wants to be informed," but most lawmakers on SSCI and HPSCI rarely attend oversight hearings.[37]

Proposed Reforms

Although there is widespread agreement that intelligence oversight reform is needed, thus far there is no consensus on the shape the reforms should take. Instead, proponents have advocated for a wide range of institutional changes that have included creating a joint committee on intelligence, strengthening oversight by vesting a single committee with both authorization and appropriation powers, or amending the reporting and intelligence-sharing provisions to incorporate a wider group of legislators into the oversight process.

A proposal to create a joint Senate and House intelligence committee has been under consideration almost immediately since the establishment of the SSCI and HPSCI.[38] Most recently, the 9/11 Commission has breathed new life into the idea as they concluded that "congressional oversight for intelligence—and counterterrorism—is now dysfunctional" and recommended that Congress either create a joint committee based upon the now defunct Joint Committee on Atomic Energy or a single committee in each house of Congress that combines both appropriation and authorization powers.[39] The creation of a joint committee would be a significant step towards integrating both houses' activities and would likely reduce costs as the congressional oversight process became more streamlined. Most importantly, a joint committee might lead the executive to be "more open and forthright with a single, small oversight body than with two with a larger, combined membership."[40]

Alternatively, Congress may opt to reform intelligence oversight by vesting both authorization and appropriation authority into a signal committee in the House of Representatives and the Senate. For example, S. Res. 164 seeks to grant appropriation authority to the Senate Intelligence Committee. Introducing the bill to the Senate, Senator Feingold observed that "the single most important step to strengthen the power of the intelligence committees is to give them the power of the purse. Without it, they will be marginalized. The intelligence community will not ignore you, but they will work around you."[41]

Thus far neither house has approved either the joint committee proposal or the single appropriations authorization alternative. Their reluctance stems from a concern that both proposals might vest too much power into a single committee and a concern that consolidating the oversight committees would remove even more legislators from the process. Perhaps more fundamentally though, any reform that dramatically alters the congressional committee system will be difficult to pass. As the 9/11 Commission Report concludes, "Few things are more difficult to change in Washington than congressional committee jurisdiction and prerogatives. To a member, these assignments are almost as important as the map of his or her congressional district."[42]

Consequently, more modest changes are currently under consideration. For example, in June 2009 the HPSCI passed the Intelligence Authorization Bill, FY 2010, which, among other things, would eliminate the president's ability to keep classified operations from any member of the intelligence committees. In effect, the "Gang of Eight briefings" (i.e., briefings that include only the two party leaders from each house, the chairs, and the ranking members of the ICs) would be eliminated as all 15 senators on the SSCI and 22 representatives on the HPSCI would have the right to be fully briefed on classified operations.[43] The shift to a more inclusive approach to intelligence oversight is consistent with House Speaker Pelosi's earlier calls to lift the restrictions on intelligence sharing among members of Congress[44] and might signal a willingness to support a more transparent and accountable process.

A Way Forward

A current running through each of the reforms review above is that intelligence oversight would be more effective if the congressional committee system was reorganized to support a "police patrolling style" of oversight where legislators would adopt a proactive role.[45] Active surveillance would simultaneously serve as a deterrent to discourage anyone from violating legislative goals and it would allow legislators to remediate a problem before a catastrophic failure occurs.

As the *9/11 Commission's Report* made clear, such reforms are badly needed. However, the drive to reform must be balanced against the need to maintain the secrecy requirements of intelligence operations and the political realities of the congressional electoral system. Any new oversight model must have the trust and confidence of the intelligence community. Moreover, reforms must be framed so that intelligence oversight augments, rather than competes, with electoral incentives.

NOTES

1. Kevin Whitelaw and David E. Kaplan, "Don't Ask, Don't Tell: Congress Gives Short Shrift to its Intelligence Oversight Duties," *U.S. News and World Report,* September 5, 2004.

2. Denis McDonough, Mara Rudman, and Peter Rundlet, *No Mere Oversight: Congressional Oversight of U.S. Intelligence is Broken* (Washington, D.C.: Center for American Progress, June 2006), 25.

3. Ibid.

4. Ibid.

5. James S. van Wagenen, "A Review of Congressional Oversight: Critics and Defenders." Posted April 14, 2007. Available at: https://www.cia.gov/library/center-for-the-study-of-intelligence/csi-publications/csi-studies/studies/97unclass/wagenen.html.

6. Loch K. Johnson, "Intelligence Oversight in the United States," in *Intelligence and Human Rights in the Era of Global Terrorism,* ed. Steve Tsang (Stanford, Calif.: Stanford University Press, 2008), 55. Also, Loch K. Johnson, "Accountability and America's Secret Foreign Policy: Keeping a Legislative Eye on the Central Intelligence Agency," *Foreign Policy Analysis* 1 (2005): 103.

7. Van Wagenen, "A Review of Congressional Oversight."

8. Pat M. Holt, "Who's Watching the Store? Executive-Branch and Congressional Surveillance," in *National Insecurity: U.S. Intelligence after the Cold War,* ed. Craig Eisendrath (Philadelphia: Temple University Press, 2000), 193.

9. Johnson, "Intelligence Oversight in the United States," 55.

10. George Pickett, "Congress, the Budget, and Intelligence," in *Intelligence: Policy & Process,* ed. Alfred C. Maurer, Marion D. Tunstall, and James M. Keagle (Boulder. Colo.: Westview Press, 1985), 157.

11. The CIA full Family Jewels report is available at: http://www.gwu.edu/~nsarchiv/NSAEBB/NSAEBB222/index.htm.

12. Johnson, "Intelligence Oversight in the United States," 55.

13. Interview with Richard Helms. May 22–23, 1978. Available at: https://www.cia.gov/library/center-for-the-study-of-intelligence/kent-csi/docs/v44i4a07p_0001.htm.

14. *The Foreign Assistance Act of 1974,* 662 (a), also known as the Hughes-Ryan Act (P.L. 93-559, 88 STAT 1795, 1804 (1974)).

15. John Hart Ely, *War and Responsibility: Constitutional Lessons of Vietnam and Its Aftermath* (Princeton, N.J.: Princeton University Press, 1995), 107.

16. Frank J. Smist, Jr., *Congress Oversees the United States Intelligence Community, 1947–1989* (Knoxville, Tenn.: The University of Tennessee Press, 1990), 27.

17. Johnson, "Accountability and America's Secret Foreign Policy," 104.

18. Elizabeth Bazan, "Electronic Surveillance Modernization Act, as Passed by the House of Representatives," CRS Report for Congress, RL33637, January 18, 2007.

19. 0 USC 1802, Sec. 102(a)(1). Available at: http://www.cnss.org/PL%2095–511.pdf.

20. Ibid.

21. Johnson, "Intelligence Oversight in the United States," 58.

22. Johnson, "Accountability and America's Secret Foreign Policy," 106.

23. Johnson, "Intelligence Oversight in the United States," 61.

24. Paul S. Rundquist and Christopher M. Davis, "S. Res. 445: Senate Committee Reorganization for Homeland Security and Intelligence Matters," CRS Report for Congress, October 15, 2004, 5.

25. Ibid, 2.

26. American Civil Liberties Union, "H. R. 6304, the FISA Amendments Act of 2008." Posted June 19, 2008. Available at: http://www.aclu.org/safefree/nsaspying/35731res20080619.html.

27. Loch K. Johnson, "Governing in the Absence of Angels: On the Practice of Intelligence Accountability in the U.S. Congress," (paper presented to the Woodrow Wilson Center Congress Project Governing Post-9/11: Congress and the President at War, Washington, D.C., May 9, 2003).

28. For example, addressing the House and Senate Intelligence Committees Director of CIA George Tenet "struck a defiant tone from the outset. Asked to limit his remarks to 10 minutes, he spoke for 50. When Sen. Bob Graham, chairman of the Senate Intelligence Committee, urged him to abbreviate his remarks, Tenet refused." John Lumpkin, "Tenet: al-Qaida Set to Strike Again," *Associated Press Online,* October 17, 2002.

29. The act goes on to exclude "(1) activities the primary purpose of which is to acquire intelligence, traditional counterintelligence activities, traditional activities to improve or maintain the operational security of the United States Government programs, or administrative activities."

30. Charles G. Coogan, "Covert Action and Congressional Oversight: A Deontology," *Studies in Conflict and Terrorism* 16 (1993): 88.

31. Jennifer D. Kibbe, "Intelligence Oversight: The Pentagon v. the Congress" (paper presented at the annual meeting of the International Studies Association, Chicago, 2007).

32. Richard A. Best, Jr., "Intelligence Authorization Legislation: Status and Challenges," CRS Report for Congress, R40240, February 24, 2009, 11.

33. David Mayhew, *Congress: The Electoral Connection* (New Haven, Conn.: Yale University Press, 1974).

34. For example, see Paul Kane, "CIA Says Pelosi Was Briefed on Use of 'Enhanced Interrogations,'" *Washington Post*, May 7, 2009, http://voices.washing tonpost.com/capitol-briefing/2009/05/cia_says_pelosi_was_briefed_on.html.

35. The National Commission on Terrorist Attacks Upon the United States, *The 9/11 Commission Report* (New York: St. Martin's Paperbacks, 2004), 597.

36. Richard Posner, *Uncertain Shield: The U.S. Intelligence System in the Throes of Reform* (New York: Rowman & Littlefield Publishers, 2006), 174.

37. Johnson, "Accountability and America's Secret Foreign Policy," 112.

38. For an overview of the evolution of proposed reforms see Frederick M. Kaiser, "Congressional Oversight of Intelligence: Current Structure and Alternatives," CRS Report for Congress, updated September 16, 2008.

39. The National Commission on Terrorist Attacks Upon the United States, *The 9/11 Commission Report*, 598.

40. Kaiser, "Congressional Oversight of Intelligence: Current Structure and Alternatives," 18.

41. S. Res. 164, 111th Cong., 1st sess., *Congressional Record*, Vol. 155 (April 23, 2009).

42. The National Commission on Terrorist Attacks Upon the United States, *The 9/11 Commission Report*, 596.

43. *Intelligence Authorization Act for F.Y. 2010*, 111th Cong., 1st sess., H.R. 2701.

44. Nancy Pelosi, "The Gap in Intelligence Oversight," *Washington Post*, January 15, 2006, B07.

45. Mathew D. McCubbins and Thomas Schwartz, "Congressional Oversight Overlooked: Police Patrols versus Fire Alarms," *American Journal of Political Science* 28, no. 1 (February 1984): 165–79.

11

Assessing the Domestic Intelligence Model and Process

James Burch

The attacks on September 11, 2001, led to renewed calls for intelligence reform and transformation. The phrase *connect the dots,* popularized by the congressional inquiry into the attacks and the 9/11 Commission, described the inability of the intelligence community (IC) to share information across organizations and to share information internally.[1] This phrase also became the rallying cry for reformers to transform the IC. These debates and emphasis towards improving domestic intelligence and security led to significant organizational change through the creation of the Department of Homeland Security (DHS), the National Counterterrorism Center (NCTC), and the Office of the Director of National Intelligence (ODNI)—specifically to oversee both domestic and foreign intelligence. During this period, there was also a revamping of the Federal Bureau of Investigation's (FBI) intelligence capability. As a result of these changes, the accomplishment of domestic intelligence functions and missions in the United States occurs within a highly decentralized approach. These reorganizational efforts at the federal level along with a renewed call for improved information sharing and the creation of State and Local Fusion Centers have resulted in significant resources, focus, and efforts dedicated to improving domestic intelligence.[2] It has also raised the issue of protecting individual liberties while ensuring domestic security.

Within a free society, the very term *domestic intelligence* raises significant questions, as well as concerns about civil liberty.[3] While collecting domestic intelligence may raise concerns about civil liberties, it also supports an equally vital need—the preservation of the nation-state. Even most libertarians will concede to the need of preventing additional terrorist attacks.[4]

Domestic intelligence, perhaps more than any other issue since 9/11, leads to several questions. What is the best organizational construct for establishing a domestic intelligence capability? Who are the stakeholders and what organizational friction will ensue as a result of transformation efforts? What is the most efficient way to establish and execute domestic intelligence? The post-9/11 debate on domestic intelligence and its potential abuse generates significant debate between individual liberties and the need to protect the homeland.

Protecting individual liberties versus ensuring domestic security is not a new issue. The 9/11 attacks have reintroduced the issue of domestic intelligence. How this issue is framed and how this capability is developed within the context of a free society is central to the public debate. As Israeli Prime Minister Benjamin Netanyahu, stated:

The governments of free societies charged with fighting a rising tide of terrorism are thus faced with a democratic dilemma: If they do not fight terrorism with the means available to them, they endanger their citizenry; if they do, they appear to endanger the very freedoms which they are charged to protect.[5]

This dilemma poses questions that lie at the very heart of the debate. Was the creation of the DHS and other initiatives the optimal organizational construct? How are individual liberties being protected with the rising domestic intelligence concerns and abuses?[6] Are there potential abuses with the implementation and proliferation of State and Local Fusion Centers?[7] These questions will continue to hamper decision makers' attempts to resolve and implement policy in the post-9/11 environment.

The Homeland Security Act of 2002 established DHS and sought to place the new organization at the center of the domestic intelligence framework. The act envisioned the new department to, "assess, receive, and analyze law enforcement information, intelligence information, and other information from agencies."[8] At its most fundamental level, DHS should be organizationally structured to maximize leverage among all agencies, federal, state, and local, involved in homeland security. Additionally, in order to realize its mandate to provide a "decisive information advantage,"[9] its organizational structure must be founded on clearly understood information-sharing mechanisms and doctrinal processes.

Challenged with developing its own organization and processes, DHS has faced the issue of being the newcomer to the IC. As Eugene Bardach explains:

The Department of Homeland Security, for instance, is poorly positioned to receive intelligence from the intelligence community agencies because it does not do intelligence collection on its own and hence will have nothing to trade. . . . Cooperation between the FBI and CIA was hampered because there was no willing enforcer.[10]

Significant organizational change, particularly during a relatively short time frame, inherently raises implementation questions. First, are these organizations functioning as intended? The creation of new agencies and missions often leads to organizational friction and uncertainty. Second, are these organizations operating efficiently? Sharing intelligence and information, historically problematic in the IC, must now be shared among a highly decentralized set of federal, state, and local customers. For information sharing, this challenge is both internal and external to DHS. Internal to DHS lays the challenge of molding 180,000 personnel from 22 agencies into a single and cohesive structure to accomplish a common purpose.[11] The DHS leadership is also faced with the challenge of integrating organizations with a long existence, highly defined mission focus, and extensive ties to the IC, such as the U.S. Coast Guard (USCG), U.S. Secret Service (USSS), and Customs, while ensuring that new ones, like the Transportation Security Administration (TSA), are integrated into a common purpose.[12]

Externally, DHS's challenge lies in fulfill its mission of supporting state and local requirements, along with the FBI and NCTC.[13] State and local intelligence support was originally charged to DHS;[14] however the creation of the NCTC in 2003 with a state and local support mission,[15] coupled with the statutory responsibility and renewed focus by the FBI to support state and local intelligence needs, has created bureaucratic competition between the three agencies. DHS has also been slow to realize its support to state and local customers.[16]

NCTC has also faced similar growth challenges with being a new organization with the unique responsibility of joint planning. For example, while successes have been realized in the defense community, the multi-faceted and integrated nature joint planning that should occur at NCTC may be problematic at best in the absence of clear guidance and poorly understood mission authorities.[17] The absence of strategic guidance for winning the war on terrorism will lead to negligible results.

Similar in function to DHS's need for leveraging a variety of intelligence sources and information from a multiple community partners, one of the primary purposes of NCTC is "to improve horizontal integration across IC agencies, but is also supposed to improve vertical integration between agencies and operations."[18] While NCTC has been charged with ensuring horizontal and vertical integration, its close access to the president has resulted in the preponderance of its analytic efforts to satisfying the White House's intelligence requirements at the expense of its other homeland security partners.[19]

One set of partners is the State and Local Fusion Centers. State and local partners have had insufficient access in terms of information sharing and tailored information.[20] As part of a renewed effort to improve the vertical dimension to provide tailored intelligence products to state and local customers, the Information Sharing Enterprise (ISE) Implementation Plan established the Interagency Threat Assessment Coordination Group (ITACG) at NCTC.[21] Although not part of the NCTC, the ITACG is located at NCTC and has representation from several federal agencies. Its primary mission is to ensure that "intelligence produced by Federal organizations within the intelligence, law enforcement, and homeland security communities is fused, validated, deconflicted, and approved for dissemination in a concise and, where possible, unclassified format."[22]

Reorganizational efforts at the FBI have also led to several mechanisms aimed at improving its domestic intelligence and surveillance capacity. The FBI established the National Joint Terrorism Task Force (NJTTF) in 2002 to coordinate its nation-wide network of Joint Terrorism Task Forces (JTTFs) throughout the country.[23] JTTFs serve as the "primary operational responsibility for terrorism investigations that are not related to ongoing persecutions."[24] They also focus on sharing information and intelligence with state and local law enforcement partners.[25] Many of the JTTFs are collocated with many of the newly formed State and Local Fusion Centers. The main effort of the FBI's intelligence reform has been the development and implementation of its Field Intelligence Groups (FIGs). Each group consists of intelligence professionals—linguists, collectors, and reports officers—that are tasked to provide focused and tactical support to law enforcement officials.[26]

The FBI also instituted the National Security Branch (NSB), which is supposed to align the FBI's national security mission under the auspices and guidance of the director of national intelligence (DNI). The NSB combined the FBI's intelligence element that previously fell under its directorate of intelligence and the counterterrorism, counterintelligence, and weapons of mass destruction elements (WMD) divisions;[27] it was also charged with providing the strategic direction to the FIGs.

The establishment of new organizations while reforming existing ones has resulted in questions to their performance. Assessing organizational performance has been the focus in the post-9/11 environment—but is it the right focus? Transformational change occurs, not only with the development or revamping of organizations, but is the product of other factors. For the purposes of this assessment, transformation is defined by four factors: *organization, processes, technology,* and a defined *end state*.[28]

There is an extensive body of post-9/11 literature that focuses on organizational approaches, such as whether NCTC and DHS are meeting their mission responsibilities,[29] whether the FBI is transforming itself into a full member of the IC,[30] or if the United States should create its own independent domestic intelligence agency.[31] There has also been extensive debate and discussion on implementing technological systems to link the disparate organizations involved in domestic intelligence and security.[32] One summary of post-9/11 reform describes these efforts as follows:

[I]ntelligence reform has largely taken the form of new organization charts in the hope and expectation that these upgraded organizations would produce new

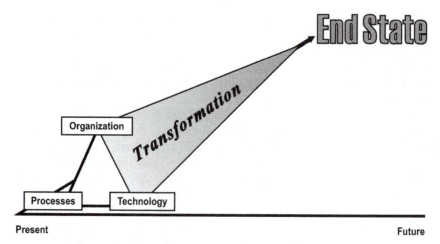

Figure 11.1 Transformation Framework

practices. Implicit in this hope was an expectation that the new forms would produce desired functions.[33]

Focusing on organizational approaches and technological solutions to streamlining domestic intelligence activities, while important, misses a larger issue. The current approach to fixing domestic intelligence shortfalls cannot be the result of assessing one or even several organizations.[34] Within a decentralized organizational construct (one that spans several levels of hierarchy and that consists of a wide variety of costumers), the importance of well-defined and understood processes becomes paramount. Process development, within the transformational framework, should become the primary focus for assessing domestic intelligence activities. To put it another way, leveraging information across several communities to create a decisive information advantage cannot occur efficiently without well-established processes.

Intelligence is not a final end state, but rather "intelligence is a *process* . . . not just a product, and systematically analyzing this process should illuminate issues, obstacles, and opportunities for effective reform."[35] Professor Gray from the University of Fayetteville and Christopher Slade from the University of Denver suggest that the intelligence cycle should be the model, that domestic intelligence activities, which span across multiple levels of government, are assessed. As they state, the primary aim of the intelligence cycle is to:

harness its collection resources to nationally developed and coordinated intelligence priorities and gaps. The intelligence cycle is just that, a cycle, in which analysts and collectors interact regularly to incorporate new information and refine intelligence collection requirements; analysts and collectors are central to the cycle.[36]

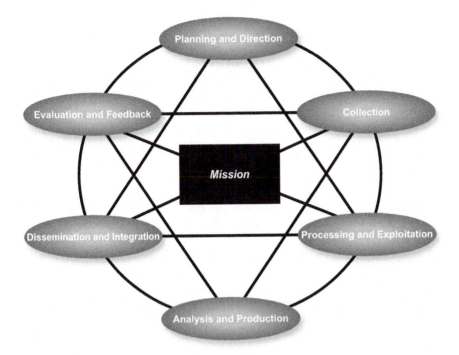

Figure 11.2 The Intelligence Cycle

Source: Joint Chiefs of Staff, *Joint Publication 2–01: Joint and National Intelligence Support to Military Operations* (Washington, D.C.: GPO, 2007), III-1.

Depending on the organization, the intelligence cycle has been defined as a five or six step process: *Planning and Direction, Collection, Processing and Exploitation, Analysis and Production, Dissemination and Integration,* and depending on the model that is used, *Evaluation and Feedback.* For the purposes of this assessment, the six-step process will be used to examine domestic intelligence activities. A depiction of the intelligence cycle is shown below.

PLANNING AND DIRECTION

The Planning and Direction phase of the intelligence cycle is the initial step that seeks to identify the nature, scope, and focus of the intelligence issue. To be effective and to ensure that the IC does not produce intelligence for its own sake, the Planning and Direction phase must be linked to the mission, the concept of operations, and/or the strategic planning process. It is also a mistake to view the intelligence cycle as a lock-step and sequential process. For example, the Planning and Direction phase may identify vital intelligence questions that do not have to be answered by additional collection. Existing data may already reside in databases and only require additional processing and exploitation, or more simply, existing analytical expertise may be able to answer the question.

For domestic intelligence activities, the Planning and Direction phase occurs at several different levels. At the federal level, the primary organizations involved in domestic intelligence activities are the NCTC, the DHS, and the FBI. By organizational charter, NCTC has been charged with the responsibility of strategic planning to synchronize intelligence activities across the foreign-domestic intelligence arenas consistent with guidance from the president, the DNI, and the Homeland Security Council (HSC).[37] This federal-level direction should incorporate regional and local inputs into the overall process, particularly for issues such as critical infrastructure and regional or local threat concerns. Planning and Direction does not imply a one-way relationship, but serves as an interactive process to refine the intelligence problem.

Counterterrorism is a complex challenge requiring knowledge and integration of capabilities that span across governmental hierarchies and the private sector.[38] From the perspective of state and local customers, there is a consensus that the federal government has been slow in providing guidance and information. Michael Lieter, the NCTC director, has acknowledged that "we have moved more slowly in our support to 'non traditional' partners such as: FBI Joint Terrorism Task Forces [JTTFs], state, local, and tribal homeland security officials, and military commanders in the field."[39] State and local customers have often categorized their relationship with DHS and JTTFs as one-sided.[40] This would seem to indicate that the overall Planning and Direction process is one sided and not iterative.

The Planning and Direction phase is also fundamental and vital to developing collection strategies and priorities for collection. The current domestic intelligence model does not effectively identify, share, or integrate concerns from a wide variety of organizations to prioritize and match them to national security objectives.[41] There is no collection requirements mechanism that spans across multiple levels of government to support the development of collection strategies and prioritization.[42] This issue is further compounded by the lack of understanding and the uncertainty as to the role of the several organizations involved in domestic intelligence.[43] The lack of a well-understood process and the continued uncertainty over organizational missions and roles are symptomatic of poor vertical and horizontal integration among federal, state, and local partners.[44]

There have been several initiatives to mitigate poor vertical and horizontal integration. An integral element of the FBI's intelligence reform resides with their efforts to fully materialize their FIGs to execute the intelligence cycle at the tactical level while ensuring its linkage to national security objectives.[45] DHS has also embedded intelligence officers at several State and Local Fusion Centers to facilitate information sharing and intelligence.[46] These initiatives, while necessary, will fall short if they are not part of a comprehensive, integrated and interagency strategy that outline a clear process. They will also fall short if state and local partners lack the capacity and guidelines to perform the intelligence cycle. As one local official stated: "[S]tandard operating procedures should reflect guidelines for intelligence collection, retention, and dissemination, but we haven't done a great job in doing so. Issues are simply talked about as they come up."[47]

COLLECTION

The purpose of the Collection phase is to identify and collect those necessary *essential elements of information* that answer an identified intelligence gap. One definition for essential elements of information (EEIs) is: "The most critical information requirements regarding the adversary and the environment needed by the commander [or decision maker] by a particular time to relate with other available information and intelligence in order to assist in reaching a logical decision."[48] These EEIs are collectable elements, do not reside in existing databases, and cannot be readily addressed by analysts. It requires a new effort to collect unknown data or validate existing assumptions. The timeliness of collection is dependent on the intelligence discipline that is utilized to satisfy the intelligence gap. For example, identifying, validating, and collecting intelligence as a result of an imagery intelligence (IMINT) requirement is often much quicker than tasking a human intelligence (HUMINT) source to gain the same information. Certain intelligence disciplines will lend themselves to satisfying particular intelligence gaps.

As noted above, for domestic intelligence activities, the term *collection* immediately brings civil liberty concerns to the forefront. The intelligence and law enforcement communities are charged with ensuring security, however, the collection and retention of data on individuals encroaches upon privacy.[49] These concerns are further compounded if the guidelines and processes governing collection activities, particularly at the state and local level, are ambiguous, vague, or nonexistent.[50] Any future collection process that integrates federal, state, and local efforts requires clear guidelines, data retention standards, and robust oversight mechanisms to make it viable.

Another issue stems from a lack of understanding about what intelligence collection entails. Intelligence collection is exploratory in nature whereas evidence gathering focuses on building cases for legal prosecution.[51] This has been one criticism of the FBI. In the absence of a clear and integrated collection process, there remain continuing concerns on the FBI's ability to perform intelligence collection.[52] If the FIGs are not empowered to direct and hold special agents accountable for collection, any FIG implementation efforts or wider FBI intelligence reform will be for naught.[53] These concerns also apply to state and local partners, where an understanding of the intelligence cycle and its processes are not uniformly understood.[54]

Concerns whether organizations with a strong law enforcement ethos are postured to perform collection activities are compounded by a larger issue—the total lack of an integrated process or underlying architecture. In a loose confederation of organizations engaged in domestic intelligence activities, this lack of process undermines any efforts to ensure precision in collection activities where collection efforts are linked specifically to a set of priorities.[55] This lack of architecture leads to a highly inefficient system. The United States possesses extremely robust and sophisticated collection systems. As a result, there is a natural tendency to over emphasize data collection.[56] There will be limited coordination, duplication of scarce resources, and potential conflicts with multiple organizations operating in a highly decentralized model and without a unified architecture.[57]

PROCESSING AND EXPLOITATION

The Processing and Exploitation phase converts collected data into a usable format for analysis. This important step focuses on ensuring data quality, common formatting, and data basing of information to ensure that it is readily accessible, retrievable, and useful for analysis. As with collection, the timeliness of processing and exploiting data can vary. Highly complex measurement and signature intelligence (MASINT) collection may require significant processing time before transforming it into a usable product. Signals intelligence (SIGINT) intercepts require translation and quality control. The end result of these tasks, however, is to make the data content relevant and usable to the customer. As a result, the customer's specification as to how the data is formatted, tagged, and presented is essential in this phase.

There have been significant discussions on intelligence fusion in the post-9/11 environment. *Fusion* is "the process of examining all sources of intelligence and information to derive a complete assessment of activity."[58] The central premise of this process is to therefore integrate disparate streams of intelligence and data.[59] It is not merely to regurgitate existing reporting or assertions, but rather to examine, evaluate, and integrate fundamental data sources to discover previously unseen relationships. As such, the fusion process is predicated on the speed and facility of access to information and data. The underlying processing and exploitation systems that format, tag, correlate, and classify data are therefore vital to supporting this process. How these systems are managed and supported is vital not only to the Processing and Exploitation step of the intelligence cycle, but to Dissemination and Integration. The implementation of processes to support these phases is driven not only by technology, but by also by policies based on a need-to-share vice need-to-know standard.

Information sharing has also been a significant post-9/11 issue. Numerous organizations have initiated well-meaning attempts to pass information; however, the lack of processes and duplication of effort have led to information overload.[60] Additionally, there are concerns with the quality of the data that is passed.[61] Merely processing and exploiting data without implementing process safeguards to prevent circular reporting and ensure the quality of the data can lead to serious consequences. The lack of validation and corroboration of data was the WMD Commission's central finding of the Defense HUMINT Service's mishandling of Curveball, the cover name for the HUMINT source who alleged that Iraq had WMD materials.[62]

Converting raw intelligence data into usable formats is integral to ensuring effective information sharing. In fact, it is the foundational basis for future retrieval, access, and database research. In a decentralized domestic intelligence model, collaboration among a wide variety of partners is predicated on common approaches to ensure data quality standards and formats. It is also based on common policies to ensure information access. Common approaches, processes, and policies also ensure greater accessibility and retrievability of data into a more usable form.

ANALYSIS AND PRODUCTION

At the core of the intelligence cycle lies the Analysis and Production phase. The development of intelligence products through various analytic techniques should be linked to the expressed requirement of the customer, whether a decision maker or another organization. To be effective, analysts must have access to monitor, evaluate, and interpret a wide array of information and data from various sources to fuse and develop analytic products. The production step of this phase prioritizes and deconflicts the creation of intelligence assessments that support various customers. Production managers ensure that the appropriate tasks are levied to the different areas of an intelligence center and track the satisfaction and completion of the product.

There are two analytic challenges in the post-9/11 era. First, is the necessity to access and evaluate large amounts of data through use of multiple analytic techniques. The challenge to accessing the wide variety of tools and databases stems from their proliferation. Many of these systems, such as the Homeland Security Information Network (HSIN), are cumbersome and duplicative.[63] The reality is also that many of these systems remain stovepiped.

Second, there is a large demand for analytic expertise. There are numerous organizations, both in the federal-state-local governments and the private sector that require homeland security analysis. Developing a professional corps of analysts to meet the diverse set of homeland security customers and varied intelligence disciplines (strategic, tactical, technical, critical infrastructure, criminal, and others) requires a long-term, sustained, and focused commitment.[64] Analysts are not created overnight and developing expertise is a product of experience and a commitment to training. To date, there has been a limited approach from the federal government to support sustained homeland security analytic training efforts.[65] There is also a limited capacity of training programs that focus on critical thinking and advanced analytic techniques to train analysts in sufficient numbers. As outlined in the Markle report: "The rich variety of analytic methods is seldom taught formally. . . . Capabilities analysis, Intelligence-target modeling, Pattern or trend analysis, Link analysis, Temporal analysis, Financial analysis, Poll-based analysis."[66] The limited training capacity is further compounded by the limited venues that exist for training.[67]

Given these limitations, the issue becomes how to rationalize the analytic tools and systems that are required for analysts to perform their tasks. Another issue centers on capacity building and ensuring that there are tailored training programs to develop the next generation of analytic expertise and in sufficient numbers to meet future needs. Ensuring the long-term development of analytic tools and technological systems while developing analysts with the right skill sets and in sufficient numbers is a long-term and strategic undertaking. It will also be a challenge to recruit and retain personnel in high demand. A recent FBI personnel retention review revealed that 65 percent of analysts might stay for five years, but were unsure because of poor human resource strategies and programs.[68]

DISSEMINATION AND INTEGRATION

A streamlined Dissemination and Integration process facilitates the timely delivery of intelligence data and products to customers. As with the Processing and Exploitation step, the rapid dissemination of intelligence is largely dependent on technology and policy. The need for rapid dissemination of intelligence and data derived from national systems to the tactical user was one of the primary lessons of the first Gulf War. In the domestic intelligence context, untimely dissemination and poor integration methods in the FBI prevented it from piecing together key intelligence elements concerning the 9/11 hijackers, even when specific messages were transmitted to the FBI headquarters.[69] The Dissemination and Integration phase requires streamlined processes that enable the customer to both *push and pull* requests for intelligence and products. A sound and well-understood dissemination architecture based on clearly understood policies supports the overall agility of the intelligence enterprise.

The 9/11 Commission found significant dissemination shortfalls, both within organizational structures, such as in the FBI, and across organizational lines.[70] In the post-9/11 environment, the key to achieving a responsive and agile domestic intelligence enterprise will be the vertical dissemination of intelligence and information from federal organizations to state and local customers and vice versa.[71] Information must be mobile so that it can span across various architectures for ready access by a wide variety of customers.[72] Additionally, it does not suffice to limit dissemination to simply share analytic conclusions. Seemingly meaningless bits of data may be the essential piece of information to another customer.[73] As such, analytic conclusions and assertions in products must be accompanied by supporting data and sources.

Dissemination initiatives since 9/11 have seen their successes and drawbacks. The NCTC has worked closely with the ITACG to improve the classified NCTC On Line Secret (NOL-S) software tool to better support state and local needs.[74] The dissemination drawbacks, however, stem from the proliferation and implementation of duplicative systems. The fielding of the HSIN is an excellent example. The push by DHS to field HSIN, despite the existence of other systems with similar functions, such as the Regional Information Sharing System (RISS), the Joint Regional Information Exchange System (JRIES), and Law Enforcement Online (LEO), and coupled with poor preplanning led to a disjointed implementation process.[75] The system's planning shortfalls were the result of an accelerated implementation timeline.[76] Additionally, there was very little training provided when the system was fielded.[77]

The implementation of dissemination systems to support information-sharing efforts can result in severe setbacks if they are not properly managed and transitioned into the field. Implementation strategies with significant stakeholder participation and input are required. The creation of the Information Sharing Establishment (ISE) under the DNI and the Information Sharing Council to support stakeholder inputs[78] will have to be sustained to realize streamlined dissemination architecture.

EVALUATION AND FEEDBACK

Some intelligence cycle models include the Evaluation and Feedback step, while others do not. As a result, this step is often the most overlooked. When viewed in its proper perspective, Evaluation and Feedback is the *only* step that completes the cycle to ensure that the IC is meeting the customer's need. Without customer feedback, the intelligence cycle becomes a linear process where customers submit requirements, but do not ultimately provide the context and customer perspective into what the IC is producing. It is ultimately the responsibility of the customer and analyst to evaluate the timeliness and content of intelligence reporting and data to determine whether the intelligence produced is meeting the customer's requirement.

Although there is an acknowledged need to evaluate and provide feedback on intelligence products, there is very little emphasis from agencies within the IC to do so. This lack of emphasis has led to serious drawbacks in collaboration and awareness. Intelligence reports from the National Security Agency (NSA) received little to no feedback from the Counter Terrorism Center (CTC), the pre-9/11 organization for counterterrorism activities. There was very little collaboration on the part of the Central Intelligence Agency (CIA) on analytic and collection efforts with the Defense Intelligence Agency (DIA) on terrorism targets.[79] In a community where information is power, there has been very little incentive to evaluate and share feedback with other agencies on intelligence, assessments, sources, and methods.

The lack of a common evaluation and feedback process, and mechanism is another drawback. Although there are several independent feedback mechanisms from agencies to solicit input on the content, timeliness, and relevancy of their products, there is no integrated process or mechanism that examines the evaluation and feedback of intelligence across organizational and intelligence functions. As a result, it is very difficult for decision makers, managers, and analysts to draw conclusions from assessments and feedback on intelligence products to determine whether they are meeting or satisfying stated requirements.

The lack of incentives and integrated processes also results in several obstacles to completing the intelligence cycle. In a decentralized domestic intelligence model characterized by multiple organizations, intelligence producers, and collectors, it is very difficult to assess whether intelligence is in fact satisfying the requirement. As a result, policy makers and customers are often dissatisfied with the intelligence they receive.

CONCLUSION

There have been significant discussions and initiatives on how to optimize the IC since 9/11. Most of these initiatives have resulted in significant organizational changes, restructuring and the creation of the ODNI, DHS, and NCTC. Other agencies such as the FBI have focused on reforming their organizations. As it has been stated: "[I]ntelligence reform, especially since 9/11, has been focused too much on the *reform* of structures and too little on the alteration of process."[80] As a recent RAND study outlines, in a decentralized domestic intelligence architecture where various intelligence capabilities are spread across multiple organizations, "preventing terrorism depends not just on the performance of individual organizations, but on how the entire system works together."[81] Merely assigning blame to one organization when there is a shortfall misses the point. The intelligence cycle is the common methodology for how the intelligence system is supposed to work together.

The organizational focus of intelligence initiatives, the creation of DHS and other agencies since 9/11 involves the application of significant resources and focus. In the case of DHS, it also resulted in the significant restructuring of formerly independent agencies under one overarching umbrella. The intent of DHS was integrative, to fuse, facilitate, and develop intelligence products aimed at strengthening homeland security. The role of DHS was further obscured by the creation of NCTC and a resurgent domestic intelligence focus in the FBI. As a result, domestic intelligence functions are not centralized at the federal level, but are largely represented by a tripartite relationship between DHS, NCTC, and the FBI.

Significant organizational change translates into significant transition costs—the disruption and refocusing of missions, reassignment of personnel, upgraded training requirements, new systems, and so forth.[82] While the establishment of policies and processes carry their own transition costs,[83] the creation of common architectures and approaches to unify the various organizations involved in domestic, or any other form of intelligence, would unify the community as a whole. It would also focus on the real issues that have plagued the IC since its inception in 1947, such as improving information sharing, creating transparency, eliminating stovepipes, and developing more of a joint approach to intelligence.

Specifically with regard to the issue of domestic intelligence, there have been numerous discussions on the creation of a single agency or an agency within an agency approach to conduct domestic intelligence activities, similar to Great Britain's MI5.[84] This was the original intent of DHS' intelligence charter. The creation of another agency, while having the benefit of focusing on one mission task, will also result in significant transition costs. A single domestic intelligence agency is not necessarily better at preventing terrorist attacks.[85] Creating another agency would result in having to resolve new organizational seams, ensure information sharing, and create additional oversight issues for Congress; the same issues that require resolution today.

The transformation model encompasses organizational reform, process mechanisms, and technological implementation. It also envisions the combination of these three elements to achieve an envisioned end state. While it may not be clear what the envisioned end-state for domestic intelligence or even homeland security might entail,[86] the guidance contained in the DNI's national intelligence strategy outlines several noteworthy objectives:

- Build an integrated intelligence capability to address threats to the homeland
- Create an information-sharing environment in which access to terrorism information is matched to the roles, responsibilities, and missions of all organizations engaged in countering terrorism
- Appropriately fund and closely integrate within the larger IC the intelligence elements of the Department of Justice and DHS
- Ensure that all IC components assist in facilitating the integration of collection and analysis against terrorists
- Connect state, local, and tribal entities and the private sector to our homeland security and intelligence efforts[87]

The vital necessity for integration efforts is specified in these objectives. The *National Strategy for Homeland Security* also emphasizes that these efforts are a shared responsibility,[88] which would imply that the various domestic intelligence capabilities residing in multiple organizations should be linked together through common processes and technologies under an enterprise approach.

The combination of networked federal agencies (DHS, NCTC, and FBI) coupled with other agencies to include state and local customers can replicate a more centralized model with a domestic intelligence agency at its hub. The key element is to network these capabilities under common standards and protocols.[89] Using the intelligence cycle and its various steps as a common point for evaluating processes and assessing future implementation strategies is ideal.

As Professor Ernest R. May stated: "Americans would be foolish to forget how little can be foreseen. When the USS Lexington was launched in 1927 almost no one imagined its need 15 years later in the Coral Sea to check the Japanese conquest of the mid-Pacific."[90] As originally envisioned, the aircraft carrier was viewed as a support element to the main striking force consisting of battleships. After striking a severe blow to battleship targets at Pearl Harbor, the aircraft carrier became the main striking force for the U.S. Navy in World War II. For domestic intelligence activities, an integrated community of agencies bounded by common processes and integrated approaches will serve to combat the present terrorism threat and unforeseen future ones.

Creating another domestic intelligence agency is not the answer. While decision makers need to ensure that the ODNI, DHS, NCTC, and FBI are appropriately resourced and focused, real transformation will only be realized through the implementation of common processes and objectives as envisioned in the *National Strategy for Homeland Security*. Common processes and technologies inherently foster information sharing and transparency. They also support the ability of oversight mechanisms to prevent *mission creep* and ensure that domestic intelligence activities are properly balanced within the spectrum bounded by the dual needs of civil liberty and domestic security.

NOTES

1. National Commission on Terrorist Attacks upon the United States, *The 9/11 Commission Report* (New York: W.W. Norton & Company, 2003), 408; U.S. Congress, Permanent Select Committee on Intelligence and Senate Select Committee on Intelligence, *Report of the Joint Inquiry into the Terrorist Attacks of September 11, 2001*, 107th Congress, 2nd Session, December 2002, S. Rept. No. 107–531, H. Rept. No. 107–792, 45; http://www.gpoaccess.gov/serialset/creports/pdf/fullreport_errata.pdf.

2. United States Government Accountability Office, *Homeland Security: Preliminary Information on Federal Actions to Address Challenges Faced by State and Local Fusion Centers*, GAO-07-1241T (Washington, D.C.: September 27, 2007), 4, http://www.gao.gov/new.items/d071241t.pdf.

3. Kate Martin, "Domestic Intelligence and Civil Liberties," *SAIS Review* 24, no. 1 (Winter-Spring 2004): 8.

4. Kim Taipale, "Rethinking Foreign Intelligence Surveillance," *World Policy Journal* (Winter 2006/2007): 78.

5. Benjamin Netanyahu, *Fighting Terrorism: How Democracies Can Defeat the International Terrorist Network* (New York: Farrar, Straus and Giroux, 1995), 30.

6. As highlighted by warrantless electronic surveillance by the National Security Agency (NSA), the monitoring of U.S. persons by the Department of Defense's (DOD) now defunct Counter Intelligence Field Activity (CIFA), and the Department of Justice's (DOJ) mishandling of National Security Letters.

7. Michael German and Jay Stanley, *What's Wrong With Fusion Centers?* (New York: American Civil Liberties Union, 2007), 6, http://www.aclu.org/pdfs/privacy/fusioncenter_20071212.pdf.

8. U.S. Congress, *Homeland Security Act of 2002*, Public Law 107-296, sec. 101 (2002), 8; Government Printing Office, http://frwebgate.access.gpo.gov/cgi-bin/getdoc.cgi?dbname=107_cong_public_laws&docid=f:publ296.107.pdf. Section 101 established the Department of Homeland Security and combined several independent agencies and personnel under its organization.

9. Department of Homeland Security, *DHS Intelligence Enterprise Strategic Plan* (Washington, D.C.: Department of Homeland Security, 2006), 3; Federation of American Scientists, http://www.fas.org/irp/agency/dhs/stratplan.pdf.

10. Eugene Bardach, "How Do They Stack Up? The 9/11 Commission Report and the Management Literature," *International Public Management Journal* 8, no. 3 (2005): 356.

11. Gregory F. Treverton, *Reorganizing US Domestic Intelligence: Assessing the Options* (Santa Monica, Calif.: RAND, 2008), 74.

12. Brian A. Jackson, *The Challenge of Domestic Intelligence in a Free Society* (Santa Monica, Calif.: RAND, 2009), 84.

13. Jim Arkedis, *Getting Intelligence Reform Right* (Washington, D.C.: Progressive Policy Institute, 2008), 5.

14. *Homeland Security Act of 2002*, Section 201 outlines the department's intelligence responsibilities.

15. Executive Order (E.O.) 13354, *National Counterterrorism Center* (Washington, D.C.: Office of the President, August 27, 2004), 2.

16. U.S. Congress, House, *Homeland Security Intelligence at a Cross-Roads: The Office of Intelligence and Analysis' Vision for 2008*, Hearing Before the Subcommittee on Intelligence, Information Sharing, and Terrorism Risk Assessment, 110th Congress, 2nd Session (February 26, 2008), 2; Federation of American Scientists, http://www.fas.org/irp/congress/2008_hr/hsintel.pdf.

17. Congressional Research Service, *The National Counterterrorism Center: Implementation Challenges and Issues for Congress*, RL32816 (Washington, D.C.: Library of Congress, March 24, 2005), 12.

18. Bardach, "How Do They Stack Up? The 9/11 Commission Report and the Management Literature," 358.

19. Treverton, *Reorganizing US Domestic Intelligence*, 33.

20. Arkedis, *Getting Intelligence Reform Right*, 5.

21. Program Manager, Information Sharing Establishment, *ISE Implementation Plan* (Washington, D.C.: Director of National Intelligence, November 2006), 28, http://www.ise.gov/docs/ISE-impplan-200611.pdf.

22. Ibid., 29.

23. Congressional Research Service, *FBI Intelligence Reform Since September 11, 2001: Issues and Options for Congress*, RL32336 (Washington, D.C.: The Library of Congress, August 4, 2004), 10; U.S. Department of State's Foreign Press Center, http://fpc.state.gov/documents/organization/39334.pdf.

24. Office of Homeland Security, *State and Local Actions for Homeland Security* (Washington, D.C.: Executive Office of the President of the United States, July 2002), 25–28, http://www.ncs.gov/library/policy_docs/State_and_Local_Actions_for_Homeland_Security.pdf.

25. United States General Accountability Office, *Efforts to Improve Information Sharing Need to be Strengthened*, GAO-03–760 (Washington, D.C.: GPO, August 2003), 38, http://www.gao.gov/new.items/d03760.pdf.

26. Congressional Research Service, *Intelligence Reform Implementation at the Federal Bureau of Investigation: Issues and Options for Congress*, RL33033 (Washington, D.C.: The Library of Congress, August 16, 2005), 21, http://www.fas.org/sgp/crs/intel/RL33033.pdf.

27. Congressional Research Service, *Homeland Security Intelligence: Perceptions, Statutory Definitions, and Approaches*, RL33616 (Washington, D.C.: The Library of Congress, August 18, 2006), 16, http://www.usis.it/pdf/other/RL33616.pdf.

28. Williamson Murray and Allan R. Millet, eds., *Military Innovation in the Interwar Period* (Cambridge, UK: Cambridge University Press, 1996), 3. Murray and Millet identify changes to organization, doctrine (i.e., processes) and technology under a clear idea of what is to be accomplished as the key elements to successful innovation.

29. Congressional Research Service, *The National Counterterrorism Center*, RL32816 (Washington, D.C.: Library of Congress, March 24, 2005), 12, http://www.fas.org/sgp/crs/intel/RL32816.pdf; United States Government Accountability Office, *Department of Homeland Security: Progress Report on Implementation of Mission Management and Functions*, GAO-07–1081T (Washington, D.C.: September 6, 2007), 3.

30. Congressional Research Service, *Intelligence Issues for Congress*, RL33539 (Washington, D.C.: Library of Congress, January 9, 2009), 18, http://www.fas.org/sgp/crs/intel/RL33539.pdf.

31. Treverton, *Reorganizing US Domestic Intelligence*, 89. Treverton weighs the pros and cons of organizational change in chapter 6.

32. Department of Homeland Security, Office of the Inspector General, *Homeland Security Information Network Could Support Information Sharing More Effectively*, OIG 06–38 (Washington, D.C.: GPO, June 2006), 11–12, http://www.fas.org/irp/agency/dhs/hsin0606.pdf; Congressional Research Service, *FBI Intelligence Reform Since September 11, 2001*, RL32336, 15; Congressional Research Service, *Intelligence Reform Implementation at the Federal Bureau of Investigation*, RL33033, 36–37. The shortcomings of deploying the DHS Homeland Security Information Network (HSIN) and the FBI Virtual Case File (VCF) system typify the technological implementation challenges in the post-9/11 era.

33. David H. Gray and Chris Slade, "Applying the Intelligence Cycle Model to Counterterrorism Intelligence for Homeland Security," *European Journal of Scientific Research* 24, no. 4 (2008): 498.

34. Brian A. Jackson, *The Challenge of Domestic Intelligence in a Free Society* (Santa Monica, Calif.: RAND, 2009), 49.

35. Gray and Slade, "Applying the Intelligence Cycle Model," 498.

36. Congressional Research Service, *FBI Intelligence Reform Since September 11, 2001*, RL32336, 23.

37. Executive Order (E.O.) 13354, *National Counterterrorism Center* (Washington, D.C.: Office of the President, August 27, 2004), 2, http://travel.state.gov/pdf/Executive_Order_13354.pdf.

38. Project on National Security Reform, *Forging a New Shield* (Arlington, Va.: Center for the Study of the Presidency, 2008), 100.

39. U.S. Congress. Senate, Select Committee on Intelligence. *Statement for the Record by Michael Lieter: Acting Director for the National Counterterrorism Center* (May 6, 2008), 3, http://www.fas.org/irp/congress/2008_hr/050608leiter.pdf.

40. U.S. Congress, Senate, Committee on Intelligence, Intelligence Reform Hearing, *Statement of James W. Spears: West Virginia Homeland Security Advisor* (January 25, 2007), 6–8, http://ftp.fas.org/irp/congress/2007_hr/012507spears.pdf.

41. Project on National Security Reform, *Forging a New Shield*, 40.

42. Gray and Slade, "Applying the Intelligence Cycle Model," 500.

43. Jackson, *The Challenge of Domestic Intelligence*, 70.

44. Project on National Security Reform, *Forging a New Shield*, 249.

45. Congressional Research Service, *FBI Intelligence Reform Since September 11, 2001*, RL32336, 21.

46. U.S. Congress, House, Committee on Homeland Security, Homeland Security Intelligence and Information Sharing, *Statement for the Record by Charles Allen: Under Secretary for Intelligence and Analysis, Department of Homeland Security* (September 24, 2008), 7, http://www.fas.org/irp/congress/2008_hr/092408allen.pdf.

47. K. Jack Riley, Gregory F. Treverton, Jeremy M. Wilson, and Lois M. Davis, *State and Local Intelligence in the War on Terrorism* (Santa Monica, Calif.: RAND, 2005), 33.

48. Joint Chiefs of Staff, *Joint Publication 1–02: Department of Defense Dictionary of Military and Associated Terms* (Washington, D.C.: GPO, March 17, 2009), 190.

49. Treverton, *Reorganizing US Domestic Intelligence*, 39.

50. Riley et al., *State and Local Intelligence*, 31.

51. Treverton, *Reorganizing US Domestic Intelligence*, 27.

52. Congressional Research Service, *FBI Intelligence Reform Since September 11, 2001*, RL32336, 19.

53. Congressional Research Service, *Intelligence Reform Implementation at the Federal Bureau of Investigation*, RL33033, 23.

54. Congressional Research Service, *A Summary of Fusion Centers: Core Issues and Options for Congress*, RL34177 (Washington, D.C.: Library of Congress, September 19, 2007), 36, http://www.fas.org/sgp/crs/intel/RL34177.pdf.

55. Congressional Research Service, *FBI Intelligence Reform Since September 11, 2001*, RL32336, 36.

56. Gregory F. Treverton, Seth G. Jones, Steven Boraz, and Phillip Lipscy, *Toward a Theory of Intelligence* (Santa Monica, Calif.: RAND, 2006), 14.

57. Treverton, *Reorganizing US Domestic Intelligence*, 30.

58. Joint Chiefs of Staff, *Department of Defense Dictionary of Military and Associated Terms*, 223.

59. Congressional Research Service, *A Summary of Fusion Centers*, RL34177, 5.

60. Riley et al., *State and Local Intelligence*, 46.

61. Treverton, *Reorganizing US Domestic Intelligence*, 32.

62. Commission on the Intelligence Capabilities of the United States Regarding Weapons of Mass Destruction (the WMD Commission), *Report to the President of the United States* (Washington, D.C.: GPO, March 31, 2005), 88–89, http://www.wmd.gov/report/wmd_report.pdf.

63. U.S. Congress, House Committee on Homeland Security, Subcommittee on Intelligence, Information Sharing, and Terrorism Risk Assessment, *Statement of William Harris: Delaware Information & Analysis Center Commander* (May 10, 2007), 3, http://homeland.house.gov/SiteDocuments/20070510132259–40476.pdf.

64. Lee S. Strickland, "The Information Shortcomings of 9/11," *Information Management Journal* 38, no. 6 (November/December 2004): 37.

65. The Markle Foundation, *Mobilizing Information to Prevent Terrorism: Accelerating Development of a Trusted Information Sharing Environment*, 3rd Report (July 2006), 30, http://www.markle.org/downloadable_assets/2006_nstf_report3.pdf.

66. Ibid., 53–55.

67. Riley et al., *State and Local Intelligence*, 38.

68. U.S. Department of Justice, Office of the Inspector General, Audit Division, *Follow-Up Audit of the Federal Bureau of Investigation's Efforts to Hire, Train, and Retain Intelligence Analysts*, Audit Report 07–30 (April 2007), iii, http://www.justice.gov/oig/reports/FBI/a0730/final.pdf.

69. U.S. Congress, *Report of the Joint Inquiry*, 117.

70. National Commission on Terrorist Attacks, *The 9/11 Commission Report*, 79.

71. Dana R. Dillon, "Breaking Down Intelligence Barriers for Homeland Security," *The Heritage Foundation: Backgrounder* 1536 (April 15, 2002): 4, http://www.heritage.org/Research/HomelandSecurity/BG1536.cfm.

72. Department of Defense, Office of the Chief Information Officer, *Department of Defense Information Sharing Strategy* (Washington, D.C.: Department of Defense, May 4, 2007), 7, http://www.defenselink.mil/cio-nii/docs/InfoSharingStrategy.pdf.

73. Department of Defense, *DoD Roles and Missions in Homeland Security* (Washington, D.C.: Defense Science Board, September 2004), 9.

74. U.S. Congress, *Statement for the Record by Michael Lieter*, 2.

75. Department of Homeland Security, *Homeland Security Information Network Could Support Information Sharing More Effectively*, 11–12.

76. Ibid., 3.

77. United States Government Accountability Office, *Homeland Security Information Network needs to Be Better Coordinated with Key State and Local Initiatives*, GAO 07–822T (Washington, D.C.: GPO. May 10, 2007), 3, http://www.gao.gov/new.items/d07822t.pdf.

78. U.S. Congress, *Intelligence Reform and Terrorism Prevention Act of 2004*, Public Law 108–458 (Washington, D.C.: GPO, December 17, 2004), 1016, http://www.nctc.gov/docs/pl108_458.pdf.

79. U.S. Congress, *Report of the Joint Inquiry*, 342.

80. Gray and Slade, "Applying the Intelligence Cycle Model," 516.

81. Jackson, *The Challenge of Domestic Intelligence*, 124.

82. Treverton, *Reorganizing US Domestic Intelligence*, 92.

83. Jackson, *The Challenge of Domestic Intelligence*, 209.

84. Treverton, *Reorganizing US Domestic Intelligence*, iii.

85. Burch, James. "A Domestic Intelligence Agency for the United States? A Comparative Analysis of Domestic Intelligence Agencies and Their Implications

for Homeland Security," *Homeland Security Affairs* III, no. 2 (June 2007): 15, http://www.hsaj.org/?article=3.2.2.

86. Bellavita, Christopher. "Changing Homeland Security: What Is Homeland Security?" *Homeland Security Affairs* IV, no. 2 (June 2008): 1, http://www.hsaj.org/?article=4.2.1.

87. Director of National Intelligence, *The National Intelligence Strategy of the United States of America—Transformation through Integration and Innovation* (Washington, D.C.: GPO, October 2005), 5–6, 11.

88. Homeland Security Council, *National Strategy for Homeland Security* (Washington, D.C.: GPO, October 2007), 4.

89. Office of the President, *National Strategy for Information Sharing* (Washington, D.C.: GPO, October 2007), A1–1.

90. Ernest R. May, "Intelligence: Backing into the Future," *Foreign Affairs* 71, no. 3 (Summer 1992): 64.

Fusion Centers and Beyond: The Future of Intelligence Assessment in an Information-Deluged Era

Guntram F. A. Werther

Fusion centers are a bureaucratic response to the intelligence community's too-slow realization that "henceforth the world will be run by synthesizers."[1] This constitutes an existential threat to many traditional intelligence community (IC) functions, if not to the IC itself. It is also the driver of IC expansion to new areas of focus, to new knowledge management arrangements, and of fundamental organizational and operational rearrangements within the IC.

What is the purpose of secret intelligence agencies, especially in addressing the large national security questions, when the information needed is almost entirely within the open world and the expertise needed to solve these complex and adaptively dynamic questions also lies in the open world? Synthesis, within a complexly adaptive world, leads to holistic ways of thinking and acting, or, barring that, to failure as reality bites. Perhaps nothing shows this complex adaptive reality better than the U.S. focus on fighting terrorism, while its economy, and the global economy, imploded in plain sight. The CIA now gives the president a daily economic brief. Society was not lacking data, but lacking understanding involving the complex interactions of many things and processes. Arguably, the self-inflicted strategic and national security damage deriving from this misunderstanding was greater than that of any terrorist event yet seen.

One could make parallel arguments, for example, involving the war on drugs. While we were so focused in Latin America, almost the whole region went Socialist and became less congenial to U.S. interests. Mexico became a national security threat on our very border that is listed on par with Pakistan's increasing national weakness in terms of national risk.

Similarly, it is now increasingly understood that reduced U.S. global power is as much, if not more, about poor U.S. education quality and institutional effectiveness as about weapons, force, and militaries. These insights are now recognized quite broadly, so that militaries are now increasingly engaged in broad social change enterprises, and intelligence organizations, both law enforcement and the IC, are broadening vistas far beyond fusion center functions.

Fusion centers are multiagency, usually task centered, information sharing and integration *operations*, created as part of much larger police, military, and IC reconsiderations of intelligence assessment and operations practices.

DROWNING IN DATA WHILE STARVING FOR WISDOM

Today's basic problem is that we are deluged by information, yet often lack individual and institutional synthesizing capacities capable of yielding holistic understanding, hence wisdom. We still focus on the trees (or parts thereof), missing the forests. We go after the sexy problem of the moment and miss yawning problems of the whole.

A holistic approach to intelligence means integrative and synthesizing orientation to information and human understanding that are more than multidisciplinary, multiagency, and/or cross-cultural but are essentially boundaryless dispositions of mind that endlessly fold in information in ways that illuminate the working of the parts within the whole, as well as the workings of the whole entity within a complex adaptive reality. A holistic view of intelligence assessment goes beyond fusing information to further tasked-for agency agendas and their operational intelligence assignments, to ask, what else happens when we do, or do not do, this or that?

With some exceptions, the IC does not typically do broad and deep studies that yield fundamental insights, largely because consumers of intelligence do not want much beyond short-term "reporting."[2] Simultaneously, the range of interests now viewed as being within the portfolio of the national state has clearly expanded, yielding complex adaptive system problems of magnitudes previously not encountered by governments. Old ways have failed to address now-necessary tasks and their changing information integration needs.

As an interim solution, fusion centers are a necessary but insufficient response to succeeding within a complex adaptive-dynamic world in which most of the expertise will reside outside of the government/intelligence community, where individual synthesizing minds are an always rare but highly necessary commodity, and where most of the changes, opportunities, and problems encountered will have such broadly holistic attributes that they are not well served by piecemeal solutions.

Success today and tomorrow requires individual synthesizing minds[3] *and* synthesizing organizations that reach far *beyond* the multiagency fusion center model.

Consequently, the fusion center is a partial solution, and then there is the *beyond*. And most of the needed attention for the early 21st century will lie in intellectually, institutionally, and operationally linking synthetic capacities located within governmental organizations, with synthetic capacities residing outside of them.

THE NEEDS OF FUSION (SYNTHESIZING) AND EXISTENTIAL IC ISSUES

This need is so fundamental that at several recent intelligence colloquia, senior IC executives almost uniformly expressed two concerns: (1) the perennial concern over hiring and retaining talent within IC agencies that are in competition for the same people with multiple other actors and (2) the future raison d'etre of intelligence services in a world both overflowing with information and where most of the multiple dimensioned talent and information resides outside of the government intelligence services. Their existential question was, who are we to be?

There is no question that agency-centered tactical and operational considerations will remain, and that in some areas secrets matter greatly. The task-centered fusion center staffed by multiagency employees and contractors is a highly useful form at this operational/tactical level.

One problem is that for more and more national security areas, the information is fluid, open-sourced, and thus secrecy, plus bureaucracy, plus exclusivity is not a virtue.[4] A second problem is that tactical and operational can get in the way of seeing the *dynamic whole*. Center-itis is only a different kind of stovepipe: a broader straw through which to view a dynamic complex adaptive world. The danger here is that a counterterrorism fusion center, or an information warfare fusion center, really will not be adequately holistic. A third problem is that in a complex adaptive world view, changing one thing can shift the whole, by way of the dynamic interconnectedness of things. When an operationally induced change is unwisely divorced from the whole view—which a task-oriented (and operational) fusion center typically will not even have a mandate to solve—very negative unintended consequences can, and will, develop.

Some recent examples include: (1) the desire of officials engaged in the war on drugs for successes countervailing even more importantly desired large-scale political-economic change agendas in places like Afghanistan-Pakistan and the Andean Rim; (2) remembering that economically developing China is also de facto politically and militarily developing China, which inevitably sets up *both* new opportunities *and* conflicts with the United States; and (3) the far less generous observation, which Elizabeth Wurtzel's *Wall Street Journal* piece termed "the march of dunces,"[5] that inevitably occurs when very smart people pursuing one desired good forget (or do not care) that their desired good is connected to everything else. Wurtzel's example here is that *very* rational people pursuing profit, while rationally offloading risk, can sink an economy.

Making sense of such dynamically adaptive complexity features within change, beyond parochial interests, is supposedly one IC future justification for its existence.[6] But, it is also a skill at which the IC is traditionally not very good. Synthesis (fusion), as in fostering broad and deep understanding and wisdom, is needed but rarely encountered within the tyranny-of-the-moment focus within the IC. Solving deep problems holistically, meaning in ways that do not make the cure worse than the original disease, is the enemy of any static bureaucratic orientation to change. Most bureaucracies are pretty well set in their ways, often because these ways worked up to this point in pursuing their tasked, parochial agenda.

Fusion as dynamically adaptive holism fosters wisdom. Fusion as a mere tactical and operational advance of a parochial agenda might do the opposite. You can use fusion centers to technologically get at people that you want to disable or kill and alienate a population to the point of threatening war. This divergence on small-scale expected and large-scale desired outcomes (tactical-operational success vs. long-term strategic success) within fusion system's orientations is fundamental to understanding whether fusion centers are a success.

The visage of managing overflowing information and ameliorating lack of understanding/wisdom is at the forefront in the question of success. Much of what the fusion center and other recent IC synthesis activity does is directed at these twins. The intelligence task, herein, involves always remembering the interconnectedness of things, and not mistaking success at a particular task with solving the problem. Problems come nested and networked into desired outcomes and into other problems. Consequently, there are fusion centers, and there are broader synthesis acts.

Fusion centers as tactical-operation efforts can be successful ways to manage complexity. Barring a mergence into holism, such an outcome cannot be proffered by fusion centers as a strategic asset. Unless fusion centers are embedded into larger thinking frameworks, they are not capable of yielding holistic integrations leading to wisdom.

THE FUSION OF THE FUSION CENTER

In a field once dominated by tactical and operational predilections (with analysis in the relative IC background), needs have shifted toward research-like and strategic orientations,[7] such that "intelligence *analysis* has become the subject,"[8] and intelligence analysis (hereafter assessment) has become progressively more open sourced, less constrained to be within government agencies, and their personnel, and more collegial. Perhaps nowhere is this better seen than in the introduction to *Global*

Trends 2025—A Transformed World, by Thomas C. Fingar, Chairman of the National Intelligence Council, who discusses the ever increasing use of non-American experts within the IC.[9] Seventy percent of intelligence is outsourced to contractors, using many boundary-blurring activities in what used to be a secrecy culture.[10]

Today, and increasingly into the future, dynamically leveraging talent and existing information is power. As a consequence, intelligence analysis is being transformed into a much more collegial affair that is not only outside the box but is outside the IC. Consequently, notions of required outreach for IC operators, the broadening of their internal IC multiagency discussion footprint via Facebook-for-spies type arrangements, and many other fusion/synthesis type activities, that lie beyond the customary boundaries of the IC, are in vogue. As a result, the concept of a task-oriented fusion center as a stand-alone solution entity of government operators/experts (whether contract or proprietary) is now, and will progressively become, ever more untenable.

FUSION CENTERS WITHIN
AN INFORMATION-DELUGED WORLD

Fusion centers, to the extent that they are narrowly task oriented (counterterrorism, organized crime, war on drugs, financial crimes, information warfare) run the risk of fostering just another kind of Balkanization of intelligence and national security activity, unless they are themselves synthesized into higher-level strategic considerations. This realization is one aspect of the *beyond* within which successful fusion centers must be embedded. It takes little insight to notice that fighting the war on drugs and war on terror in places like Afghanistan, the Andean Rim, and so forth, enfolds adaptive complexity features where advancing toward one aim impacts success on the other. Add in ever-shifting multidimensional political, economic, and strategic national security concerns, and the notion of the unlinked task-oriented fusion center too often degrades to fostering very problematic efforts.

The issue that Przeworski and Teune (1982) raise as an analytical fusion problem is that "a change in one element of these syndromes would bring about not only a change in the other elements, but a change in the entire pattern . . . [analysis must be such that] an entire set of interconnected phenomena can be handled at the same time."[11] The issue here is that, for example, whereas the U.S. legal system is a syndrome within the whole of U.S. society, changing one or a few aspects of the legal system can have far-reaching impacts not only on that syndrome (e.g., secrecy in surveillance; indefinite detention of suspects), but also on the pattern of the whole society.

Rand scholars Gregory F. Treverton and C. Bryan Gabbard (2008) further noticed that "every agency has a separate set of research priorities and product lines. . . . Yet none of the agencies knows much of what its colleagues do. . . . For all the language about the importance of intelligence analysis, data sharing, fusion priorities, and the like, the price of doing better is seen as too high for the likely results."[12]

A number of efforts toward building deep understanding and holistic futures forecasting insight are maturing in the IC. It remains true that any task-oriented fusion center must have a focus in order to be effective at its assigned task. Thus, the issue of maintaining focus in both large-scale and small-scale fusion tasks looms large, because it is also true that a change in one element can shift the entire system. We *must* think holistically to understand *any* dynamic syndrome's shifting.[13] We have not solved this.

Finally, linked to each of these points is the truth that "analysts are imprisoned not by organizations or sources, but, rather, by tools."[14] Not only do we not have many analysts that are high-level synthesizers,[15] we also have few assessment tools that work when the world is actually changing. There has been a generic meltdown of cutting-edge forecasting models during our current global political economic situation. The cutting edge in forecasting models and technology usage is not nearly adequate, leading both to conclusions that support the primacy of building up human assessment capacity and/or building up better mechanical tools, or some best practice fusion of both realms.[16] Fusion centers, as a simple and primarily operational solution to managing complexity, will simply fail. Their success hinges upon bolstering human talent.

FUSION CENTERS AND TALENT MANAGEMENT

Along with these several themes, it is therefore useful to address the functionality and limits of fusion centers. Given that the expertise necessary to understand and solve complex national security challenges almost certainly does not reside and will never *be able* to reside within the intelligence organization or the fusion center as narrowly understood, the question arises, "Do intelligence agency officers become contract monitors?"[17] There is quite a bit of evidence that this is occurring under the fusion/synthesis requirements of the current, and future, intelligence workday world. One professional IC officer commented to the author that the only thing contracting out had done was raise the price of talent. The salient point is that the *talent* the IC increasingly needs to address complex adaptive situational and future interests is now so broad that it cannot possibly reside solely within the IC agencies. It follows that if the IC increasingly outsources and develops talent-farming relationships to the point that they become contract monitors for outside talent, the raison d'etre question looms again.

Fusion in this broad sense can lead to a kind of organizational extinction for cold-war-modeled IC services, the point senior IC executives were making. Supporting this view, the ODNI's *2008 Intelligence Community*

Centers for Academic Excellence Seminar revealed that serving (proprietary) intelligence officers will increasingly be working with outside researchers, including graduate students, in ongoing collaboration on projects.[18] The ODNI's National Intelligence Council's *Global Trends 2025* reflects that intelligence research will further reach outside of the government. It is commonplace that a modern IC seminar is indistinguishable from an academic or business one; many of the same people are there. At what point, save as purchaser, can much of this fusion work simply be done elsewhere?

There is a horns-of-the-dilemma issue here: If necessary fusion activity opens up the IC to the extent that they increasingly become contract administrators and organizers of outside talent, they face relevancy issues. If fusion center activities remain relatively limited, special purpose operational, and tactical entities, they guarantee relevancy questions of another kind in an interconnected world with complex adaptive features, syndrome shifting attributes, and melding organizational/personnel boundaries.

The previous discussion ought to have awakened the notion that fusion centers cannot save anything. If they are highly necessary to success in a complex world, then the proprietary and secrecy feature of IC agencies is hard to maintain above relatively narrow tactical-operational agendas.

FUSION CENTERS, CAPACITY, AND INTELLIGENT REFORM

Fusion centers are mainly a bureaucratic response to "stove piping," having the correct information *within the agencies*, but in the wrong bureaucratic places.[19] The real world does not conform to agency mission statements; thus, the emerging broader usage of information fusion within that real world forms the horns of the IC institutional dilemma. The intelligence and national security/police service "legacies," as General Cartwright[20] calls them, are confronting larger change management problems.

Peacekeeping and stability operations, like many of the newer IC efforts, are already multidimensional and multiorganizational affairs. If national economic weakness, lost intellectual property, or low domestic literacy rates can be as much of a national security threat as some guy with a bomb, then the fusion of fusion centers into *the beyond* takes on a meaning far beyond building up tactical and operational synergy.

But we have a technical capacity problem here. We need fusion, but in his classic, *A Random Walk Down Wall Street,* Princeton economist Burton Malkiel concluded that a blindfolded chimpanzee throwing darts at the *Wall Street Journal* could select stocks as well as a money manager can. Predicting the future, whether inside or outside of government, pretty much has the same record.

You can have a fusion center, with all kinds of fusion (synthesis) activity up and down the IC and with related national security/police agencies. But, if you cannot do fusion well beyond the tactical and operational levels, because of the poor state of the forecasting assessment art, then both at the level of analyst skill and at the level of assessment tool capacity, you are in trouble. We are in deep, deep trouble. Changing this holistic incapacity is now a major focus within the IC.

WHAT KIND OF PERSON BELONGS IN A FUSION CENTER

The fusion center seems the natural habitat of the rarest-of-rare persons: the high-level and naturally multidisciplinary/cross-disciplinary integrating thinker—the true synthesizer. You have probably fired or not hired several of these people and almost certainly do not have a career path for them within the organization, because they do not fit. Most people, even most geniuses, are excellent at one thing, and thus they can be task fitted to agency needs and goals. The synthesizer, however, seeks an understanding of the multiplicity of forms and processes and thinks at multiple levels about interconnectedness and change. Because this skill set takes much longer to learn, such people are older.[21] Furthermore, since we mostly do not even try to teach such things,[22] advanced-level synthesizers are usually self-taught. Advanced synthetic thinking cannot in fact be taught.[23] Such ability requires what Gardner calls "the synthesis of synthesizing;"[24] and one does not teach that.

People like this get into trouble within our standardizing, mission-specific, short-answer, and too often paint-by-numbers and just-do-your-job society. Many critics of modern intelligence have bemoaned precisely this unreal, agenda-driven, disconnected, static, nonstrategic, and short-answer reporting style of doing intelligence that remains too prevalent. They notice that such foci eschew the deeply complex and dynamic understanding that advanced synthesis-of-synthesizing talents pursue across boundaries. That observation does not, however, mean that we are going to give up our mental buckets in favor of doing truly holistic thinking.

One of the more humorous, and utterly doomed, exercises currently advanced in response to decades of national hyperspecialization policies is the new organizational bundling of existing specialized experts already on staff to form new multidisciplinary centers, where the terms synthesis and integration, like the term *holistic,* are now upon many lips.[25] Constructed integration and synthesis work of this kind of *Frankenstein construction* involves the building up of wholes from disconnected parts on hand. The institutional hope here is that three buckets of paint and three brushes working in committee can make a Rembrandt. This is the opposite of thinking whole and cannot be further from the truth.[26]

Fundamental researchers and scientists are a situational necessity, as are outside experts, but are not appropriate to a *fusion* center, which is about fusion, and not about finding the building blocks of the universe. It is not even clear that having too much formal scientific training is useful in a fusion endeavor, as compared with a broad and deep understanding of the world.

Subject experts can be farmed (prenetworked to some degree), but not to such a degree that they acquire the institutional affiliation mind-set and associated biases of your organization. Leave them in the waters where you found them! Avoiding the proprietary asset predilection of the cold war spy games.

We see again, regarding both formational developmental types, that the fusion center internally contains little of what it needs to function effectively beyond tactical and operational levels, because deep synthesis talent *must* mostly reside outside of it. But, the point is larger. Contracting with outsiders that *you think you need* in some sense becomes a Frankenstein construction too; you are looking for answers to your problem as you have framed or preframed it.

REALITY BITE BACK

The reality of where we are within the IC and related agencies is far different from this level of attainment as a common thing. An assessment at the ODNI 2008 summer seminar rated the average analyst's ability within the IC at 1.5 on a 5-scale (holistic integration being 5); the fusion and holistic forecasting performance in the academic and private sector is not much better. That result is simply one measure of the status of the U.S. fusion/synthetic thinking effort, with idiosyncratic exceptions to this rule. Partly this outcome is the result of 50 years of hyperspecialization focus in academics and business, and partly it is due to a coemergent primary focus on methods and models (tools) that simply are not up to the task of holistically forecasting the behavior of dynamically adaptive, human-involved complex systems.

The author's judgment is that machines and methods will never accomplish high-order fusion-quality insight, largely for the reasons Sir Isaiah Berlin expressed: it is a species of direct acquaintance. This suggests that attaining singularity is "chimera."[27]

METHODS, TOOLS, AND THE HUMAN ELEMENT IN FUSION ACTIVITY

If the fusion center cannot be about true consilience (unity of all knowledge) or about singularity (man-machine mergence), what can it be?

The problem is *both* with the hammerhead and with the hammer. The quality of analysts is low when graded on their integration ability, *and* the performance of machines and models is low in critical situations. Machines and models are best at synthesis and forecasting when nothing fundamental is changing and typically fail systemically when anything fundamental is changing. Thus machines and models can fuse vast volumes of information, which will be of a great deal of use in static or stable environments. Real-world problems are not static. That fact was Przeworski and Teune's critical insight into the syndrome-shifting nature of complex adaptive wholes, which effective fusion activity, and hence the effective fusion center, must attempt to understand. A change in one variable can change the whole pattern. Now, which change dynamic merges from which pattern shift?

The point is that fusion must take place within the individual mind as a holistic comprehension, and that fusion is not about organizational sharing at all. If the wrong kinds of people are present, nothing beyond increased tactical and operational effectiveness can be expected. It is the sequential experience of the ODNI that not only are the correct people for higher-level synthesis not in the IC agencies, they are not even in the country. This is the fundamental realm of *the fusion center and beyond* motif that is being presented herein for the reader's consideration.

The *Techno-social Predictive Analytics Initiative* symposium for Spring 2009 of the Department of Homeland Security's National Visualization and Analytics Center sums up the matter this way: "There is now increased awareness among subject matter experts, analysts, and decision makers that a combined understanding of interacting physical and human factors is essential in estimating plausible futures for real-world scenarios . . . More specifically, Techno-social Predictive Analytics will define, develop, and evaluate novel modeling algorithms that integrate domain knowledge about interacting physical and human factors."[28] The question is, can this be done with modeling algorithms?

Secretary of Defense Robert Gates warns, "Never neglect the psychological, cultural, political, and human dimensions of warfare, which are invariably tragic, inefficient, and uncertain. . . . Be skeptical of systems analysis, computer models, game theories, or doctrines that suggest otherwise."[29]

Pilkey and Pilkey-Jarvis (2007), in their provocatively named *Useless Arithmetic: Why Environmental Scientists Can't Predict the Future*,[30] join numerous others in noting that the state of the arithmetic modeling science simply is not up to understanding complex adaptive system's behavior, whether natural or human involved.

The ODNI *Global Trends 2025* specifically avoids prediction,[31] settling for the mere presentation of trends for precisely these reasons. That sad endpoint is the state of the fusion discipline, and thinking about fusion centers and the beyond involves making headway holistically on all fronts: mechanical, modeling, and human analyst skills based.

CONCLUSION

There are things that governments need to keep secret, but in a largely open-sourced world of free-flowing information, where synthesis is the key to wise understanding, fusion centers need to be as open an affair as they can be. Not only in the necessary expertise likely to be outside of the intelligence organization, but the increasingly research-like tradecraft of intelligence[32] and the folding-in logistic of proper futures forecasting both mitigate against a narrow and task-specific mind-set for fusion centers, except perhaps in their tactical and operational iterations. Where strategic insight and deep understanding are the purpose of fusion centers, they must be open.

NOTES

Ideas presented herein on holistic intelligence assessment from a complex adaptive systems approach were presented at the Office of the Director of National Intelligence 2008 IC Centers for Academic Excellence Program, to senior executive seminars at Exxon-Mobil and Alcatel-Lucent, to the Association of Foreign Intelligence Officers, and at several private salons on intelligence futures during 2008/2009.

1. Wilson, Edward O. 1998. *Consilience: The Unity of Knowledge*. New York: Alfred A. Knopf, 269.

2. Treverton, Gregory F. and C. Bryan Gabbard. 2008. *Assessing the Tradecraft of Intelligence Analysis*. Santa Monica, Calif.: Rand Corporation, 6.

3. Werther, Guntram. 2008. *Holistic Integrative Analysis of International Change: A Commentary on Teaching Emergent Futures*. Carlisle, Penn.: National Intelligence University, Office of the Director of National Intelligence, and The U.S. Army War College Center for Strategic Leadership (Proteus Monograph Series Vol. 1, Issue 3): 1–10.

4. United States Joint Forces Command. 2008. *The Joint Operating Environment 2008; Challenges and Implications for the Future of Joint Force*. https://us.jfcom.mil/sites/J5/j59/default.aspx.

5. Wurtzel, Elizabeth. "Twelve Years Down the Drain." *Wall Street Journal*, April 8, 2009, Opinion Page.

6. Ibid. Treverton and Gabbard, *Assessing the Tradecraft of Intelligence Analysis*, 45.

7. Cartwright, General John. "Culture and Dynamics of Change" (lecture, Unrestricted Warfare Symposium, Johns Hopkins University, Baltimore, Md., March 20, 2007).

8. Ibid. Treverton and Gabbard, *Assessing the Tradecraft of Intelligence Analysis*, iii.

9. Fingar, Thomas C. 2008. *Global Trends 2025—A Transformed World*. NIC 2008–003. http://www.dni.gov/nic/NIC_2025_project.html.

10. Moynihan, Daniel P. 1998. *Secrecy: The American Experience*. New Haven, Conn.: Yale University Press.

11. Przeworski, Adam and Henry Teune. 1982. *The Logic of Comparative Social Inquiry*. Malabar, Florida: Robert E. Krieger Publishing Company, 29.

12. Ibid. Treverton and Gabbard, *Assessing the Tradecraft of Intelligence Analysis*, xi–xii.

13. Ibid. Werther, *Holistic Integrative Analysis of International Change*, 6–9.

14. Ibid. Treverton and Gabbard, *Assessing the Tradecraft of Intelligence Analysis*, xi.

15. Gardner, Howard. 2006. *Five Minds for the Future*. Boston: Harvard Business School Press, 45–76.

16. Werther, Guntram. Forthcoming. Proteus Management Group. Carlisle: Office of the Director of National Intelligence, National Intelligence University, and US Army Center for Strategic Leadership.

17. Ibid. Treverton and Gabbard, *Assessing the Tradecraft of Intelligence Analysis*, 16.

18. Anonymous. Office of the Director of National Intelligence. *Intelligence Community Centers for Academic Excellence Seminar* (July 2008). College Park, Md.

19. Moynihan, Senator Daniel P. 1998. *Secrecy: The American Experiment*. New Haven, Conn.: Yale University Press.

20. Cartwright, "Culture and Dynamics of Change."

21. Ibid. Gardner, *Five Minds for the Future*, 73.

22. Ibid. Gardner, *Five Minds for the Future*, 47.

23. Ibid. Werther, *Holistic Integrative Analysis of International Change*, 48–50.

24. Ibid. Gardner, *Five Minds for the Future*, 67.

25. Alsop, Ronald. "M.B.A. Programs Blend Disciplines to Yield Big Picture: M.B.A. Track/Focus on Academics and Other B-School Trends." *Wall Street Journal*, July 11, 2006.

26. Werther, Guntram. 2006. *Profiling International Change Processes: Introducing A Holistically Integrated and Socio-Psychologically Grounded Approach to Emerging Trends Prediction*. In *Proteus Futures Digest*, ed. John Auger and William Wimbish, 161–81. Carlisle: Proteus Management Group, Office of the Director of National Intelligence, National Intelligence University, and the U.S. Army War College Center for Strategic Leadership, 2006.

27. Kurzweil, Ray. 2006. *The Singularity in Near: When Humans Transcend Biology*. New York: Penguin Books.

28. http://predictiveanalytics.pnl.gov/about.stm.

29. Gray, Andrew. "Technology No Cure-all, Gates Tells Military." September 29, 2008. http://www.reuters.com/articleID=USTRE48S4XK20080929.

30. Pilkey, Orrin, and Linda Pilkey-Jarvis. 2007. *Useless Arithmetic: Why Environmental Scientists Can't Predict the Future*. New York: Columbia University Press.

31. Ibid.

32. Ibid. Cartwright, "Culture and Dynamics of Change."

Disrupting Human Networks: Ancient Tools for Modern Challenges

Jeffrey H. Norwitz

The future of war, conflict, and societal unrest will be increasingly defined by nonstate actors who reject traditional notions of sovereignty, national identity, and international norms of behavior. This chapter suggests applications for human source intelligence in order to neutralize emerging challenges from dangerous armed groups and related movements.[1] Second, it explores ways to influence decision makers who lead criminal and terror organizations, so as to effectively inhibit their ability to operate. Then, it discusses how individuals within the group can be manipulated causing friction or fissures between members, thereby reducing group cohesion and effectiveness. Organizational and group behavior provides a perspective on where to find or develop these fissures. Operational human intelligence techniques provide the leverage to exploit these fissures in order the break the structure.

Let us be clear about the outcome. Outright destruction, annihilation, or eradication of armed groups is probably impossible. We can, however, influence the behavior of organizations and their members. This is an ongoing struggle with long-term objectives. Continued vigilance is part of any influence strategy. Methods must be uninterrupted. Tactics must be relentless. And victory is only temporary.

HUMAN NETWORKS ARE GROUPS

Understanding group dynamics begins with the leader. In any group, someone is in charge. They may appear to share power, but upon close examination, there will be a dominant decision maker. If we are to effectively influence how the group behaves, we need to first identify the leader, study their background, what they believe, where they get their information, and how they relate to others. Influencing the activities of leaders cannot be achieved without understanding what makes them tick.

Studies of leaders in the human factors context suggest there are four distinct considerations dealing with how leaders receive, and are therefore influenced by, information.[2] The first consideration looks at *personal characteristics* and focuses on the leader's self-image to include confidence, ideology, philosophy, motivation, beliefs, values, as well as likes and dislikes. Other personal characteristics deal with background and skills. Among them are age, where the leader was born, raised, and relevant socialization factors. Also included are marital status, the nature of the marital relationship, and relationships with immediate and extended family, and the nature of those relationships. Interests, schooling, including the type of student the leader was, focus of study, former positions held, and key personal associates are also important to know. It's crucial to understand the leader's norms that include their views on how individuals should behave, impertinent behaviors, words or phrases that can be insulting, and views of the role of minority or majority groups.

The second consideration looks at the leader's *operating environment*. This includes how the leader came to power, groups or individuals that constrain the leader, and whether or not the leader challenges restraint. Incorporated in this are perceptions about others, the leader's degree of ethnocentrism, and distrust for others. We want to know how the leader views others and also how others view the leader. The focus is on existing perceptions about the leader on a variety of perceptual planes and, at a more basic level, whether the leader is liked or disliked and by whom. Also relevant is how the leader views his/her defined constituency or followers. Finally, the leader's operating environment includes sources of finance and likelihood of corruption.

The third consideration deals with the leader's *advisory system*. Some of the most significant people are the leader's advisors. When examining the leader it is important not to become caught up in the formality of line and block charts, because they may not really tell us who is influential. Rather, we have to look at the leader's formal and informal network of advisors who may change over time. For a variety of reasons advisors can also fall out of favor or new ones may emerge. When the most influential advisors are identified, the potential spin, personal agenda, or filtering of information by advisors should also be discerned. Some leaders may not even care about advice from others. As a result, they may pay lip service to their advisors and, instead, consider themselves the ultimate authority on all issues. Last is the degree of control the leader needs over the policy process and their interest and level of policy expertise.

The final consideration looks at the leader's *information environment*. This involves the degree of complex thinking the leader exhibits. For example, some individuals are open to information, deal well with ambiguity, and have an ability to grasp nuance. These types of leaders usually want diverse information. Those who lack in cognitive complexity are black-and-white thinkers. They are essentially closed to conflicting information, do not seek out alternative views, and do not care about supplementary information. Whether complex or not, the type of information the leader pays attention to, the sources of this information, and how the leader prefers information to be presented, will aid in designing an influence strategy.[3]

Contemporary circumstances demand additional discussion of *religion* as it pertains to how leadership thinking is shaped. Within the context of this chapter, spiritual convictions have their origins in all aforementioned areas of consideration for how leaders receive information. For instance, personal characteristics of upbringing, family, values, and socialization are strongly influenced by the presence or absence of religious principles. The operating environment as evidenced by a leader's view of others, constituency, and followers can reveal religious influence, or lack thereof. Dogmatic or strident rule sets of a leader's advisory system may echo prescriptive righteous devotion. Likewise, a leader may deal with complexity by turning to pious spiritual doctrine as a way of managing ambiguity. This chapter is concerned with the degree to which religion drives a leader's decision making because, if we are going to influence leadership behavior, we must consider the extent that theology drives behavior.

HUMAN INTELLIGENCE ABOUT HUMAN NETWORKS

Armed groups and criminal enterprises are human-centric activities. In other words, while groups may embrace technology in weapons and communications, they are essentially *humans* doing things that *humans* do in ways that *humans* do them. Psychology, sociology, and anthropology inform us on human behavior in general. But particulars about a leader, group, and its members must be specifically discerned. Human intelligence is the answer. Human intelligence, commonly abbreviated as HUMINT, is that which is derived from human sources. In contrast to intercepted phone conversations (signals intelligence, or SIGINT), photos (imagery intelligence, or IMINT), and other technical or scientifically derived intelligence; HUMINT is the cornerstone of intelligence work and reveals secrets of the mind. Mark Lowenthal, with 27 years of experience as an intelligence official in the executive and legislative branches of government and in private sector offers the following on HUMINT:

HUMINT is espionage—spying—and is sometimes referred to as the world's second-oldest profession. . . . Spying is what most people think about when they hear the word "intelligence," whether they conjure up famous spies from history such as Nathan Hale or Mata Hari (both failures) or the many fictional spies such as James Bond.

HUMINT largely involves sending agents to foreign countries, where they attempt to recruit foreign nationals to spy. Agents must identify individuals who have access to the information that we may desire; gain their confidence and assess their weaknesses and susceptibility to being recruited; and make a "pitch" to them, suggesting a relationship.

For intelligence targets where the technical infrastructure may be irrelevant as a fruitful target—such as terrorism, narcotics, or international crime, where the "signature" of activities is rather small—HUMINT may be the only available source.

HUMINT also has disadvantages. First, it cannot be done remotely, as is the case with various types of technical collection. It requires proximity and access and therefore must contend with the counterintelligence capabilities of the other side.

Some critics argue that [HUMINT] is the most susceptible to deception. The "bona fides" of human sources will always be subject to question initially and, in some cases, never be wholly resolved. Why is this person offering to pass information—ideology, money, revenge? Is this person a double agent who will be collecting information on your HUMINT techniques?[4]

HUMINT provides an otherwise unattainable window into the personality, emotional makeup, and innermost secrets of those who are being targeted for influence operations. HUMINT is unmatched in its ability to uncover this often private, subtle, and privileged information about individuals and groups who we want to influence. According to Lowenthal,

HUMINT involves the manipulation of other human beings as potential sources of information. The skills required to be a successful HUMINT collector are acquired over time with training and experience. They basically involve psychological techniques to gain trust, including empathy, flattery, and sympathy. There are also more direct methods of gaining cooperation, such as bribery, blackmail, or sex.[5]

As it pertains to recruiting sources inside armed groups, experience shows that regardless of culture, language, age, gender, political, religious, or educational background; the four most common motivators for people to deceive trusted comrades are (1) greed, (2) anger or revenge, (3) thrill or excitement, and (4) visions of self-importance (ego, vanity). Others simply volunteer their services for ideological motives. HUMINT officers perfect ways to exploit each of these scenarios and literally develop scores of persons acting as psychological hostages. Even in those relationships that seem to start with full cooperation, a measure of coercion will be contrived in order to hook the source lest he or she develop remorse.

Professional intelligence officers who specialize in human source intelligence are customarily called *HUMINTers*. They are not intelligence analysts nor are they staffers who write reports. Rather, HUMINTers are operational people, specially trained and highly skilled to blend into any environment wherein human relationships are the essence. Human source intelligence work is part clinical psychologist and part theatrical actor. As you read this, throughout the world, thousands of men and women are quietly gathering intelligence, manipulating human relationships, assessing likely informants, and influencing leaders.

Thus the world of HUMINT is in a continuous reciprocating ballet of spy versus counterspy, sometimes using very different rule sets. For example, a democratic nation will, by the very nature of the form of government, follow a set of norms embodying rule of law and human dignity, unlike some adversaries, which justify ends by any means. Therein emerges a tension when armed groups violently attack democracies. Yet measured state responses are a necessary moral obligation.

One of the quintessential thinkers on intelligence matters and democratic norms of behavior is Stansfield Turner, retired navy admiral and former director of central intelligence (1977–1981). Citing a perceived "lack of discussion of how our democracy affects and is affected by what we do to deter terrorism," Turner wrote a book on the very subject.[6] His conclusions:

> One of the key elements for us in combating terrorism is international cooperation . . . If we are going to defeat international terrorism—not just Osama bin Laden but the broader sweep—we will need an analogous multinational program that will put pressures on the movement of individual terrorists and on their bases of support in our societies. Only when we truly analyze which alternatives promise the best payoffs will we begin moving towards a long-run solution to terrorism. And only then will we deserve the respect that we'll need to lead the responsible nations of the world in a coordinated campaign to suppress this scourge against mankind. Terrorists are not invincible: the Zealots, Assassins, and others were suppressed in time. Today many countervailing strengths come from the very fact that we have a democratic system. But that means we need public understanding of our options for curtailing the current wave of terror and the wisdom to avoid actions that might undermine the democratic process we are defending.[7]

Security professionals must be proactive to frustrate threatening organizations. We have to go after the group, not wait for the group to attack us. We are often too reactive in our dealings with armed groups. Yet we cannot allow open society and freedoms to become a force-multiplier for our enemies. For example, democracies and representative forms of government are characterized by: transparency, free press, the ability to dissent, accountability, rule of law, and international responsibilities under treaties and other sovereign obligations. An enemy that is committed to an opposite political and moral framework can cleverly operate with impunity in an open society enjoying the tolerance of democratic laws and norms. At the time of their choosing an enemy can emerge from within the populace having planned, recruited, resourced, and executed an attack right under the noses of the target population. Because of the constraints faced by representative democracies that recognize the rule of law, those nations are often perceived as weak by the adversary who follows no set of laws.[8] Furthermore, proactive approaches, especially those using human source networks to attack human source networks, require the utmost in secrecy. And this runs counter to a free, open press and an informed population. Nonetheless, the ability to break armed groups will be proportional to the ability for security forces to operate clandestinely within a legal framework.

THINKING ABOUT THE LAW

In point of fact, based on abuses in the past, there are laws and presidential orders that clearly define how America conducts intelligence activity and still protects constitutional underpinnings. Some of the key legal boundaries by which American intelligence agencies must adhere are articulated in Executive Order 12333, "United States Intelligence Activities"; DOD Directive 5240.1 DOD, "Intelligence Activities"; the National Security Act of 1947 (50 U.S.C. §401); and the Foreign Intelligence Surveillance Act (FISA) of 1978 (50 U.S.C. §§1801–11, 1821–29, 1841–46, and 1861–62).

But what about the future as it relates to the law? Do we have the necessary legal tools to disrupt human networks that pose a national security threat? Shortly after the September 11, 2001, attacks, I wrote a foretelling article entitled, "Combating Terrorism: With a Helmet or a Badge?" In it, I examined the underlying challenges of treating terrorism as a crime and thereafter the efficacy of America's concept of judicial justice in the face of 9/11.[9] The article begins with a fictitious scenario wherein bin Laden, with a team of defense attorneys, surrenders himself to American authorities and thereafter starts a cascade of legal challenges in court. Eight years after I wrote the article, the potential for that vexing scenario remains unfortunately very real. A former U.S. Attorney, speaking at the U.S. Naval War College, opined that America was today no closer to clarifying constitutional complexity dealing with detained terrorism suspects than on 9/11. For example, even after the Supreme Court rendered opinions in *Rasul v. Bush*,[10] *Hamdi v. Rumsfeld*,[11] and *Hamdan v. Rumsfeld*,[12] they seemingly confused the matter even more in *Boumediene v. Bush*.[13]

Craig H. Allen, Judson Falknor Professor of Law at the University of Washington and formerly the Charles H. Stockton Chair in International Law at the U.S. Naval War College, writes about the future legal challenges posed by enemy human networks.

The threats posed by armed groups plainly challenge our traditional paradigms for preventing and controlling large-scale violence. Conflicts with armed groups such as Al Qaeda—whose members are not found on the battlefield, who "hide in plain sight" among civilians, and who flout the principles of distinction and humanity that are so central to the law of armed conflict—do not fit nicely into the "war" construct, and yet the magnitude of the risk posed by those groups does not fit within our traditional understanding of "crime." In short, the threat is too lethal to be treated as a mere crime and too private to be called a war.

Perhaps it is time to reject the binary thinking that fuels the present destructive debate and acknowledge that the existing regimes do not, individually or collectively, adequately address the present needs for an ordered approach to the myriad forms of contemporary large-scale violence by armed groups. Such a declaration is, perhaps, the indispensable first step in formulating a new and more flexible regime that will allow us to harness law as an ordering force in what has become an increasingly disordered world.

But many are reluctant to take seriously any reform proposals, whether at the international or national level. They argue that there is not sufficient international will or cohesion to develop and ratify a new international regime. Perhaps they also fear that an admission that the existing regime does not cover the present situation would be an invitation to an unprincipled nation or its executive to exploit the gap, while arguing that the law does not constrain it. On the national level, the fierce and debilitating partisan divide and the dizzying sine curve of public opinion cast serious doubt on the prospects for any reform, particularly one that would establish a basis for preventive detentions and provide for criminal trials with fewer protections than those afforded to ordinary criminal defendants.

In the final analysis, program analysts and policy makers must determine which approach best provides the optimal level of security, liberty, and protections for the accused. More than a half century ago Abraham Maslow reminded us that in the hierarchy of human needs none is more fundamental than security. If security is defined as the freedom from violent acts, an effective security regime must do more than merely respond to attacks; it must also prevent them when possible—particularly those that might include unleashing a weapon of mass destruction.[14]

NEUTRALIZING ARMED GROUPS

At some point in an individual's life, he or she joins a group. This can be a weekly coffee get together with friends or colleagues, the boy scouts, a political party, or the military, or anything else that brings people together for a common purpose. Individuals seek interaction with others and want a shared identity. One way to achieve this is to join a group. Once a person is part of a group they acquire a shared group identity. This comes with constraints, obligations, responsibility, and commitments. While personal identity is still important, the member also adopts a group identity. Outward evidence may be clothing, tattoos, distinct language, or even ways of walking. Even though groups are made up of individuals, certain group dynamics can and do affect the behavior of individuals. The group is a powerful shaping force.

According to some social psychologists, when individuals join groups, previous group identities are stripped away. Moreover, individuals who join groups attain a level of anonymity. Personal accountability and responsibility shifts from the individual to the group. Group members often behave in ways very different from when they were unaffiliated. Sometimes when individuals join secretive groups, they are pressured to sever certain outside connections. The main reason is to protect the group from unwanted scrutiny. When individuals are being assessed for recruitment, group indoctrination is important, and group propaganda is central to this indoctrination. The group central messages are constantly reinforced. Indoctrination is an ongoing process, and individuals are expected to put the group above everything else.

The clandestine group, with its like-minded members, becomes the individual's identity, and the group is now the new family for the recruit. There are indeed perceptions about what a prototypical member should be. Therefore, a recruit is expected to conform to and obey the norms of the group and participate in group behavior. These norms are usually articulated by those in central leadership positions, while pressure to conform comes from all levels and members. However, for some, their attraction to the group fades. Their level of commitment dissipates. They become marginalized and no longer feel a sense of camaraderie. These are the potential deviants we can exploit, and skillful human intelligence tells us who they are.

GROUP FISSURES

Groups are not perfect entities and they often suffer from fissures. The most significant fissure points that derail the functioning of groups are *conflicts between members*. Research suggests that group dissention can lead to power struggles between members and that differences of opinion can result in factional disputes. These power struggles cause factions to emerge. Power struggles can result in splits so severe that individuals leave one group and form another, often with competing agendas. Furthermore, power struggles can destroy a group causing members to turn on one other and even eliminate rivals. But conflict between individuals is not necessarily always because of power. Members can have basic personality conflicts and may become marginal or even deviant affiliates that threaten group cohesion. At some point individuals seek to leave the group if this tension exists, or may be pressured to leave by other more prototypical members. Thus, any type of individual conflict in the group is an exploitation opportunity for an informational influence campaign because when tension occurs, the level of commitment of certain members may be shaken. Any type of unhappiness is exploitable, and where none exists, it can be created.

Groups that must maintain a high security posture go to great lengths to ensure internal security. Groups warn members that they are always the target of security forces and must be vigilant to protect against such penetration. Groups tend to continually watch their members for potential betrayers. Armed groups tend to create their own counterintelligence wings not only to stop penetration from the outside, but to find betrayers within. This can and does create a potential for serious mistrust among members. We can seize and exploit mistrust that already exists, and we can also create distrust among members.

Research further suggests that there are often considerable policy and procedural fractures in groups. Unless the group is highly cohesive, there are often disagreements about the way things are done and the methods and goals of the group. These disagreements create rifts between members of groups. From there, cliques may form, and members will compete with each other. However, more dominant cliques or individuals may also have the power to expel others. On the other hand, individuals may leave the group, form another, and press forward with their agenda. Thus we can facilitate the fracture, exploit it, destabilize a group, and if new groups are formed, ultimately cause them to turn on each other.

Identifying marginal and deviant members is extremely important to any informational influence campaign. Groups have norms and members are expected to follow them. Marginal and deviant group members are problematic because they do not conform and therefore threaten the cohesiveness of the group. They also threaten the obedience of other members and promulgate irregular behavior. Additionally, marginal members and deviants often bring negative attention to the group. On occasion, group norms require participation in violence as a vetting process. Members may fail or refuse to take part. Marginal members and deviants who cannot be rehabilitated are dealt with through conformity measures, expelled, or killed.

Once questions are raised, groups tend to want to find the answers. Suspicion is then cast on members of the group, which in turn heightens the sense of threat. Members tend to turn on each other. Turncoats are not taken lightly in armed groups. They violate norms and challenge the cohesion of the group. They are the betrayers.

Marginal members and deviants are the dream of an influence operator. For one, deviants are always on the fence. While the group may tolerate them, there will come a point when they push the limits too far. The reasons for their behavior vary, but the bottom line is that they do not like to follow the rules. It is important to find out why and then use these deviants to cause dissention in the group. Again, human intelligence informs us of the situation.

STRATEGIES FOR EXPLOITATION

One of the first jobs of an influence planner is to identify those weak links in the group. We can exploit these fissures in various ways. We can seize upon already deviant behavior and twist the circumstances to our advantage. Or, we can encourage such behavior that can result in group dissension and individual defection from the group. Or, we can create the appearance of deviance, even when none exists. Imagination and deviousness are all that are necessary to exploit fissures.

One of America's most successful yet unheralded HUMINT intelligence officers is Duane R. "Dewey" Clarridge, retired senior official of the Central Intelligence Agency (CIA). For 32 years, Clarridge was a legendary CIA operations officer deeply involved in many of the CIA's most important covert actions in the cold war.[15] Clarridge ran some of the most clandestine yet indispensable campaigns of the 20th century to disrupt, influence, and, in some cases, totally destroy armed groups with aims inimical to the United States. Commonly referred to a covert action, Clarridge's activities showcase the effectiveness and efficacy of disruption and influence campaign strategy.[16] Working against the deadly Abu Nidal Organization (ANO), Clarridge headed the CIA Counter Terrorism Center (CTC) in 1986. Based on the recruitment of an ANO member and good analysis, Clarridge's shop developed superb intelligence about Abu Nidal himself. Writing in the first person, Clarridge shares a rare glimpse into the mind of a master of influence operations.

Abu Nidal had an extensive commercial network in Eastern Europe, Greece, Cyprus, Yugoslavia, and to a lesser extent, Western Europe. Under the umbrella of these "legitimate" businesses, the ANO could move and hide funds, acquire and transport weapons, and arrange meetings and liaisons.

I arrived at the conclusion that the best way to attack Abu Nidal was to publicly expose his financial empire and his network of collaborators. Governments in Europe squirmed, but they terminated their dealings with Abu Nidal. We decided to make recruitment pitches to ANO personnel in various countries. Most of the approaches did not result in agent penetrations of the ANO . . . but our pursuit of Abu Nidal's organization and personnel eventually paid off in a very different way.

Seeing his financial empire under attack and listening to reports of CIA efforts to recruit his cadres, Abu Nidal was aware that we were coming after him and his people. He, like many in his line of work, was paranoid. CIA fueled his hysteria over plots against him—feeding fear to a paranoid is something we know how to do. Not surprisingly, Abu Nidal panicked. Those who reported having been approached by us were not rewarded for their loyalty, because Abu Nidal never quite believed that anyone in his group had turned us down. Their loyalty was suspect thereafter, and punishment was torture and death.

By 1987, a fearful Abu Nidal had turned his terror campaign inward. The ANO was starting to drown in the blood of its disciples. A simple allegation was sufficient; usually there was no investigation. Accused followers were tortured to confess, then executed on the basis of the confession. After the effective ANO apparatus in southern Lebanon fell under suspicion, over three hundred hard-core operatives were murdered on Abu Nidal's order. On a single night in 1987, approximately 170 were tied up and blindfolded, machine-gunned, and pushed into a trench prepared for the occasion. Distrust reached high into the politburo ruling the ANO. Even his lieutenants began to believe he was insane. Abu Nidal's paranoia, fed by our crusade against him, caused him to destroy his organization.[17]

Creating fissures with marginal members or deviants, involves fabricating the aura of dissension, even when it does not necessarily exist. We are going to play upon the penchant of individuals to distrust the activities of others when security is paramount. The perception merely needs to be created that something is not quite right with the members of the group.

For example, suppose we want to create an atmosphere of suspicion around a member who has access to the group leadership but, for some reason, is not considered part of the inner circle. Our goal is to drive him into our camp by causing him such chaos within the group that he has no choice but to seek sanctuary with us. We start our influence operation with surveillance by which we establish his routine so we can predict his travel patterns. If he uses a car, we are in luck. Choosing a spot where there will be plenty of witnesses, we arrange for a police car to stop our subject in what appears to be a normal traffic stop for some sort of moving violation. It will be important that such a traffic stop create as much commotion as possible cleverly designed to draw the public's attention to the activity. Disrupt the traffic flow. Use lights and siren. Use loud speakers. Next, our collaborating police officer is seen walking back and forth from the subject's car to the police car. The officer is seen talking to the subject for an inordinate amount of time. The subject is asked to join the officer in the police car where they are seen talking even more. As they walk back to the subject's car, our theatrical officer is seen laughing and patting the subject on the back after which the subject drives away (totally confused) but with the officer waving at him.

If the scenario is played out with the right audience, word of the event will quickly get back to the group and thereafter, the subject member we have targeted will be under great suspicion—totally unable to explain the police behavior. This will make him appear even more traitorous. If a similar contrived "friendly" association with law enforcement can be repeated, the target member will eventually realize he is being manipulated by police, but it will be too late to convince his group peers. With the proper incentive and approach, there is a good likelihood he will become our asset in return for protection. The seeds of doubt will have been planted in the group it will cause them to look at other members as suspect, perhaps the member's confidants, allies and so forth.

A final word about implementation strategies. Nothing can match the value of having a witting or unwitting person inside a secretive organization. This provides an otherwise unattainable window into the personality, emotional make-up, and innermost secrets of those who are being targeted for influence operations. Human intelligence is unmatched in its ability to uncover this often private, subtle, and privileged information about leaders and groups that we want to disrupt.

Operational tactics to break armed groups often, at some point, demand direct contact with a group member who our analysis suggests is most vulnerable to recruitment or can be manipulated to our advantage. Finding and vetting likely candidates is an ongoing process for human intelligence officers. The more recruited sources one has, the greater success at having the right source at the right time. In summary, strategies to exploit individual and group fissures in order to disrupt armed groups most often leverage the skills and operational tactics of human intelligence practitioners.

CONCLUSION

The future is full of uncertainty and the implications are grave for the stability of security of nations who cherish freedom and the rule of law. Globalization and interconnectedness will fuel discontent in some regions, while dissuading disputes in others. Armed groups are merely one vestige of mankind's struggle in an increasingly smaller world. Prevention of hostilities and rapid resolution thereof demands new solutions. This chapter suggests human intelligence can inform us about armed group leaders and become an enabler to disrupt groups, thereafter neutralizing the danger from criminal and terrorist networks where, in all likelihood, the most serious threats will emerge. This is not new, but it foreshadows the nature of future substate conflict. George Will, the Pulitzer Prize–winning author and political scientist, said, "The future has a way of arriving unannounced." The purpose of this chapter is to prepare ourselves for when we discover, unexpectedly, that the future is here.[18]

NOTES

The views expressed in this chapter are the author's and do not represent those of the Defense Department, Naval Criminal Investigative Service, the Naval War College, or the Federal Law Enforcement Training Center.

1. As used herein, an armed group refers to classic insurgents, tribal warlords, terrorists, guerrillas, pirates, militias, and organized criminal syndicates.

2. The author acknowledges the contribution of Dr. Elena Mastors who collaborated on research for this chapter. Scholarly discussion of leader considerations and strategies to influence their decision making as highlighted in this chapter can be found in Elena Mastors and Jeffrey H. Norwitz, "Disrupting and Influencing Leaders of Armed Groups," in *Armed Groups: Studies in National Security, Counterterrorism, and Counterinsurgency,* ed. Jeffrey H. Norwitz (Newport, R.I.: Naval War College, 2008), 323–41. See http://www.JeffNorwitz.com.

3. For further discussion, see Martha Cottam, Beth Dietz-Uhler, Elena Mastors, and Tom Preston, *Introduction to Political Psychology* (Hillsdale, N.J.: Lawrence Erlbaum and Associates, 2004).

4. Mark Lowenthal, *Intelligence: From Secrets to Policy*, 2nd ed. (Washington, D.C.: CQ Press 2003), 74 –77.

5. Ibid., 211.

6. Stansfield Turner, *Terrorism and Democracy* (Boston: Houghton Mifflin, 1991), xii.

7. Stansfield Turner, *Ten Steps to Fight Terrorism Without Endangering Democracy* (College Park: Center for International and Security Studies at Maryland School of Public Affairs, 2001), 18.

8. A superb treatment of the challenges facing democracies to deter nonstate actors is found in Yosef Kuperwasser, "Is It Possible to Deter Armed Groups?" in *Armed Groups: Studies in National Security, Counterterrorism, and Counterinsurgency*, 127–33.

9. Jeffrey H. Norwitz, "Combating Terrorism with a Helmet or a Badge?" in *American Defense Policy*, 8th ed., Paul J. Bolt, (Baltimore, Md.: Johns Hopkins University Press, 2005), 424–32.

10. *Rasul v. Bush*, 542 U.S. 466, 500–501 (2004), http://www.law.cornell.edu/supct/html/03–334.ZS.html.

11. *Hamdi v. Rumsfeld*, 542 U.S. 507, 538 (2004), http://www.law.cornell.edu/supct/html/03–6696.ZS.html.

12. *Hamdan v. Rumsfeld*, 548 U.S. 557 (2006), http://www.law.cornell.edu/supct/html/05–184.ZS.html.

13. *Boumediene v. Bush*, 553 U.S.; 128 S.Ct. 2229; 2008 WL 2369628; 2008 U.S. Lexis 4887 (2008), http://www.law.cornell.edu/supct/html/06–1195.ZS.html.

14. Craig H. Allen, "Armed Groups and the Law," in *Armed Groups: Studies in National Security, Counterterrorism, and Counterinsurgency*, 89–113.

15. Duane Clarridge, "Speech about Covert Action before Smithsonian Associates," January 27, 1997, http://bss.sfsu.edu/fischer/IR%20360/Readings/Clarridge.htm (accessed May 16, 2009).

16. Duane Clarridge, interview by author, July 2007.

17. Duane Clarridge, *A Spy For All Seasons: My Life in the CIA* (New York: Scribner, 1997), 334–36.

18. Jeffrey H. Norwitz, "Introduction," in *Armed Groups: Studies in National Security, Counterterrorism, and Counterinsurgency*, xxvi.

Epilogue

Since the terrorist attacks of 9/11, there have been significant changes within the intelligence community (IC), and significant challenges remain. On December 25, 2009, there was a failed attack on a flight from Europe to the United States. But for the incompetence of the terrorist and the initiative of the passengers and crew on that flight, there may have been devastating results. As several of the writers have shown, some of the same problems still exist within a system that should have prevented this terrorist from even boarding a plane. All the "dots" were not properly connected. With a forecast of things to come within the IC, on January 7, 2010, the Director of National Intelligence sent the following message to the employees of the IC.

Colleagues

The President has completed his preliminary review and briefed the nation regarding the Abdulmutallab attempted terrorist attack on December 25. He has directed me to lead the Intelligence Community's work in improving our procedures and systems to detect and prevent a similar attempt from succeeding.

That Mr. Abdulmutallab boarded Northwest Flight 153 for Detroit was a failure of the counterterrorism system. We had strategic intelligence that al Qa'ida in the Arab Peninsula (AQAP) had the intention of taking action against the United States. We did not direct more resources against AQAP, nor insist that the watch-listing criteria be adjusted. The Intelligence Community analysts who were working hard on immediate threats to Americans in Yemen did not understand the fragments of intelligence on what turned out later to be Mr. Abdulmutallab, so they did not push him onto the "no fly" list.

We will take a fresh and penetrating look at strengthening both human and technical performance and do what we have to do in all areas. I have specifically been tasked to oversee and manage work in four areas:

- Assigning clear lines of responsibility for investigating all leads on high-priority threats, so they are pursued more aggressively;
- Distributing intelligence reports more quickly and widely, especially those suggesting specific threats against the U.S.;
- Applying more rigorous standards to analytical tradecraft to improve intelligence integration and action; and
- Enhancing the criteria for adding individuals to the terrorist watchlist and "no fly" watchlist.

While the December 25 attempt exposed improvement needs and flaws in coordination, it did not expose weakness in the concepts of intelligence reform or suggest that its progress should be redirected. The Intelligence Reform and Terrorism Prevention Act (IRTPA) and the progress of the past five years will continue to guide our future improvements.

As the White House review stated, "the work by America's counterterrorism (CT) community has had many successes since 9/11 that should be applauded . . . On a great number of occasions since 9/11, many of which the American people will never know about, the tremendous, hardworking corps of analysts across the CT community did just that, working day and night to track terrorist threats and run down possible leads in order to keep their fellow American safe." I strongly agree. The review also recognizes the barriers to information sharing that existed just five years ago, which we have worked so hard to dismantle, have indeed been broken down.

The job of collecting, analyzing, and integrating information on a global scale is difficult, and this community performs that work at high levels every day. We will sustain our dedication and professionalism to the tasks we now face. We will leverage this challenge to emerge even stronger and more able to provide the support to national security that President Obama hailed as critical to our future.

We will meet this challenge. I am confident that together we will deliver to the President the improvements he has called for.

Dennis C. Blair

Source: U.S. Director of National Intelligence, www.dni.gov.

Index

About the Editor
and Contributors

EDITOR

Keith Gregory Logan is an Assistant Professor in the Department of Criminal Justice at Kutztown University; he teaches courses in Homeland Security and Defense, Criminal Law and Procedure, and Contemporary Issues. He holds an undergraduate degree in political science, a master's degree in criminal justice, and a law degree. He is a member of the District of Columbia Bar and the Virginia State Bar. A former federal law enforcement officer and security officer, he also served as a Special Assistant United States Attorney in the District of Columbia and the Eastern District of Virginia (EDVA), and represented the United States Attorney's Office, EDVA, before the Fourth Circuit Court of Appeals. His initial federal service started as a Congressional Staff Assistant for a New York congressman, and he later served with the following agencies during his career: Drug Enforcement Administration, Agency for International Development, General Services Administration, Department of Interior, Department of Education, Environmental Protection Agency, and the Nuclear Regulatory Commission. He has received numerous awards during his federal service. In 2007, he was a guest lecturer on the American Criminal Justice System and Homeland Security at the Russian Federation Diplomatic Academy in Moscow. While a member of the U.S. Army Reserves, he achieved the rank of Major, Military Police Corps and was a nuclear, biological, chemical/chemical, biological, radiological (NBC/CBR) defense instructor.

He has presented the following research: *Motor Vehicle Search Incident to Arrest: Will the Court Move in a New Direction?* at the 2008 Annual

Conference of the American Society of Criminology, and *Fiction as a Didactic Tool in Teaching Criminal Justice/Homeland Security* at the 2007 Annual Conference. Several of his recent publications include "Son of Sam Laws," in *Victimology and Crime Prevention*, ed. Bonnie S. Fisher and Steven P. Lab; "United States v. Booker and United States v. Fanfan," in *Race and Crime, Vol. 2*, ed. Helen Taylor Green and Shaun L. Gabbidon; "People v. Lee," in *Forensic Science*, ed. Any Embar-Seddon and Allan D. Pass; and "Foreign Intelligence Surveillance Act," in *Battleground: Criminal Justice, Volume 1*, ed. Gregg Barak. He is also a member of the editorial board of the *Encyclopedia of U.S. Intelligence*, scheduled for publication in late 2010.

CONTRIBUTORS

Ryan K. Baggett is the Deputy Director, Technology and Information Services at the Justice and Safety Center, and an Adjunct Instructor Department of Criminal Justice and Police Studies, Eastern Kentucky University. He holds a Bachelor of Science in Criminal Justice and a Master of Science in Criminal Justice. He recently coauthored *Homeland Security and Critical Infrastructure Protection* (2009) with Pamela Collins, and he has participated in numerous presentations at national conferences.

Stephanie Cooper Blum is an attorney for the Department of Homeland Security (DHS) where she advises on issues of civil rights and civil liberties. She previously served as a member of the Department of Justice's Task Force on Detention Policy, worked as an employment litigator for the Transportation Security Administration, and served as a law clerk to three federal judges. Ms. Blum is the author of *The Necessary Evil of Preventive Detention in the War on Terror: A Plan for a More Moderate and Sustainable Solution* (2008). She holds a master's degree in security studies from the Naval Postgraduate School, a JD from University of Chicago Law School, and a bachelor's degree in political science from Yale University. Ms. Blum has written various articles on homeland security issues and is an instructor at Michigan State University's Criminal Justice School.

James Burch, LCDR, and a Cryptologist retired from the Navy in 2009; he was most recently assigned to NORAD, U.S. Northern Command as the Deputy Chief of Collection Management within the Intelligence Directorate. Prior to that he had been assigned to Cruiser Destroyer Group Two as part of the George Washington Battle Group from 2001–2003; after 9/11 he participated in Operations Enduring and Iraqi Freedom. He attended the U.S. Army's Command and General Staff College (CGSC) in Leavenworth, Kansas; the Naval Command and Staff College; and the Joint Forces Staff College. LCDR Burch's educational background consists of a B.S. in Marine Transportation from the U.S. Merchant Marine Academy, an M.A. in Military History from CGSC, and an M.A. is Security Studies in Homeland

Security and Defense from the Naval Postgraduate School. He has published "A Domestic Intelligence for the United States? A Comparative Analysis of Domestic Intelligence Agencies and Their Implications for Homeland Security," *Homeland Security Affairs* III, no. 2 (June 2007); he presented "The Domestic Intelligence Gap: Progress Since 9/11?" at the 2008 CHDS Alumni Association Conference.

Michael W. Collier is an Assistant Professor in the Department of Safety, Security, and Emergency Management, College of Justice and Safety, Eastern Kentucky University. Previously, he was a Professor of National Security and Intelligence Studies at American Military University, Charles Town, West Virginia. He is also a former Director of Research and Academic Programs at Florida International University's Latin American and Caribbean Center. He holds a Ph.D. in International Relations from Florida International University (2000), an M.S. in Strategic Intelligence from the U.S. Defense Intelligence College (1986), and a B.S. from the U.S. Coast Guard Academy (1974). In a U.S. Coast Guard career, he was a specialist in law enforcement and military intelligence. He served as Coast Guard and Police Attaché in the U.S. Embassy, Bogotá, Colombia; Commanding Officer, USCGC *Thetis* (WMEC 910); and Deputy Director of Intelligence, Joint Interagency Task Force East, Key West, Florida. His books include *Political Corruption in the Caribbean Basin, Constructing a Theory to Combat Corruption* (2005); *Terrorism Preparedness in Florida, Improved Since 9/11, but Far from Ready* (2005); and *Security and Intelligence Analysis* (forthcoming).

Pamela A. Collins is a Professor in the Safety, Security and Emergency Department at Eastern Kentucky University and the Executive Director of the Justice and Safety Center. She holds a Bachelor of Science in Security and Public Safety, Master of Science in Criminal Justice, and a doctorate in Educational Policy Studies and Evaluation. She also serves as a Principal Investigator and Program Manager with the National Incident Management System Support Center and was appointed by the Governor of Kentucky to represent the Council on Post Secondary Education with the Kentucky Wireless Interoperability Executive Committee. She recently authored *Homeland Security and Critical Infrastructure Protection* (2009) and co-authored *Women in Law Enforcement: Public and Private Security* (2001) with Kathryn Scarborough, as well as several other books and book chapters.

Gary Cordner is a Professor of Criminal Justice at Kutztown University of Pennsylvania and a Commissioner with the Commission on Accreditation for Law Enforcement Agencies (CALEA). Previously, he was Police Chief in St. Michaels, Maryland, and Dean of the College of Justice & Safety at Eastern Kentucky University, where he helped establish a B.S. in homeland security degree program in 2007. He also served on the Kentucky Law Enforcement Council, the Kentucky Criminal Justice Council, and the

Lexington/Fayette County Civil Service Commission. Cordner is coauthor of three books: *Police Administration* (2007), *Police & Society* (2008), and *Planning for Criminal Justice Organizations and Systems* (1983); he is also the co-editor of several anthologies. He is past-president of the Academy of Criminal Justice Sciences and past-editor of *Police Quarterly* and the *American Journal of Police*. He earned his Ph.D. from Michigan State University.

David M. Keithly has published several books, most recently *The USA and the World 2008,* and over 75 articles in journals and magazines. He is the American editor of *Civil Wars.* He teaches at the American Military University and the National Defense Intelligence College. He has twice been a Fulbright fellow in Europe and was a fellow of the Institute for Global Conflict and Cooperation at the University of California; a scholar-in-residence at the Friedrich Naumann Foundation in Bonn, Germany; and a legislative fellow in the parliament of the German state of Thüringen. He is president of the Fulbright Association's Southeast Virginia chapter. He has a Ph.D. from Claremont Graduate School and an M.A. from the German University of Freiburg. He was designated a Navy "National Reserve Officer of the Year" in 1993 and received the annual faculty research award at the Joint Military Intelligence College in 2001. A retired reserve officer, he held field-grade rank in two services.

Louis H. Liotti is a civil trial attorney specializing in maritime, construction, product liability, and insurance defense matters. He spent almost 10 years in law enforcement, first as an attorney for the United States Customs Service and then as an Assistant District Attorney for Westchester County, New York. He also served as a Special Assistant U.S. Attorney for the Eastern District of New York. He attended the United States Naval Academy; received a B.A. degree in Political Science, with a specialization in International Relations, from Hofstra University; and earned a J.D. from Hofstra University School of Law. He served as a Brigade Naval Gunfire Officer with the 2d Air-Naval Gunfire Liaison Company (ANGLICO), Force Troops, Fleet Marine Force. He is presently active in the U.S. Coast Guard Auxiliary.

Gregory Moore is Director of the Center for Intelligence Studies as well as the Chair of the Department of History and Political Science at Notre Dame College in Cleveland, Ohio. He earned a B.A. in History from Ashland College in 1969 and completed his doctorate at Kent State University in 1978, where he was a teaching fellow. His area of interest is in American Diplomatic History with an emphasis on American-Asian relations. He has taught courses in American Diplomacy, Chinese History, Japanese History, Middle Eastern History, the Cold War, Terrorism, International Relations, and International Law. Moore has been named to *Who's Who in American Education* and *Who's Who Among American Teachers.* He currently serves as Vice-chair of the International Association for Intelligence Education. Moore is the coauthor of *The War Came to Me: A Story of Hope and Endurance* (2009) and is the editor-in-chief of the *Encyclopedia of U.S. Intelligence,* scheduled for publication in 2010.

Nadav Morag is a Professor at the Center for Homeland Defense and Security (CHDS) at the United States Naval Postgraduate School. He teaches senior federal, state, and local homeland security officials selected and funded by the Department of Homeland Security within the context of the center's M.A. in Homeland Security program. He previously served as Senior Director for Domestic Policy and subsequently as Senior Director for Foreign Policy at Israel's National Security Council, where he was responsible for producing policy recommendations on matters of national security for then prime minister Ariel Sharon and his cabinet. At the Israeli NSC, he worked with a team of other senior officials from the Israeli military, ISA, Mossad, foreign ministry, and the police developing policy recommendations based on intelligence and other sources on matters including counterterrorism policy, bilateral security relations with a number of regional countries and Europe, and the development of a homeland security policy for the Israeli national police. He has authored articles on terrorism, strategy, and the Middle East, including "The Economic and Social Effects of Intensive Terrorism: Israel 2000–2004," *Middle East Review of International Affairs* 10, no. 3 (2006); "Measuring Success in Coping with Terrorism: The Israeli Case," *Studies in Conflict and Terrorism* 28, no. 4 (2005); "The National Military Strategic Plan for the War on Terrorism: An Assessment," *Homeland Security Affairs* 2, no. 2 (2006); and "Unambiguous Ambiguity: The Opacity of the Oslo Peace Process," in *Israel: The First Hundred Years, Volume II: From War to Peace?* ed. Efraim Karsh (2000).

Jeffrey H. Norwitz is presently an instructor with the Counterterrorism Division at the Federal Law Enforcement Training Center. He is a retired federal special agent with 35 years experience in complex criminal, counterintelligence, and counterterrorism investigations. Following army service, he entered civilian law enforcement in Colorado Springs as a patrol officer, SWAT team sniper, and commander of the bomb squad. He later joined the Naval Criminal Investigative Service (NCIS) and served tours around the world, including counterintelligence supervisory special agent for New England. For eight years he was visiting professor of National Security Studies at the U.S. Naval War College where he held the John Nicholas Brown Chair of Counterterrorism. He earned a graduate degree in National Security Studies from the Naval War College and was voted Eastern Kentucky University's Distinguished Alumnus in 2006. His scholarly work appears in *Terrorism and Counterterrorism: Understanding the New Security Environment* (2003); *American Defense Policy,* 8th ed. (2005); *Practical Bomb Scene Investigation* (2006); *Defending the Homeland: Historical*

Perspectives on Radicalism, Terrorism, and State Responses (2007); and *Armed Groups; Studies in National Security, Counterterrorism, and Counterinsurgency* (2008).

John Riley is an Assistant Professor in the Political Science Department at Kutztown University. He has served as the Senior Research Director of the Post Conflict Reconstruction Project (a joint project sponsored by the Center for Strategic Studies and Role of American Military Power), which explores more-effective strategies to reconstruct war-torn states. He is the Co-Director of the Kenyan Democratization Project, which measures the Kenyan public's support for human rights and democratization. He has presented in numerous national and international conferences; served as the Associate Editor of the *Political Handbook of the World*; and published in the fields of U.S. foreign policy, international law, and social science methods.

Kathryn Scarborough is on leave from her position as a Professor in the Department of Security, Safety, and Emergency Management at Eastern Kentucky University. She is coauthor of textbooks on police administration and women in law enforcement (*Women in Law Enforcement: Public and Private Security* [2001] with Pamela Collins), and has directed several projects focused on law enforcement technology, cybercrime, and police intelligence. She worked as a police officer in Virginia and earned her Ph.D. in criminal justice from Sam Houston State University.

Mary Kate Schneider is a Ph.D. student in the Department of Government and Politics at the University of Maryland. She is a research assistant for the Minorities at Risk (MAR) Project at the Center for International Development and Conflict Management (CIDCM), a project that tracks the status and conflicts of politically active groups throughout the world. She holds an M.A. in political science from Lehigh University; has conducted fieldwork in postconflict Serbia and Kosovo; and has presented work on nationalism, state building, and the European Union at conferences throughout the United States.

Guntram F. A. Werther, Ph.D., earned his doctorate from Washington University in St. Louis (1990), having it nominated as the best work in comparative politics nationally (APSA Gabriel Almond Prize nominations for both 1991 and 1992). His emerging international futures forecasting work was selected as winner of the 2007 Proteus Management Group (complex adaptive systems) International Monograph Competition. In 2008, this work was featured at the Intelligence Community Centers of Academic Excellence Program Summer Seminar (ODNI). His 2006 complex systems "International Change Profiling" essay was competitively selected for another new 2008 Proteus/ODNI book. Since 1986,

Werther has taught at four major universities, has consulted at the senior executive levels of multiple Fortune 100 firms and governments (Asia, Europe, Middle East, and Latin America primarily), and has developed cutting-edge holistically integrative, multidisciplinary, and cross-cultural programs in both online and standard formats. Currently, he is Executive in Residence at Thunderbird—The School of Global Management and Associate Faculty (MBA—Strategy) at Arizona State University's W. P. Carey School of Management. Werther's 1992 comparative study of conflict styles and the mirroring management approaches of governments dealing with ethnic national self-determination movements was reviewed as the best work in its field.

CPSIA information can be obtained
at www.ICGtesting.com
Printed in the USA
LVOW03*0012271215

467675LV00001BB/17/P

9 780313 376627